Transactions of the Royal Historical Society

SIXTH SERIES

XX

CAMBRIDGE
UNIVERSITY PRESS

Published by the Press Syndicate of the University of Cambridge
The Edinburgh Building, Cambridge CB2 8RU, United Kingdom
32 Avenue of the Americas, New York, NY 10013–2473, USA
477 Williamstown Road, Port Melbourne, VIC 3207 Australia
C/Orense, 4, planta 13, 28020 Madrid, Spain

A catalogue record for this book is available from the British Library

First published 2010

ISBN 9781107008687 hardback

SUBSCRIPTIONS. The serial publications of the Royal Historical Society, *Royal Historical Society Transactions* (ISSN 0080–4401) and Camden Fifth Series (ISSN 0960–1163) volumes may be purchased together on annual subscription. The 2010 subscription price (which includes print and electronic access) is £113 (US$190 in the USA, Canada and Mexico) and includes Camden Fifth Series, volumes 36 and 37 (published in July and December) and Transactions Sixth Series, volume 20 (published in December). Japanese prices are available from Kinokuniya Company Ltd, PO Box 55, Chitose, Tokyo 156, Japan. EU subscribers (outside the UK) who are not registered for VAT should add VAT at their country's rate. VAT registered subscribers should provide their VAT registration number.

Subscription orders, which must be accompanied by payment, may be sent to a bookseller, subscription agent or direct to the publisher: Cambridge University Press, The Edinburgh Building, Shaftesbury Road, Cambridge CB2 8RU, UK; or in the USA, Canada and Mexico; Cambridge University Press, Journals Fulfillment Department, 100 Brook Hill Drive, West Nyack, New York 10994–2133, USA. Prices include delivery by air.

SINGLE VOLUMES AND BACK VOLUMES. A list of Royal Historical Society volumes available from Cambridge University Press may be obtained from the Humanities Marketing Department at the address above.

Printed and bound in the United Kingdom at the University Press, Cambridge

CONTENTS

Transactions of the RHS 20 (2010), p. v © Royal Historical Society 2010
doi:10.1017/S0080440110000022

EDITORIAL NOTE

The slightly more diverse fare in this year's *Transactions* reflects two developments. First, the Society has adopted a new format for its regional visits. Whereas previously the visits to UK Higher Education Institutions were accompanied by a formal paper reading by a speaker nominated by the Society, it has been decided to offer our support to regional symposia, preferably involving more than one institution, from which we will publish a selection of papers. The first of these symposia on the subject of 'Poverty and Welfare in Ireland, c. 1833–1948' hosted by the Queen's University Belfast and Oxford Brookes University was held at the Institute of Irish Studies at the Queen's University Belfast on 26–7 June 2009, and three of the papers presented are published here. We have also decided that the Gresham Lectures for the Public Understanding of History founded in memory of Colin Matthew deserve a wider audience, and if appropriate, we propose to publish them in *Transactions*. Charles Saumerez Smith's lecture on the institutionalisation of art in the nineteenth century therefore appears in print here.

Transactions of the RHS 20 (2010), pp. 1–26 © Royal Historical Society 2010
doi:10.1017/S0080440110000034

TRANSACTIONS OF THE
ROYAL HISTORICAL SOCIETY
PRESIDENTIAL ADDRESS

By Colin Jones

FRENCH CROSSINGS: I. TALES OF TWO CITIES

READ 27 NOVEMBER 2009

ABSTRACT. Under the general title, 'French Crossings', the presidential addresses over the next four years will explore intersections and relationships between cultures, periods, disciplines, approaches, historiographies and problems, all within the general field of early modern and modern French history. 'Tales of Two Cities' takes as its approach both comparative history and *l'histoire croisée*. It compares and contrasts the very differing cultural impact on each side of the Channel of one of the most influential British novels about Franco-British political culture, namely, Charles Dickens's *A Tale of Two Cities* (1859). The novel has been conventionally hailed in England, especially from the end of the nineteenth century, as a parable unfavourably contrasting France's revolutionary tradition with the allegedly more humane political evolutionism of England. In France, the novel has been largely ignored or else viewed as a Burkean rant. Yet Dickens's personal attitudes towards France and in particular Paris suggests a more ambiguous and complicated history. For Dickens, modern Paris, as regenerated under Haussmann, was a brilliant success story against which he contrasted both Paris in the 1790s and the social and political circumstances he claimed to detect within English metropolitan culture in the recent past and present. Dickens views the radical and disinherited workers' suburb of the Faubourg Saint-Antoine less, it is suggested, as quintessentially French than as quintessentially plebeian, and the prospect of a slide into revolutionary politics as a lurking threat within England as well as France.

At his recent Regius Professorial Lecture at Cambridge, published in fuller form as a book, *Cosmopolitan Islanders*, Richard Evans made the excellent point that British university history departments are often more diverse in their scholarly interests than their peers in other European countries. By his calculation, scholars of foreign history account for some 44 per cent of a sample group of history departments – and of this cohort, 10 per cent are historians of France.[1] I am proud and happy to number myself among them. But I am also aware that this situation makes me unusual among presidents of this Society. Since the late nineteenth century, the majority of presidents (with some very distinguished exceptions) have been historians of England, and they have used the generous canvas of four successive presidential addresses as an opportunity to explore the state of a key issue or else to offer a synthesis in regard to some knotty problem or major theme in, usually, English history.[2] My approach will not follow this model. This also owes something to the fact that my range of academic interests is quite diverse. After a combined honours degree in History and French at Oxford, I started, and continue, research as a historian of the French Revolution. I feel most comfortable in the eighteenth century, but have strayed much wider, writing general histories of France and of Paris. The history of medicine is a strong area of engagement, as is the study of historiography. Recent work ranges into the history of the emotions, of physiognomy, caricature, surrealism and literature. With this kind of approach to French history, multi-period as well as cross-disciplinary, it seemed that if I ranged more widely and more disparately than is the presidential custom I would play to any strengths I may have. So, sacrificing homogeneity and synthesis, I will follow my interests.

'French Crossings' is the title I have taken for my set of presidential addresses and in this and in future years, I will be crossing periods, crossing approaches, crossing disciplines and crossing problems. These crossings will always involve France and its history, since France provides the framework and the focus for all my work. In this paper, I shall be dabbling in comparative Anglo-French history, even though I am somewhat sceptical about that genre. Comparative history is too often set within the framework of the nation-state and privileges social-structural methodologies. Although laudably aiming at a better understanding of two societies, it often works in practice with an internally stable and homogenised notion of those societies – and so ends up freezing and fortifying national stereotypes rather than undermining or subverting them. This looks problematic in an era of globalisation, especially too among historians eager to take the so-called cultural turn. Though there will be a comparativist aspect to my paper, my main inspiration comes from what Germanist scholars Michael Werner and Bénédicte Zimmermann have called, in contradistinction to comparative history, *l'histoire croisée* – intercrossing or entangled history.[3] *L'histoire croisée*

---

[1] Richard J. Evans, *Cosmopolitan Islanders. British Historians and the European Continent* (Cambridge, 2009), 12–13, 16. The statistics are not very reliable, but probably do give rough approximations.
[2] For a full list, see the website of the Society, http://www.royalhistoricalsociety.org (10 Jan. 2010).
[3] Michael Werner and Bénédicte Zimmermann, 'Beyond Comparison: *Histoire Croisée* and the Challenge of Reflexivity', *History and Theory*, 45 (2006), 30–50; *De la comparaison*

highlights accounts conducted below the waterline of the nation-state and using varying frames and scales of reference. It also seeks to register the ways in which acts of crossing and intercrossing generate effects, repercussions and impacts on the societies involved, and also on the things (individuals, practices, objects) that do the crossing. Far from remaining intact and identical in form, these are transformed in the process of crossing. *L'histoire croisée* is also open to a principle of reflexivity: that is, it encompasses how historians are personally implicated – entangled in fact – within the process of their historical investigation.

What I shall be doing in this paper is simply to follow a person and an object in their crossings of the Channel over time. The person is Charles Dickens; and the object, his novel, *A Tale of Two Cities*.[4] The time frame for my analysis, which will combine both comparative history and *l'histoire croisée*, is the last 150 years: very precisely so, for the novel was published in 1859. The last weekly instalment of the novel in Dickens's periodical, *All the Year Round*, was issued on 26 November 1859, 150 years ago.[5]

As is well known, crossing, passing and doubling are fundamental features of the plot of a novel whose characters are always in the 'habit of passing and repassing between France and England' (*ATOTC*, 68). Yet in many ways, as we shall see, the novel generally has been viewed as reinforcing national stereotypes. Dickens is invariably seen as a one of the greatest and most quintessentially English of writers – *The Times* saluted him on his death as 'the Great Commoner of English Literature'.[6] His novel's very title has become almost a charter for comparative, contrastive

à l'histoire croisée, ed. *idem* and *eadem* (Paris, 2004); *Le travail et la nation: histoire croisée de la France et de l'Allemagne*, ed. Bénédicte Zimmermann, Claude Didry and Peter Wagner (Paris, 1999); *Transferts. Les relations interculturelles dans l'espace franco-allemand (XVIIIe–XIXe siècles)*, ed. Michel Espagne and Michael Werner (Paris, 1988); Deborah Cohen and Maura O'Connor, 'Introduction: Comparative History, Cross-National History, Transnational History – Definitions', in *Comparison and History: Europe in Cross-National Perspective*, ed. *eadem* and *eadem* (2004) ix–xxiv; H. G Haupt and J. Kocka, 'Comparative History: Methods, Aims, Problems', and Nancy L. Green, 'Forms of Comparison', both in *ibid.*, 23–39, 41–56; Deborah Cohen, 'Comparative History: Buyer Beware', *GHI Bulletin*, 29 (2001), 23–33; Stefan Berger, 'Comparative History', in *Writing History: Theory and Practice*, ed. Stefan Berger, Heiko Feldner and Kevin Passmore (2003), 161–79.

[4] Michael Slater's definitional biography, *Charles Dickens* (2009), supersedes earlier lives. This paper also draws heavily upon Dickens's correspondence and journalism, for which I have used the authoritative *The British Academy Pilgrim Edition of the Letters of Charles Dickens*, ed. Graham Storey *et al.* (12 vols,, Oxford, 1965–2002), and *The Dent Uniform Edition of Dickens' Journalism*, ed. Michael Slater and John Drew (4 vols., 1994–2000). For the novel, I have used the Penguin Classics edition, ed. Richard Maxwell (new edn, London, 2003). To lighten the footnotes I will henceforth bracket references to these in the text as follows: *Letters*; *Journalism*; and *ATOTC*, indicating volume and page numbers.

[5] By chance, the lecture on which this paper is based was delivered on 27 November 2009, making it 150 years plus a day after 26 November 1859. 27 November 2009 was 150 years to the day when English readers awoke to discover that Sydney Carton had had his head cut off.

[6] Cited in Slater, *Charles Dickens*, 618.

history at macro, nation-state level. It is a novel set in two cities, Paris and London, but through them it has been taken to be in essence about two contrasting political cultures – France's revolutionary tradition, and England's evolutionary trajectory.[7] The equation between London as social order incarnate, Paris as insurrectionary ferment, reflects a growing complacency within England about the two societies which then, in the 1850s, was just hardening into mid-Victorian orthodoxy. By seeming to offer a tale of two contrasting political pathways, a tale of two civilisations, *A Tale of Two Cities* accrued a persistent, talismanic cultural and emotional presence around which national identity crystallised. The novel became, in sum, an English 'site of memory' – or *lieu de mémoire* – as French historian Pierre Nora would put it.[8]

A Tale of Two Cities has almost certainly been more influential in shaping British culture's view of the French Revolution than the work of any mere historian. For every one reader of Thomas Carlyle's *French Revolution* (or even William Doyle's, for that matter), there must be a hundred who will have sampled *A Tale of Two Cities* in some form. There was indeed a time when every British schoolchild could recite (and every stand-up comedian could bowdlerise) the opening lines of this arch-English *lieu de mémoire* – 'it was the best of times, it was the worst of times' – and the punchline of its closing peroration, as tragic hero Sydney Carton goes self-sacrificially to the guillotine doubling, passing, as another man, with indeed (since we are going to be talking about such things) a second identity, 'it is a far, far better thing that I do now than I have ever done'. Writing in 1940, George Orwell observed that the novel must bear much of the responsibility for the fact that 'the average Englishman' still viewed revolution as 'no more than a pyramid of severed heads'.[9]

I shall argue that there is much more that is interesting and ambivalent about the novel than this (as Orwell was indeed aware). There are, I hope to show, quite a number of tales to tell about *A Tale of Two Cities*.

Before we look at the novel, however, I shall confess – with a nod towards the reflexivity highlighted in *l'histoire croisée* – my own 'entanglements' in the subject of this paper: to note that my own crossings – my

[7] See e.g. Claire Hancock, *Paris et Londres au XIXe siècle: représentations dans les guides et récits de voyage* (Paris, 2003), esp. 167ff; C. Dever, '"An Occult and Immoral Tyranny": The Novel, the Police and the Agent Provocateur', in *The Literary Channel: The International Invention of the Novel*, ed. C. Dever and M. Cohen (Princeton, 2002), 225–50, esp. 229ff.

[8] Pierre Nora, 'Between Memory and History: *Les Lieux de Mémoire*', *Representations*, special issue, 'Memory and Counter-Memory', 26 (1989), 7–24. Nora was introducing to an Anglophone audience a publishing project later conveniently issued in three volumes as *Les lieux de mémoire* (Paris, 1997). Parts have been translated into English and the project has spawned a veritable exegetical tradition – to which I hope to return in a future address.

[9] George Orwell, 'Charles Dickens', in *idem, Inside the Whale and Other Essays* (1940), 1–85, at 25.

own 'habit of passing and repassing between France and England' – have inevitably influenced what I have to say. My own serious and serial French crossings began when I was a student, guided by my doctoral supervisor, the late Richard Cobb. Cobb's approach to doctoral supervision was very simple: he wanted his students to get across the Channel as fast as possible, to stay there, dug into the archives, for as long as they could, and to develop as swiftly as they might be able what he, describing his own experiences as 'an Anglo-French historian', called 'a second identity'.[10] What Cobb detested above all were historians who wrote from their Oxbridge colleges or London clubs, who rarely crossed the Channel and who invariably ended up retailing national sterotypes. Admiration for one particular scholar was irreparably damaged when Cobb learnt that he had only ever been to the Archives Nationales once, sat in the *salle de lecture* for a single morning – and found the experience so alienating and intimidating that he ran back to London and never repeated the experience.

Cobb regarded national stereotypes much as Lucien Febvre, the great founder of the *Annales*, regarded anachronism: namely, as the historian's cardinal sin above all others.[11] It was Cobb's belief that immersion within French society and culture would proof us against any tendency towards national stereotyping – and help us produce better history. His antidote against stereotyping was to invite us to view our encounter with France as an anthropological field trip to an alien culture – but it was anthropology with a difference, for we were encouraged to believe that that alien culture was in many respects superior to our own. It was also Cobb's particular point of pride that, because of his excellent accent and his frequent presence in France, he could invariably pass as French (something most of us can only envy). The supreme achievement of understanding French men and women was thus to be able to pass as one; and Cobb recorded how on crossing the Channel to France he would find that when he was talking his hands and mouth strangely started to do different things from when he was in England. Cobb the cultural anthropologist thus doubled the talented impersonator – crossing mixed with passing.[12]

---

[10] Richard Cobb, *A Second Identity: Essays on France and French History* (Oxford, 1969), esp. the Introduction, 'Experience of an Anglo-French Historian', 1–50. For more on Cobb, Colin Lucas, 'Richard Charles Cobb', in *New Oxford Dictionary of National Biography;* and my essay, 'Olwen Hufton's "Poor", Richard Cobb's "People" and the Notions of the *Longue Durée* in French Revolutionary Historiography', in *The Art of Survival: Gender and History in Europe, 1450–2000*, ed. Ruth Harris and Lyndal Roper, Past and Present Supplement 1 (Oxford, 2006), 178–203.

[11] Lucien Febvre, *Le problème de l'incroyance au XVIe siècle. La religion de Rabelais* (Paris, 1947 edn), 6: 'le péché des péchés – le péché entre tous irrémissible'.

[12] Cobb, *A Second Identity*, 50. Cobb prided himself as being a latter-day *sans-culotte* (the subject of his studies), and he shared with them a taste for rhetorical violence and exaggeration, irreverently nonconformist behaviour and wild drinking.

Richard Evans's *Cosmopolitan Islanders* devotes some colourful pages to Cobb, yet while noting his achievement as a historian, it concludes that at bottom Cobb and those who derived inspiration from his example remained 'fundamentally British'.[13] This is an unsatisfactory description, and Evans seems fundamentally to miss the point. Cobb's notion of a 'second identity' was grounded in the belief that by dint of crossing and re-crossing the Channel between England and France, he became a different individual. It was not just about hand-and-mouth gestures; it was about how to think and how to write – indeed how to be. In these post-modern times we can surely accept a more fragmented, fluid and generous sense of identity and subjectivity than Evans allows. In this paper, I shall be writing if not as a fully fledged 'Anglo-French historian' as Cobb claimed to be, then at least as an 'entangled' historian, an historian 'inter-crossing' so to speak, whose quality of perception and whose historical judgement have been altered by prolonged exposure to another culture – by French crossings in fact. And I will be focusing on an author, Charles Dickens, who is less 'fundamentally British' than he is accounted, and a novel which, I shall argue, plays more complicatedly with national stereotypes than is usually realised.[14]

A Tale of Two Cities made a huge impact on its appearance in 1859, enjoyed instant popularity and received considerable critical acclaim. Yet it appears to have been at the very end of the nineteenth century that it really established itself in the British national consciousness. What elevated it to another level as an emblem of national identity, as a *lieu de mémoire* in effect, was the production in February 1899 of a play based on the novel entitled *The Only Way* that the theatrical impresario John Martin-Harvey presented at London's Lyceum Theatre – with himself in the starring role of Sydney Carton. As Joss Marsh has shown,[15] the play nailed down its place in the national imagination when, several months later, in the Boer War, the English commander at the siege of Mafeking, General (later Über-Scout) Robert Baden Powell kept up morale among the troops by staging a production of *The Only Way*. Sydney Carton's final, dying words on the scaffold – 'it is a far, far better thing' – seemed apt for that Mafeking moment. Baden-Powell's stroke of imperial *sangfroid* helped to ensure Martin-Harvey's play lasting success, and won him, like

---

[13] Evans, *Cosmopolitan Islanders*, 153 (and more generally 142–53).

[14] Some of these ideas are explored in *Charles Dickens, A Tale of Two Cities and the French Revolution*, ed. Colin Jones, Josephine McDonagh and Jon Mee (Basingstoke, 2009), 'Introduction', 1–23.

[15] In discussing the play and its resonance, I draw heavily on Joss Marsh's essay, 'Mimi and the Matinée Idol: Martin-Harvey, Sydney Carton and the Staging of *A Tale of Two Cities*', in *Charles Dickens and the French Revolution*, ed. Jones *et al.*, 126–45. Further details are in *The Autobiography of Sir John Martin-Harvey* (1933); Nicholas Butler, *John Martin-Harvey: Biography of an Actor-Manager* (Colchester, 1997); and H. Philip Bolton, *Dickens Dramatized* (1987).

Baden-Powell, the status of national hero. Martin-Harvey's entry to the salons of dukes and duchesses was assured, race-horses were named after him, posters of the guillotine scene proliferated and music-hall comedians did impressions of him as Sydney Carton. The ultimate accolade was quasi-plagiarism: Sydney Carton's popularity at the *fin de siècle* helps explain the great popular success enjoyed by the Baroness d'Orzcy's much inferior *Scarlet Pimpernel*, first in 1903 as a play and then from 1905 as a novel.

In the Great War, Martin-Harvey would play his Carton to British footsoldiers in the trenches, with bombs whistling round his ears. It was for 'their beloved *Tale of Two Cities*', he noted in his memoirs, that 'they always called'.[16] Troops idolised the final guillotine tableau with its 'far, far better thing' eclipsing even a strong challenge from the 'Once more unto the breach' of Shakespeare's Prince Hal. Both these scenes, incidentally, represented Britain's allies, the French, as the enemy – but no one seemed to mind, or maybe even notice. What was crucial about the play and particularly the final scene was less the precise national identity of Carton's executioners than the opportunity the death-scene afforded for the construction of a melodramatic yet peculiarly potent form of stoical, calm, self-sacrificial, stiff-upper-lip English masculinity. Paradoxically it is Sydney Carton's capacity to lose his head while others all around him were keeping theirs which marks him out as a model Edwardian, Kipling-esque man.[17]

Sir John Martin-Harvey would play in around 2,500 theatrical performances of *The Only Way*, continuing during the interwar period, and occurring throughout the English provinces, in Ireland – James Joyce's Molly Bloom caught the show when it hit Dublin, the final monologue of *Ulysses* reveals – and into Canada and north America.[18] The eminence of a play that its author hailed as 'the popular masterpiece' of English theatre was confirmed by a film version in 1925. '*The Only Way*', the movie magazine, *Variety*, noted in September 1925, 'marks a gigantic forward movement in British film production... Never in the history of a picture shown in this country has an audience deliberately refused to leave the theatre and called insistently for the leading actor and producer.'[19] The play's extraordinary hold on the broad Anglophone

[16] *Autobiography*, 483; Butler, *John Martin-Harvey*, 106.
[17] For Edwardian masculinity generally, see John Tosh, *Manliness and Masculinities in Nineteenth-Century Britain* (Harlow, 2005).
[18] Though Martin-Harvey claimed to have played 5,000 performances, his biographer Nicholas Butler has documented 2,475 (5). For Dublin, cf. James Joyce, *Ulysses* (9th reimpression, London, 1960), 911.
[19] Cited in Marsh, 'Mimi and the Matinée Idol', 142 n. 3. For other studies on Dickens on film, see Judith Buchanan and Alex Newhouse, 'Sanguine Mirages, Cinematic Dreams: Things Seen and Things Imagined in the 1917 Fox Feature Film *A Tale of Two Cities*', and

public was strengthened by the appearance in 1935 of another Hollywood version of *A Tale of Two Cities*, this time with the actor and quintessential stage Englishman Ronald Coleman putting in an Oscar-nominated performance as Sydney Carton. His interpretation was definitional, and successors in the role – including Dirk Bogarde in the 1958 British film of the novel – have tended to impersonate Ronald Coleman as much as to play Sydney Carton. By the time of Coleman's appearance, Martin-Harvey had already grown rich and fat in the lead role of the play, *The Only Way*, well after he was aesthetically or athletically equipped for it. He was seventy-six years old in his final, 2,465th performance in the role in Newcastle at another high moment of English patriotism: May 1939, the eve of war. 'It was a far, far better thing' seemed apt in an odd, proto-Churchillian way – and indeed Martin-Harvey was developing a Churchillian chubbiness. Never in the course of British theatre history had an actor owed so much fame and repute to so little plausible resemblance to the dashing young character he was playing.

But what did the French make of all this? What was the reception of Dickens's novel in France? In effect, under the comparativist lens, *A Tale of Two Cities* has been a tale of two receptions: one warm and impassioned, the other, as we shall see, quizzical and rejecting. The French reading public, it must be said, did not dislike Dickens. On the contrary. He was very popular across the Channel, his journalism and extracts from his novels appearing in French periodicals from the late 1830s. In 1856, he signed a contract with Hachette which gave that publishing house translation options over all his novels and short stories. Dickens was soon being recognised by strangers in the streets on visits to Paris, and he rejoiced to discover his novels available in translation 'at every railway station, great or small' (*Letters*, X, 151).[20] Yet the appearance of the French translation of *A Tale of Two Cities* in 1861 failed to ignite public interest across the Channel. Significantly, Dickens refrained from performing in France public readings of his abbreviated version of *A Tale of Two Cities*, preferring to expose his Parisian audience to *David Copperfield*, *Christmas Carol*, *Dombey and Son* and the *Pickwick Papers*.[21]

Charles Barr, 'Two Cities, Two Films', both in *Charles Dickens and the French Revolution*, ed. Jones *et al.*, 146–65, 166–87, and, more generally, Jason W. Stevens, 'Insurrection and Depression-Era Politics in Selznick's *A Tale of Two Cities (1935)*', *Literature Film Quarterly* (2006), 176–94; and Pascal Dupuy, 'La diffusion des stéréotypes révolutionnaires dans la littérature et le cinéma anglo-saxons, 1789–1989', *Annales historiques de la Révolution française* (1966), 511–28.

[20] For reception details, see also *Letters*, III, 399, 502n, VII, 39–40, VIII, 726–7.

[21] *Charles Dickens. The Public Readings*, ed. Philip Collins (Oxford, 1975). For the abbreviated version of *ATOTC* (which was never in fact performed), see Michael Slater, '"The Bastille Prisoner": A Reading Dickens Never Gave', *Études anglaises*, 23 (1970), 190–6.

For the next 150 years, the French tale has been one of neglect.[22] *David Copperfield* has gone into scores of French translations and versions since its publication in French; *A Tale of Two Cities* has scarcely reached double figures. Comically symptomatic of the failure of the novel to capture the national imagination has been an almost pathological inability to agree on a title for it in French. From the outset, the literal translation – *Un conte de deux villes* – was rejected, presumably on grounds of dysphony (that ugly 'de deux'), and for most of its history, it traded under the title *Paris et Londres en 1793*. The difficulty of finding a way to treat the novel sympathetically is also evident in the frequent omission of the opening and closing lines of the novel. An English-language version of the novel without 'best of times, worst of times' and 'far, far better thing' would be viewed as an evisceration of a national treasure.[23] In France, such cuts have been par for the course.

In one way it is supremely easy to understand the negativity of French responses. For the images that the novel presents of the French Revolution, and notably of the Reign of Terror in 1793 when it climaxes, are notoriously negative. Dickens presents his tale as a parable in which 'myriads of small creatures, the creatures of this chronicle among the rest' (*ATOTC*, 7) face up to and survive an oppressive and terroristic foreign regime.[24] The most sympathetic French characters are in fact naturalised Englishmen: notably Doctor Manette, imprisoned in the Bastille under the Ancien Régime, before beginning life anew in London's Soho; and Charles Darnay, nephew and heir of the marquis de Evrémonde, the latter an aristocrat of a gratuitous viciousness rarely found outside the pages of Jean-Paul Marat. Darnay thwarts the bloodlust of the ghastly Madame Defarge – probably in fact the least unsympathetic French character in the book (though this is certainly not saying much) – and is rescued from the guillotine and spirited back to London with his wife, Lucy Manette, as a result of a prison cell substitution by the self-sacrificial Sydney Carton. Some of the Parisian set-piece scenes in the novel have become classics of political nightmare: the dank, dungeon chill of Manette's cell in the Bastille; the Kafka-esque atmosphere of the Revolutionary Tribunal; the hideous account of the Carmagnole revolutionary dance, with

[22] See the excellent, if now dated, article, Annie Sadrin, 'Traductions et adaptations françaises de *A Tale of Two Cities*', in *Charles Dickens et la France: Colloque international de Boulogne-sur-Mer, 3 juin 1978*, ed. Sylvère Monod (Lille, 1979), 77–91. Cf., extending and updating this article, Jones *et al.*, 'Introduction', esp. pp 7–8.

[23] Symptomatically, the first paragraph was retained virtually verbatim even in the much scaled-down reading version.

[24] It has been convincingly argued that Dickens was also moved in this regard by sympathy for English settlers caught up in the 1857 Indian Mutiny. Grace Moore, *Dickens and Empire: Discourses of Class, Race and Colonialism in the World of Charles Dickens* (Aldershot, 2004). Thanks to Margot Finn on this point.

tricolor-bedecked *sans-culottes* shrieking frenetically as the guillotine blade is sharpened; Madame Defarge counting the stitches in her knitting as heads fall; and the revolutionary mob 'all armed alike in hunger and revenge', 'headlong, mad and dangerous' and primed for maximum atrocity (*ATOTC*, 224, 222, 230). And hovering menacingly over it all: the grim, personalised Faubourg Saint-Antoine, home of Parisian revolutionary bloodlust, site of hunger, poverty and neglect, whose 'lords in waiting on the saintly presence' were, in Dickens's enumeration, 'cold, dirt, sickness, ignorance and want' (*ATOTC*, 32).

From the start, French audiences found *A Tale of Two Cities* difficult to stomach. The overt politics of the novel proved more than enough to offend French audiences of whatever political stripe. The Left were appalled by Dickens's blood-swilling account of radicals in the reign of Terror; while Right-wing nostalgics for the Ancien Régime were upset by the virulent representation of the aristocracy. For 150 years (and counting), French readers have shunned the novel on, evidently, the mildest and most superficial knowledge. What knowledge they do have has easily fitted into national stereotypical responses every bit as crude as the chauvinistic British reading that I have evoked. French readers have tended to prefer their Dickens full of loveable characters, jocular, quintessentially English humour, whimsical dialogue and mawkishly sentimental highspots. These benign qualities of Dickens's *œuvre* were viewed as his predominant characteristics in the respectful if condescending praise which the literary historian Hippolyte Taine accorded him from the 1860s in his canonical four-volumed *Histoire de la littérature anglaise*.[25] In the event, however, Dickens could not have had a more problematic literary supporter. For after the Paris Commune in 1871, Taine developed a second identity as a rabid counter-revolutionary analyst of the French Revolution in general and Parisian crowds in particular.[26] Ever since, Dickens's politics have been tarred with an ultra-reactionary brush in France. This has been an enduring legacy. In 2007, for example, the distinguished historian, Jean-Noel Jeanneney, went out of his way bitterly to regret the fact that French schoolchildren wanting to find out about the French Revolution on the World-Wide Web might be reduced to reading authors from

[25] Hippolyte Taine, *Histoire de la littérature anglaise*, started to be published in 1863, being added to and going into numerous later editions. I have consulted the 1881 edition, with 5 volumes. Also on late nineteenth- and early twentieth-century reception in France, see Floris Delattre, *Dickens et la France: étude d'une interaction littéraire anglo-française* (Paris, 1927), and, more generally, *Dickens, Europe and the New Worlds*, ed. Annie Sadrin (Basingstoke, 1999).
[26] Hippolyte Taine, *Les origines de la France contemporaine* (Paris, 1876–94). The volumes concerning the Ancien Régime (vol. I) and the Revolution (vols. II–IV) appeared in 1876, 1878 and 1885. For Taine, Le Bon and other analysts of crowd behaviour in this period, see Susanna Barrows, *Distorting Mirrors: Visions of the Crowd in Late Nineteenth-Century France* (New Haven, 1981).

within the English anti-revolutionary historiographical tradition. He took this evidently baleful filiation back to Edmund Burke, passing thereafter through Thomas Carlyle, Charles Dickens and the Baroness d'Orczy to end up... in the pages of Simon Schama. *Quelle galère*, one might be tempted to say: *quelle galère* 'fundamentally British' even – if we were talking only of national stereotypes.[27]

Analysis of the reception of Dickens's great novel on the two sides of the Channel thus reveals the French and British in paradoxical agreement. French hatred balances British love – but both audiences have concurred in seeing in *A Tale of Two Cities* as counter-revolutionary, probably Francophobic and thoroughly jingoistic. It is tempting to accept this judgement. Yet there is, I believe, something more complicated and more interesting going on here which merits further exploration. And it is Dickens himself who cues us in. In May 1860, he wrote to his French publishing house thanking them for accepting the novel for translation. He concluded the letter in French, 'Voila [*sic*] un de mes espoirs les plus ardents en l'écrivant' (*Letters*, IX, 249). He had already in fact approached his friend the French actor François Régnier about the possibility of putting on in Paris a stage version of the novel which, he hopefully stated, would be of interest 'because it treats of a very memorable time in France'. Régnier quashed the proposal politely and smartly – and for Dickens the penny quickly dropped (*Letters*, IX, 132 and 163). This was not something that French theatre audiences would wish to see.

This apparent conundrum – that Dickens initially imagined that *A Tale of Two Cities* would be well received in France – is worth exploring in more detail, for it militates against the simplistic interpretations which have characterised the novel's reception in French and English culture. In what remains of this paper, I want to propose an alternative way of thinking about the novel, and to tell a different tale about this tale of two cities, which subjects the novel to the interpretative grid of *l'histoire croisée*, and which avoids the crudities of national sterotyping. For indeed if anyone in Victorian culture was subject to French crossings, it was the archetypically, 'fundamentally' English novelist, Charles Dickens.

> I see a beautiful city and a brilliant people rising from this abyss, and in their struggles to be truly free, in their triumphs and defeats, through long years to come, I see the evil of this time and of the previous time of which this is the natural birth, gradually making expiation for itself and wearing out. (*ATOTC*, 389)

Thus Sydney Carton on the scaffold, leading on to his climactic final words. This 'beautiful city', rapturously foreseen, was – I think it is safe to say – the Paris that Charles Dickens loved, and this

---

[27] Jean-Noel Jeanneney, *Google and the Myth of Universal Knowledge: A View from Europe* (Chicago, 2007); and esp. *idem*, 'Quand Google défie l'Europe', *Le Monde*, 24 Jan. 2005, 13.

'brilliant people' were the French men and women whose friendship he cherished. The author of this putatively Francophobic novel was more cosmopolitan than chauvinistic, more Francophile than Francophobe, and less 'fundamentally English' – I would suggest – than many of his biographers and literary critics. Dickens excoriated those of his compatriots who, basing their prejudices on ancient anti-revolutionary caricatures, viewed the French as 'benighted frog-eaters' (*Journalism*, III, 332). His very first acquaintance with Paris in 1844 had sparked love at first sight. Paris was 'the most extraordinary place in the world', he wrote. 'I walked about the streets, in and out, up and down, backwards and forwards – and every house and every person I passed seemed to be another leaf in the enormous book which stands wide-open there' (*Letters*, IV, 166–7). He lived in the city for nearly a year in 1846–7, resided in Boulogne for nearly as long in the 1850s and made in total at least twenty visits to France, most of them to Paris.[28] He developed enormous respect for French art, theatre, culture and civility, saluting the French as 'in many high and great respects the first people in the universe' (*Letters*, V, 42). And he prided himself as 'an accomplished Frenchman' on understanding and speaking in French, which he referred to as 'le langage des dieux et des anges' (*Letters*, V, 42, 256–7). His son wrote of him that 'he used to say laughingly that his sympathies were so much with the French that he ought to have been born a Frenchman' – indeed on one occasion, again jocularly, but again revealingly, he signed himself 'Charles Dickens, Français naturalisé, et Citoyen de Paris'.[29] He seems to have felt as comfortable with this ascription as with the moustache which he grew at about the same time. This was, he noted, 'the pride of Albion and the admiration of Gaul'.[30] Clearly, this was a man so thoroughly versed in Channel-crossing that even his moustache boasted a second identity.

For the rest of his life, Dickens remained alert to Paris's sensual charms. 'I want to be pleasant and gay and to throw myself *en garçon* on the festive diableries of Paris', he told a friend in 1855 (*Letters*, VII, 522). Paris was, he remarked on other occasions, 'as bright and wicked and as wanton as ever', 'a wicked and destestable place though wonderfully attractive' (*Letters*, IV, 665–6, 669; cf. X, 200). 'In Paris', Dickens noted, 'I seem to be a rather free and easy superior vagabond' (*Letters*, VII, 542). And it was as a 'superior vagabond' that Dickens cavalierly penetrated the 'wide-open', feminised city, wicked but devilishly attractive, naughty but oh-how-so-very nice. This marks him out as a variant of the *flâneur*, that characteristic

---

[28] *Dickens on France: Fiction, Journalism and Travel Writing*, ed. John Edmondson (Oxford, 2006), vii. The number was almost certainly higher because of secret jaunts to the city with his mistress, Ellen Ternan. Cf. Slater, *Charles Dickens*, 531.

[29] Henry Fielding Dickens, cited in *Dickens on France*, ed. Edmondson, vii.

[30] *Letters*, VII, 60: as cited in Slater, *Charles Dickens*, 356.

figure of urban spectacle and modernity imagined by the poet Charles
Baudelaire at this very time in Paris's history, to describe the wandering
walker, wallowing in the vista of 'poetic and marvellous subjects', observing, yet mentally detached from the crowd.[31] Dickens's most frequent
visits to the French capital in the 1850s and 1860s coincided with one of
the most dynamic periods in the city's history and he – like Baudelaire –
was a witness to the transformation effected on the built environment
under the direct influence of Napoléon III and his prefect of Paris, Baron
Georges Haussmann.[32] Baudelaire, proto-theorist of *flânerie*, reacted to
the changes in ways which nurtured Parisian nostalgia for a lost world –
'the shape of a city changes more quickly, alas! than the human heart' was
his plangent view of Haussmannisation.[33] Dickens's attitude in the face of
Parisian urban development and boulevardisation was, in contrast, akin
to awe and wonderment. In 1853, he remarked to his wife that

> Paris is very full, extraordinarily gay and wonderfully improving. Thousands of houses
> must have been pulled down for the construction of an immense street now in the making
> from the dirty old end of the Rue de Tivoli [*sic*], past the Palais Royal, away beyond the
> Hôtel de Ville. It will be the finest thing in Europe. (*Letters*, VII, 163)

By 1862, he was marvelling at all that had been achieved: 'Wherever I
look I see astounding new works, doing or done' (*Letters*, X, 151).

A Tale of Two Cities contrasts 'the beautiful city' of its author's experiences
and that of its hero's envisioning with the Faubourg Saint-Antoine of the
1790s, hotbed of radicalism and sedition, home of poverty and vice. The
neighbourhood had lost nothing of its radicalism throughout the period
of Dickens's acquaintance with the city – the insurrectionary disturbances
of 1830, 1848, 1851 and 1871 were reminders of that.[34] Dickens presents
a grim personalised depiction of the neighbourhood. The last chapters
of the novel read as a deadly duel between it and Sydney Carton, a duel
which powerfully recalls the challenge that Eugène de Rastignac threw

[31] The *flâneur* has become a major focus of nineteenth-century scholarship since the
rediscovery several decades ago of the work of Walter Benjamin. See in particular his *The
Arcades Project*, trans. Howard Eiland and Kevin McLaughlin (Cambridge, MA, 1999). See
too T. J. Clark, *The Painting of Modern Life: Paris in the Art of Manet and his Followers* (Princeton,
1984), and Vanessa Schwartz, *Spectacular Realities: Early Mass Culture in Fin de Siècle Paris*
(Berkeley, 1998). The gender politics of the *flâneur* are discussed in Lynda Nead, *Victorian
Babylon: People, Streets and Images in Nineteenth-Century London* (New Haven, 2000). On Dickens
and the *flâneur*, see M. Hollington, 'Dickens, *Household Words* and the Paris Boulevards', in
Dickens, Europe and the New Worlds, ed. Sadrin, 22–33.
[32] For an overview of Haussmannisation, see Patrice Higonnet, *Paris, Capital of the World*
(Cambridge, MA, 2002), and Colin Jones, *Paris: Biography of a City* (2004), esp. ch. 9.
[33] The quotation comes from Baudelaire's poem, 'Le Cygne' ('The Swan') from *Les fleurs
du mal*.
[34] A good overview of how this the revolutionary tradition played out in French culture is
provided by Priscilla Parkhurst Ferguson, *Paris as Revolution: Writing the Nineteenth-Century City*
(Berkeley, 1994).

down to Paris at the end of Balzac's *Père Goriot: A nous deux maintenant!* [35] So vividly characterised is Dickens's description of that neighbourhood that one assumes that this connoisseur of mid-century Paris knew these turbulent areas well. But did he?

In order to get a grip on this question, I have closely scrutinised Dickens's correspondence and his voluminous journalism for all references to his movements around the city. The map and the Appendix

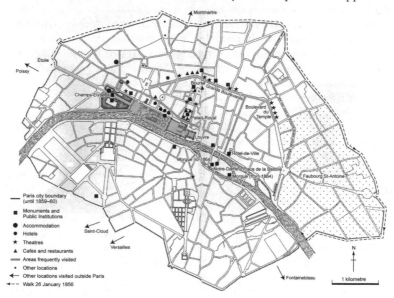

indicate locations where Dickens stayed and places he visited. For residing any time in the city Dickens always plumped for the chic neighbourhoods of the Right Bank – especially around the Champs-Élysées, the Palais-Royal and the Grands Boulevards. This was classic English tourist territory: the hotels, shops, cafés and restaurants of the right bank and the west end and not at all the poorer and more disinherited peripheral neighbourhoods, including the Faubourg Saint-Antoine. A glance at the map suggests a total lack of first-hand experience of the poor northern, eastern and southern extremities of the city, areas that contemporary guidebooks viewed as zones of repulsion for well-heeled travellers, wandering tourists and dedicated *flâneurs*.[36] On one occasion, Dickens claimed to take 'colossal', 'two-hour' walks in the city and to have visited

[35] The personalisation of the Faubourg evident earlier (e.g. *ATOTC*, 191–4, 228–35) becomes mesmerically insistent from 318 until the end of the novel. Balzac's novel was published in 1835.

[36] Hancock, *Paris et Londres au XIXe siècle*, esp. 57ff.

'all the spots made memorable by the first Revolution' (*Letters*, V, 13). Yet these simply do not appear to have included the Faubourg Saint-Antoine. The closest he appears to have come was in January 1856, when he records how he had gone out to the Barrière de l'Étoile to the west of the Arc de Triomphe and walked north then eastwards around the city walls looping round till he reached the river Seine – and then 'entered Paris beyond the site of the Bastille' (*Letters*, VIII, 37). This itinerary skirted the Faubourg Saint-Antoine; it did not penetrate within.

The location that Dickens did regularly visit that brought him close to the revolutionary neighbourhood that constituted the villain of his novel's plot was the Boulevard du Temple in the north-east of the city, widely known as the Boulevard du Crime, 'the boulevard of crime'. This suggests that Dickens here at least might have rubbed shoulders with the underworld of poverty and vice. But this was far from the case. The street got its nickname from the popular theatres which were crowded along it and which served up crime-laden popular melodramas of which Dickens was a great aficionado – he sometimes went to the theatre in Paris twice or three times in a single evening (*Letters*, VII, 540).[37] The Boulevard du Crime offered only representations of crime and other passions on stage, not outside. This was the milieu represented in Marcel Carné's great film melodrama *Les enfants du paradis*, released in 1945. It was a terrain as far removed from real paradise as the Boulevard du Crime was from real crime.

It would appear that the heartland of Parisian poverty and distress, which plays such a big part in *A Tale of Two Cities*, represented something that Dickens did not know at first hand, or did not really chose to get to know. There is a massive mismatch between his spatial appropriation of the city through his personal experience on one hand and, on the other, the imagined topography in evidence in his novel – between, to borrow the vocabulary of the urban theorist Henri Lefebvre, Dickens's 'spatial practice' and his 'representational space'.[38] His spatial practice suggests that he knew absolutely nothing of the Faubourg Saint-Antoine, which was a major protagonist in his novel, and the poverty and radicalism still to be found in it. His correspondence is silent on popular suffering in the French capital, even as in the late 1840s, one of the worst economic crises of the nineteenth century thus far was building up, producing unemployment, dearth and high prices across the city and the country at large. And at that very same time, Friedrich Engels – an aficionado of Palais Royal cafés like Dickens – was busy making contact with

---

[37] Pierre Gascar, *Le boulevard du crime* (Paris, 1980). This theatre district was much reduced by Haussmannisation from the 1860s in fact.

[38] See Henri Lefebvre, *The Production of Space*, trans. Donald Nicholson-Smith (Oxford, 1991).

revolutionary cabinet-makers in the Faubourg Saint-Antoine.[39] Only when Dickens witnessed a mugging close to the Porte Saint-Denis did he become aware of precariousness in popular living standards, which he interpreted as a mark of insecurity (*Letters*, IV, 676). He soon after decamped back to England. He was not around for the February or June *journées* of the 1848 Revolution – and he died before the Paris Commune of 1871. He never experienced a Parisian crowd with its dander up, let alone mobilised for revolt.

Overall, Dickens's representations of space within Paris in the 1790s seem to offer little overlap with his own spatial practices on his frequent visits to the city from the 1840s onwards. If we can rule out personal, first-hand experience, what were, then, the sources of *A Tale of Two Cities*'s memorable depictions of the Parisian poor and dispossessed and of revolutionary street radicals? On what materials is based his imaginative construction of the Faubourg Saint-Antoine?

I shall suggest five vectors of influence and zones of engagement. The first of these is obvious enough: Dickens read widely on the subject, devouring 'cartloads of books'[40] from the period relating to the revolutionary period, and for a time by his own admission perusing 'no books but such as had the air of the time in them' (*Letters*, IX, 245). Literary scholars have traced a great many references, most prominent among them what Dickens referred to as 'a curious little book printed in Amsterdam, written to make out no case whatever and tiresome enough in its literal dictionary-like minuteness' (*Letters*, IX, 259). The work so condescendingly referred to was the *Tableau de Paris* of Louis-Sébastien Mercier. Mercier is perhaps most famous among British audiences for having made one of the truly worst predictions in world history. Writing in 1788, in the final volumes of his *Tableau de Paris*, he had written: 'dangerous rioting has become a moral impossibility in Paris. An attempt at sedition here would be nipped in the bud. Paris never need fear an outbreak such as the late Lord George Gordon recently led in London'.[41] Mercier was here referring to the 1780 Gordon Riots in London which saw hundreds die and much property destroyed in an orgy of anti-Catholic violence. But it was less Mercier the lamentably bad political prophet than Mercier the analyst of Parisian street life that appealed to Dickens. Literary critics

---

[39] Marxists Internet Archive: http://www.marxists.org/archive/marx/works/1846/letters/46_09_16.htm (consulted 7 Jan. 2010). For Dickens, ct., for example, the correspondence at *Letters*, V, 15, where he affects to know nothing of what was taking place within Paris except at the theatre.

[40] Slater, *Charles Dickens*, 473.

[41] Louis-Sébastien Mercier, *Tableau de Paris* (12 vols., Amsterdam, 1788; Slatkine reprint, Geneva, 1970), VI, 26. There is an excellent modern edition edited by Jean-Claude Bonnet (Paris, 1994). For Dickens's sources more generally, see esp. Andrew Sanders, *Companion to A Tale of Two Cities* (1988); and *ATOTC*, Appendix 3.

have traced a number of important plot incidents back to passages in Mercier – the death of a child under the carriage wheels of a heartless aristocrat is a famous example.[42]

If Dickens's research on the Faubourg Saint-Antoine derived much from the second-hand experience furnished by contemporary writings and accounts, a second vicarious source for his accounts of Parisian violence may be found in the lifeless relics on view at the Paris Morgue, situated until 1864 on the Quai du Marché-Neuf on the Left Bank and then shifted to the eastern edge of the Île de la Cité. Dickens was an inveterate habitué of this gothic institution, even on high days and holy days (a Morgue visit was one year, for example, the delightful Christmas present he gave himself).[43] 'Whenever I am in Paris', he noted, 'I am dragged by an invisible force into the Morgue' (*Journalism*, IV, 88). Here, unidentified bodies – fished bloated out of the Seine, discovered lying in the gutter, abandoned in some cheap hotel – were laid out for any passer-by to view and, hopefully, identify. Like a hardened *flâneur*, Dickens compared his viewing of corpses to a shopping trip to a department store, another choice venue for Parisian *flânerie*: 'all the bodies lie on inclined planes within a great glass window as though Holbein should represent Death in his grim Dance, keeping a shop and displaying his goods like a Regent-Street or Boulevard linen-draper' (*Journalism*, III, 375; cf. IV, 221). Dickens admits to having been literally haunted by the images of violent death which he encountered at the Morgue – some of whose features he would delineate in the bloodier scenes of *A Tale of Two Cities* (*Journalism*, III, 93). The faces of the wild Saint-Antoine crowd are 'cadaverous' (*ATOTC*, 531). Similarly the bloated features of the bodies in the Morgue were echoed in the 'bloated' gaoler at the La Force prison on the edge of the Faubourg Saint-Antoine, every one of whose wards was despatched to violent death on the scaffold and who 'looked like a man who had been drowned and filled with water' (*ATOTC*, 267, 291).[44]

[42] See Sanders and *ATOTC*, as cited in the previous note. Mercier's depiction of the faubourgs is gloomy, but he does not highlight Saint-Antoine, which was far from being the most disinherited neighbourhood in 1789. In this respect, see Thomas Stammers, 'The Faubourg Saint-Antoine and the French Revolution of 1789' (BA dissertation, University of Cambridge, 2004).

[43] *Journalism*, IX, 88. See esp Vanessa Schwartz, 'Public Visits to the Morgue on the Thomas Cook Itinerary', in *idem, Spectacular Realities*, 45–88. (For comparisons with shopping, see 59.)

[44] In the notes of *ATOTC*, Richard Maxwell states that originally Dickens placed Darnay in the prison in the Luxembourg palace, only later relocating him to La Force, where particularly gruesome massacres took place in September 1792 (*ATOTC*, 476). Compelling also is the fact that unlike the Luxembourg, La Force is on the very edge of the Faubourg Saint-Antoine. Prisoners sentenced to death by the Revolutionary Tribunal were transferred to the Conciergerie prison on the Ile de la Cité.

On one occasion in the 'dismal' Morgue, 'looking mortally ashamed of itself and supremely wicked', he was struck by the corpse of an old man – 'a body horribly mutilated with a musket-ball in the head and afterwards drowned' (*Journalism*, IV, 220; *Letters*, VI, 120). His experience of witnessing this horror, he recounted, 'looking at something which could not return a look', was 'like looking at a waxwork without a catalogue and not knowing what to make of it' (*Journalism*, IV, 223). And Dickens knew all about waxworks. He was as keen on the lifeless and hopefully lifelike figures of the famous waxworks established in 1835 by Madame Tussaud at London's Baker Street Bazaar as he was as of the Parisian Morgue. As we are talking of French crossings and second identities let us remind ourselves that the woman known to the English as Madame Tussaud was Marie Grosholtz, heir, mentee and alleged niece of the great Parisian waxworks impresario, Curtius (whose pre-revolutionary establishment had been, incidentally, on the Boulevard du Temple).[45] On decamping to England under Napoleon's Consulate, she brought with her a grisly legacy – the death-masks of the famous revolutionary figures, Marie-Antoinette, Marat and Robespierre among them, which she had made at the height of the Terror. From 1846, these and other vestiges of revolutionary violence were the object of a ghoulish *mise-en-scène* in the so-called and still visitable 'Chamber of Horrors'. They included a waxwork image of one of the seven prisoners in the Bastille released on 14 July 1789 – an image which seems clearly to have been in Dickens's head as he was recounting that episode.[46]

As was the case with the Morgue corpses, Dickens found the spectacle of the waxworks unsettling, since he felt he was 'looking at something which could not return a look' (*Journalism*, IV, 223). That vacant, unengaged stare is a familiar one in *A Tale of Two Cities*. It is the 'watchful eye that seldom seemed to look at anything', the eye in fact of the sinister Madame Defarge before the Terror who 'leaned against the doorpost knitting and saw nothing', but who marked all down for the revolutionary reckoning when vacant eyes would become those of an avenging 'tigress' (*ATOTC*, 35, 52, 375). Dickens was beset by the horrible anxiety that such apparently lifeless simulacra on view at the Morgue or waxworks might reinvigorate themselves and come menacingly to life. And coming to life is, of course, one of *A Tale of Two Cities*'s great themes – as in Manette's 'return to life' from the Bastille, or in the grave-digging 'resurrectionist' Jerry Cruncher. Indeed Dickens even once jocularly referred to himself as a Cruncher-like 'resurrectionist'.[47]

[45] Pam Pilbeam, *Madame Tussaud and the History of Waxworks* (2003).

[46] This is discussed in Keith Baker, 'A Genealogy of Dr Manette', in *Charles Dickens and the French Revolution*, ed. Jones *et al.*, 64–74.

[47] See below, pp. 1–39. A. D. Hutter, 'The Novelist as Resurrectionist', *Dickens Studies Annual*, 12 (1983), 23. According to anecdote, the young Dickens, when asked to provide

Where else did Dickens have his imagination shaken and stirred in ways that allowed him to make of a Faubourg Saint-Antoine that he seems never once to have visited a place so vividly memorable? After reading, attendance at the Morgue and visits to the waxworks, the fourth source of Dickens's inspiration is the Parisian theatre. As the literary critic Annie Sadrin has noted, there is a pervasive theatricality about every aspect of the novel – a theatricality of cruelty, vengeance, rage, desire.[48] Dickens owned up this influence pretty directly: the plot of *A Tale of Two Cities* was 'a story in two periods, with a lapse of time in between, like a French drama'. By 'French drama', of course, Dickens meant the melodramas which were launched into popularity by the French Revolution in fact, and which were most typically played in the theatres which ran along the Boulevard du Temple, the 'Boulevard of Crime' that we have already evoked, and that we know that Dickens frequently attended.[49] Though Dickens's comments on theatre performances are rather summary, we can identify specific examples to support the generic claim of influence. One will have to suffice.

In January 1847 Dickens wrote from Paris to a correspondent,

> There is a melodrama called *The French Revolution* now playing at the Cirque in the first act of which there is the most tremendous representation of a people than can well be imagined. There are wonderful battles and so forth in the piece, but there is a power and massiveness in the Mob which is positively awful. (*Letters*, V, 19–20)

The play in question had been written by one Fabrice Labrousse, a prolific author in the genre; and it was played by the famous Franconi troupe at the Cirque-Olympique theatre, itself located on the Boulevard du Crime. The troupe specialised in epic equestrian shows called hippodramas which combined a melodramatic plot with spectacular special effects. Dickens, a keen circus fan, heartily loved the genre. *Galignani's Messenger*, the English-language Paris newspaper for the expatriate community, described the production of *La Révolution française* as 'seasoned with guns, trumpets and drums' and recommended it as suitable for what it called 'children of larger growth' (*Letters*, V, 14n).[50] This latter category evidently included

---

a calling-card, wrote out 'CHARLES DICKENS. Resurrectionist. In search of a subject'. *Ibid.*, 32n.
   [48] Annie Sadrin, *Dickens ou le roman-théâtre* (Paris, 1992), esp. 198–9.
   [49] F. Kaplan, ed., *Charles Dickens's Book of Memoranda* (New York, 1981), 1855, no. 21 (no pagination); Peter Brooks, *The Melodramatic Imagination. Balzac, Henry James, Melodrama and the Mode of Excess* (1876), is the classic study.
   [50] François Labrousse and Julien de Mallian, *La Révolution française* (Paris, 1847). Labrousse's numerous other dramas included *La Bastille* (1837). This production was the last to be played at the Cirque Olympe with both a stage and a ring – thereafter the ring was removed and additional seating installed. This must have made the production particularly impressive. A. H. Saxon, *Enter Foot and Horse. A History of the Hippodrama in England and France* (1968), 131. Franconi was a favourite of Dickens: see *Letters*, e.g. VI, 117, VII, 541, VIII, 95. For this world more generally, see Caroline Hodack, 'Du théâtre équestre au cirque: commercialisation

Charles Dickens. A letter that Dickens wrote to Lady Blessington provided more detail.

> At the Cirque there is now a new showpiece called the French Revolution in which there is a representation of the National Convention and a series of battles (fought by some 500 people who look like fifty thousand) that are wonderful in their extraordinary vigour and truth. (*Letters*, V, 14)

Let us now switch to the description in *A Tale of Two Cities*, some twelve years later, of the revolutionary dance, the Carmagnole, which represents the Parisian mob at its most sanguinary and irrational. 'There could not be fewer than 500 people', the novel recounts, 'and they were dancing like 5,000 demons' (*ATOTC*, 288). To Lady Blessington he had said '500 people [who look like] 50,000'. This seems to me a very striking resemblance. And, taken with the other evidence I have supplied, it suggests that in his depiction of the Paris mob and the revolutionary Faubourg Saint-Antoine, Dickens, drawing little on first-hand experience, in essence imagined the French Revolutionary Terror not only in his library, but also at the Morgue, in Madame Tussauds waxworks, in the theatre and at the circus.[51]

There is, however, one final source of inspiration for Dickens's Faubourg Saint-Antoine that cries out for inclusion. For that he did not have to cross the Channel himself, since it was altogether closer to home. It was the poorer neighbourhoods and the destitute classes of his own metropolis. I have suggested a stark contrast between Dickens's own 'spatial practice' in regard to Paris and the 'representational space' portrayed in his novel. Yet when we look at his relationship with London, there is a much tighter fit between personal psycho-geography and fictional representation. Dickens knew the London that was the setting for most of his novels, as one friend put it, 'from Bow to Brentford'. His passion for London walks – which grew in length from five to ten miles a day towards twenty miles or more – and also for night walking made him someone who, he later boasted, knew London 'better than any one other man of all its million'. London walking was an ontological necessity for Dickens: 'If I couldn't walk fast and far I should just explode and perish', he noted.[52] Dickens drew heavily on this rich assembled knowledge in his writings. His London – on the page and in soon-established tourist trails – left few stones unturned.

---

des loisirs et théâtralisation de l'histoire en France et en Angleterre, c. 1760–c.1860' (doctoral thesis, École des hautes études en sciences sociales, 2004).

[51] The metaphorical transmutation of wine into blood in the famous opening scene in the novel is recalled by Dickens's excited record of a melodrama in which the famous Lemaître, playing a murderer, was transfixed by the thought that his glass of wine contained blood (*Letters*, VIII, 536).

[52] Slater, *Charles Dickens*, 28; M. Andrews, *Charles Dickens and his Performing Selves* (Oxford, 2006), 117; R. Bodenheimer, *Knowing Dickens* (Ithaca, NY, 2007), 178ff; and generally Jeremy Tambling, *Going Astray. Dickens and London* (2009).

The London that Dickens knew so well and represented so capaciously in his writings often, however, disappointed him and caused him to vent his spleen. London was, he grumbled in 1851, 'a vile place. I have never taken to it since I lived abroad. Whenever I come back from the country now and see that great heavy canopy lowering over the housetops I wonder what on earth I do there except on obligation' (*Letters*, VI, 287). He deplored 'the shabbiness of our English capital'. It was 'hideous to behold', its ugliness 'quite astonishing'.[53]

> The meanness of Regent Street set against the great line of the Boulevards in Paris is as striking as the abortive ugliness of Trafalgar Square set against the gallant beauty of the Place de la Concorde . . . No Englishmen knows what gaslight is, until he sees the Rue de Rivoli and the Palais Royal after dark. (*Journalism*, IV, 279)

Whatever he made of revolutionary Paris, the comparison between contemporary London and contemporary Paris invariably – as here – went in Paris's favour. The 'astounding new works, doing or done' which, as we have seen, bowled him over in Paris were conspicuous by their absence in the capital of his own country. Dickens was struck, and indeed infuriated, by the contrast between his native London and Paris 'the beautiful city' that Sydney Carton foresaw and that he, Dickens, experienced at first hand. An article he commissioned for his periodical *Household Words* in 1855 made the contrast even more direct:

> The citizens of London and the citizens of Paris can be compared and contrasted in almost the same terms as the cities themselves. [T]he one [is] sombre, heavy, large, continually expanding, seldom changing; the other bright, compact, open, lively and ever improving. The pace of London improvement is that of the overgrown alderman or of his beloved turtle . . . While the wise men of the East have been haggling about one little piece of open ground at the base of St Paul's cathedral, a considerable portion of the capital of the great French empire has been not only razed but rebuilt.[54]

A Tale of Two Cities presents a pre-Haussmannian Paris of the 1790s clogged up in the 'cold, dirt, sickness, ignorance and want' that were the tutelary deities of the Faubourg Saint-Antoine. Yet Dickens found these urban features literally unlocatable in Haussmann's efficient, centralised, 'brilliant city' of the 1850s and 1860s. In that sense maybe *A Tale of Two Cities* is a tale of two chronologically distinct Parises. Yet much more evidently, those grim features of the plebeian urban landscape were traceable in Dickens's imagination to London's East End, a terrain more than familiar to him through his night walks and restless perambulations. Here lurked an old-style poverty, kept in place by an inert local government system which blocked change in all its forms. Furthermore, although Dickens never saw a Parisian crowd with its anger roused, he had a close and sometimes uncomfortable knowledge of English collective

---

[53] Slater, *Charles Dickens*, 400.
[54] 'Paris Improved', *Household Words*, Nov. 1855, 361.

violence with crowds acting 'like herds of swine' (*Journalism*, II, 28).[55] It was in London, not Paris that he witnessed public executions alongside its customary rough, plebeian audience. The tumbrils he had seen came out of the Old Bailey courtyard not the Conciergerie prison. And it was Newgate gaol that he knew from personal experience, not the La Force prison on the edge of the Faubourg Saint-Antoine, where Charles Darnay was imprisoned; La Force had been closed down before Dickens arrived in Paris – its demolition began in 1845.

I am arguing that Dickens's depiction of the Parisian mob and revolutionary collective violence of the 1790s was pieced together vicariously and from Anglo-French sources. Among them, in fact, one should also note that his earlier work. *Barnaby Rudge*, his other great historical novel, which he published in 1841 – three years before his Parisian *coup de foudre* – was set in London in the 1780s. Its centre-piece is a long, vivid description of the same Gordon Riots that had put the fear of God into Louis-Sébastien Mercier – who had actually witnessed them at first hand, and who felt thereafter that Parisian crowds were tame and anaemic in comparison.[56] If one is looking for Dickensian descriptions of blood-curdlingly violent, fleetingly psychopathic, loomingly monstrous renditions of mob violence, one looks in fact more to *Barnaby Rudge* than to *A Tale of Two Cities*. One looks in other words – as Dickens did, as Mercier had done – less towards Paris, and more towards London. To update my argument: Charles Dickens imagined the Terror in his library, at the Morgue, in Madame Tussauds, in the theatre and at the circus, yes: and also while walking the dark, dangerous streets of London.

I am thus rejecting the widespread notion of *A Tale of Two Cities* as a comfortable Victorian political parable contrasting English stability with French turbulence. For Dickens, mob violence and the threat from below did not stop at Dover. Indeed there was a danger that it was there that they might start. Whereas for Dickens spectacular urban improvement was attentuating the Parisian revolutionary tradition, in London complacency and insouciance towards the social question among an Ancien Régime-style ruling class impervious to the need for reform was, he feared, fertile soil for mob violence. Popular violence was not at all un-English in scope. Indeed in the Gordon Riots, London had already given a master-class in it, which pre-dated the French Revolution. And for Dickens that English past was still potentially present. His image of revolutionary Paris in the 1790s stands proxy for the nightmare vision of a future London gripped by popular violence triggered by ruling-class complacency and heartlessness. His depiction of the English popular classes is not at all of the people

[55] Cited in Slater, *Charles Dickens*, 55.
[56] *Parallèle de Paris et de Londres. Un inédit de Louis-Sébastien Mercier*, ed. Claude Bruneteau and Bernard Cottret (Paris, 1982), 10–12.

set in Victorian aspic or freeze-dried into constitutional deference. On the contrary, the people for Dickens was formed in the wax of his own nightmarish imagination on his visits to the Morgue and to Madame Tussauds – fears of the lifelike springing to life, of the mortiferous made animate, of fantasy turned scarily into reality, of the English mob, in sum, to use the language of our novel, resurrected and rudely returned to life.

In recent years it has become common in France to refer to certain disputes and issues as 'franco-français' – 'Franco-French' thus denoting something that is essentially for internal consumption and which does not lend itself well to foreign export. I suppose I have been proposing a reading of *A Tale of Two Cities* which is essentially – by parallel – 'Anglo-English'. 'Crush humanity out of shape . . . under similar hammers and it will twist itself into the same tortured forms' (*ATOTC*, 385). This was the general moral which Dickens implanted in his novel, and it was not addressed to the French: it was part of a very English debate in which Dickens felt he was striking a radical blow. In this particular tale of two cities, the Parisian setting of the novel is merely a theatrical backdrop to English action – quite literally so in some respects, as I have shown. This talismanic text of British chauvinistic nationalism was thus a wake-up call for social reform directed at the English upper classes.[57]

Given the domestic, 'Anglo-English' orientation of the novel, one begins to understand why Dickens imagined, even if only fleetingly, that it could be successfully adapted for Parisian theatre audiences. He may even have thought that his visceral attack on the English crowd in *Barnaby Rudge* had proofed him against the charge that in attacking the *sans-culottes* he was being somehow anti-French. In his own eyes, his beef was with the crowd *sui generis*, and not specifically with the French crowd.[58] As things turned out, French readers have quite understandably and probably irreparably failed to warm to a novel whose vision of the city they had, however, influenced. It may have been of some comfort to French readers to think they were not the target of attack, but only small comfort if they realised that they were ammunition in someone else's battle. The French consequently took their cues (for once) from the English, despising as a reactionary and Francophobic text what English audiences prized as a national icon.

Running against the grain of Anglo-French unanimity over the values incarnated by the novel, I have tried to suggest, is the *l'histoire croisée* of Charles Dickens himself. Dickens's acquaintance with France

---

[57] This was especially the case in that at this time Dickens was highly suspicious of Napoleon III's aggressive foreign policy. See J. P. Parry, 'The Impact of Napoleon III on British Politics, 1851–80', *Transactions of the Royal Historical Society*, 11 (2001), 147–75.

[58] This was highlighted for me by Peter Mandler.

changed him. The idea that the novelist remained always and forever 'fundamentally' English ignores the extent to which his outlook was transformed by his immersion in French cultural and political life and Paris's metropolitan sociability. The Paris that Dickens brought back in his suitcase and in his head was not the revolutionary Paris seemingly depicted in his novel (for crowd violence was something he had learned from his earliest years in London). Rather it was the vision of a Haussmannian city whose pleasures he relished and which offered a way ahead from the drably menacing pre-modernity of the English capital.

By the same token, the future which Dickens imagined was one in which England and France's differences were merged rather than accentuated. The hints are pretty obvious if we care to take them. The principal families in the novel, Dickens's 'small creatures' in this universalist morality tale, share an everyman character emblazoned in their names which have a symptomatically hybridic form. There are the Evrémondes (English 'every' plus a trace of the French 'tout le monde') and the Manettes (English root, French diminutive suffix – 'little men' or indeed 'small creatures'). Furthermore, the future that Dickens imagines is one of international harmony or even of transnational hybridity: Lucy Manette and Charles Darnay's little daughter is depicted 'dressing a doll at her mother's footstool, chatter[ing] in the tongues of the Two Cities that were blended in her life' (*ATOTC*, 219) – as they were blended, of course, in the *histoire croisée* that was the life of Charles Dickens.

APPENDIX: DICKENS'S PARIS

Dates are only assigned when they are known, a number of references in Dickens's journalism refer to visits without dates and often at an earlier time.

PLACES OF RESIDENCE (all on Right Bank)

Rented rooms:
48 Rue de Courcelles: *Letters*, IV, 666ff (1846)
49 Champs-Élysées: *Letters*, VII, 719ff (1855)
Hotels:
Brighton: *Letters*, IV, 666 (1846)
Bristol (Place Vendôme): *Letters*, IV, 230 (1844)
Helder (Rue du Helder): *Letters*, X, 178 (1862), XI, 89–90 (1865), XII, 124ff (1868)
Londres (Rue Castiglione): *Letters*, VII, 162 (1855)
Meurice (Rue Saint-Honoré): *Letters*, IV, 228 (1844), V, 1 (1847)
Windsor (Rue de Rivoli): *Letters*, VI, 115 (1851)

THEATRES

Boulevard du Temple
    Ambigu: *Letters*, VII, 536 (1855), VIII, 11, 78, 82 (1856), XII, 703–4 (1865), *Journalism*, III, 359
    Cirque-Olympique: *Letters*, V, 14–15 (1847), V, 26 (1847), VII 540 (1855), *Journalism*, III, 359
    Folies Nouvelles: *Letters*, VII, 690 (1855), VIII, 28 (1856)
    Funambules: *Letters*, VI 120 (1850)
    Gaieté: *Letters*, VI, 289 (1851), VII 756 (1855)
    Lyrique: *Letters*, X, 163 (1862), 295 (1865), *Journalism*, III, 359
    Porte Saint-Martin: *Letters*, V, 14–15 (1847), VII, 540 (1855), VIII, 23, 28 (1856), *Journalism*, III, 359
    Variétés: *Letters*, V, 14–15 (1847), VIII, 17 (1856), *Journalism*, III, 359
    Vaudeville: *Journalism*, IV, 365
Cirque d'Été: *Letters*, VI, 116 (1850)
Comédie-Française: *Letters*, V, 14 15 (1847), VI, 540, 749, 756 (1855), VIII, 95 (1856)
Comédie-Italienne: *Letters*, IV, 238 (1847)
Gymnase: *Journalism*, III, 359
Odéon (Left Bank): *Letters*, IV, 138 (1844), VIII, 78, 82 (1856)
Opéra: *Letters*, XII, 703–4 (1868)
Opéra-Comique: *Letters*, VII, 540 (1855), *Journalism*, III, 359

CAFES AND RESTAURANTS

Bains Chinois: *Journalism*, III, 34–5
Café de Paris: *Letters*, IV 686 (1846), VII, 752 (1855), *Journalism*, III, 499
Café Véry: *Journalism*, III, 499
Café Voisin: *Letters*, X, 158 (1862)
Champeaux (Bourse): *Journalism*, III, 499
Maison Dorée ('Golden House'): *Journalism*, III, 499
Trois Frères (Provençaux): *Letters*, IV, 674, 686 (1846), V, 3 (1847), VI, 116 (1850), VII, 752 (1855), VIII, 95 (1856), *Journalism*, III, 499
Vaudeville: *Letters*, XII, 124 (1865)
Véfour: *Letters*, VII, 752, 756 (1855), *Journalism*, III, 499

MONUMENTS AND PUBLIC BUILDINGS

RIGHT BANK (WEST)
    Tuileries: *Journalism*, I, 322
    Place de la Concorde: *Letters*, VIII, 78 (1856)
    Champs-Élysées: *Journalism*, III, 499
    Universal Exposition (1855): *Letters*, VII, 535 (1855)
    Jardin d'Hiver: *Letters*, VIII, 28 (1856)
    British Embassy: *Letters*, V, 23 (1847), X, 178ff (1862)

Palais Royal: *Letters*, V, 14–15 (1847), V, 26 (1847), *Journalism*, III, 34–5
Bibliothèque Royale: *Letters*, V, 113 (1847)
Bourse: *Letters*, VIII, 94 (1856)

RIGHT BANK (EAST)
Bastille: *Letters*, VIII, 1
Hôtel de Ville: *Journalism*, IV, 224
Saint-Jacques de la Boucherie: *Journalism*, IV, 224
Boulevard Sebastopol: *Journalism*, IV, 225

RIGHT BANK (NORTH)
Porte Saint-Martin: *Journalism*, III, 359
Porte Saint-Denis: *Letters*, IV, 676 (1846)

ILE DE LA CITÉ
Notre Dame: *Journalism*, IV, 220
Hôtel-Dieu: *Letters*, V, 13 (1847)
Morgue (1): *Letters*, IV, 676 (1847), V, 13 (1847), VI, 120 (1850), *Journalism*, III, 93–4, 369ff, IV, 88ff, 220ff

LEFT BANK
Beaux-Arts: *Letters*, V, 26 (1847)
Conservatoire: *Letters*, V, 13 (1847)

OTHER LOCATIONS
9 Rue des Capucines : *Letters*, IV, 678
26 Rue Chaptal (Ari Scheffer's studio): *Letters*, VII, 758 (1855), VIII, 18 (1856)
Rue de Douai (home of Viardot): *Letters*, VIII, 33 (1856)
Rue Ville l-Évêque (D'Orsay's atelier): *Letters*, VI, 289 (1851)
Maison Victor Hugo (Place des Vosges): *Letters*, V, 15
Rue de Rivoli: VI, 115 (1851)
Barrière de l'Étoile: VIII, 11, 37 (1856), *Journalism*, III, 34–5

OUTSIDE PARIS
Poissy: *Letters*, VI, 267, 289 (1851), *Journalism*, I, 322
Saint-Cloud: *Letters*, V, 13 (1847)
Versailles: *Letters*, V, 13 (1847)
Fontainebleau: *Letters*, VI, 116 (1850)
Montmartre: *Letters*, VI, 267, 289 (1851), *Journalism*, I, 336
Grenelle, *Journalism*, I, 366.

Transactions of the RHS 20 (2010), pp. 27–55 © Royal Historical Society 2010
doi:10.1017/S0080440110000046

LIVING LIKE THE LAITY? THE NEGOTIATION OF RELIGIOUS STATUS IN THE CITIES OF LATE MEDIEVAL ITALY*

By Frances Andrews

READ 25 SEPTEMBER 2009

ABSTRACT. Framed by consideration of images of treasurers on the books of the treasury in thirteenth-century Siena, this article uses evidence for the employment of men of religion in city offices in central and northern Italy to show how religious status (treated as a subset of 'clerical culture') could become an important object of negotiation between city and churchmen, a tool in the repertoire of power relations. It focuses on the employment of men of religion as urban treasurers and takes Florence in the late thirteenth and early fourteenth centuries as a principal case study, but also touches on the other tasks assigned to men of religion and, very briefly, on evidence from other cities (Bologna, Brescia, Como, Milan, Padua, Perugia and Siena). It outlines some of the possible arguments deployed for this use of men of religion in order to demonstrate that religious status was, like gender, more contingent and fluid than the norm-based models often relied on as a shorthand by historians. Despite the powerful rhetoric of lay–clerical separation in this period, the engagement of men of religion in paid, term-bound urban offices inevitably brought them closer to living like the laity.

In the late 1250s, an anonymous Sienese painter produced a miniature of a now obscure monk, Ugo, from the major Cistercian abbey of San Galgano in southern Tuscany (Figure 1).[1] He is portrayed with his white habit and tonsure, sitting at a desk or *cathedra*, presenting an open book. It is the conventional pose known to art historians as the author-portrait,

---

* The research for this paper was generously funded by Villa I Tatti and the Arts and Humanities Research Council. Thanks are also due to numerous people who either heard or read earlier versions and offered precious criticisms: the valiant members of the St Andrews Institute of Mediaeval Studies 'in-progress' group (Ian Johnston, Chris Jones, Simon Maclean, James Palmer and Clive Sneddon), Louise Bourdua, George Dameron, David d'Avray, Trevor Dean, Katharine Park, Hamish Scott and the audience at the Royal Historical Society meeting who put up with some remarkable technical hitches. I am also very grateful to the postdoctoral fellow on the AHRC project Dr Agata Pincelli and to Drs Eleonora Rava and Sarah Tiboni.
[1] A. Canestrelli, *L'Abbazia di San Galgano* (Florence, 1896); Laura Neri, 'L'Abbazia di San Galgano e Siena (1181–1320). Per una storia dei rapporti fra i Cistercensi e la città' (MA thesis, Università di Siena, 1991/2).

Figure 1 Anonymous, Ugo, monk of San Galgano. Tavola di Biccherna, Siena, Archivio di Stato, 1 (July–December 1258), detail. Reproduced by permission of the Archive.

used to present an Evangelist, a scribe or perhaps a Master.[2] What makes this image unusual is that the book is not held open to reveal a biblical quote or an appropriate monastic text, but is furnished simply with dates: 'i(n) a(nno) d(omini) mcclviii mense iulii', confirming that this is not a book of the Bible or a monastic chronicle, nor even a text for classroom use. Instead, it is a representation of the author as treasurer (*camerarius*). Ugo's image has been painted on what was originally the wooden cover of one of the books of the Biccherna, the treasury of the commune of Siena, about sixteen miles across the hills from his remote, rural monastery. The dates on the open book, combined with what remains of the larger inscription framing his depiction, identify this as the communal account book for which he had been responsible in the second semester of 1258.[3]

[2] Don Denny, 'Author portrait', in *Grove Dictionary of Art*, ed. Jane Turner (34 vols., London and New York, 1996), I, 835–7. For images of Masters (though rather later), see, for example, R. Grandi, *Monumenti dei dottori e la scultura a Bologna (1267–1348)* (Bologna, 1982), 266 fig. 84, 351 fig. 188, 353 fig. 195, 358 fig. 213.

[3] Giorgia Corso, 'Siena Archivio di Stato, 1', in *Le Biccherne di Siena. Arte e finanza all'alba dell'economia moderna*, ed. Alessandro Tomei (Siena, 2002), 108–11. On the financial offices of Siena see William M. Bowsky, *The Finance of the Commune of Siena, 1287–1355* (Oxford, 1970).

If this image is unexpected, it is because the Cistercians, like most medieval monks professing the rule of Benedict, are conventionally defined in terms of their commitment to a life of chastity, obedience and personal poverty in a more or less inaccessible and enclosed monastic community. Most historians would acknowledge that this is shorthand for a more complex social reality, but one that is justified as a categorisation by the normative texts produced by the monks themselves.[4] In terms of such texts, Ugo must count as an anomaly. There is nothing in the rule of Benedict, or the constitutions used by the Cistercians, to indicate that its author expected his monks to serve as treasurers in a city such as Siena, one of the major centres of the Italian mercantile world; still less that they should be portrayed gripping a book of urban accounts. Nor is there any such indication in the various 'institutes' or customs adopted to supplement the succinct language of other monastic rules. Yet, though the form of this particular image is apparently unique, Ugo the monk-treasurer was by no means unusual as an *ante-litteram* public servant. He is just one of countless men of religion, most of them inevitably recorded in texts rather than visual images, on whom, from the middle of the thirteenth century, cities increasingly relied to fill key administrative and financial roles. The evidence for this phenomenon can be used to construct hypotheses about why the monk Ugo was to be found in this position, and some of these will be outlined below.[5] The main focus here will, however, be on the way in which it allows a more nuanced understanding of the varying expectations of clerical and, in particular,

[4] For example, C. H. Lawrence, *Medieval Monasticism: Forms of Religious Life in Western Europe in the Middle Ages*, 2nd edn (1989).

[5] Luigi Zanoni, *Gli Umiliati nei loro rapporti con l'eresia, l'industria della lana ed i comuni* (Milan, 1911); Norbert Kamp, *Istituzioni comunali in Viterbo nel medioevo: Consoli, Podestà, Balivi e Capitani nei secoli 12 e 13*, trans C. A. Agnesotti (Viterbo, 1963) see also (originally published as Norbert Kamp, 'Konsuln und Podestà, Balivus Communis und Volkskapitän in Viterbo im 12. und 13. Jahrhundert', in *Biblioteca degli Ardenti della città di Viterbo. Studi e ricerche nel 150° della fondazione*, ed. Augusto Pepponi (Viterbo, 1960), pp. 51–127); Bowsky, *Finance*, 7; Raoul Manselli, 'Gli Umiliati, lavoratori di lana', in *Produzione, commercio e consumo dei panni di lana (nei secoli xii–xviii)*, Atti della seconda settimana di studio, Prato, 1970, ed. M. Spallanzani (2 vols., Florence, 1974), II, 231–6; Richard C. Trexler, 'Honor among Thieves. The Trust Function of the Urban Clergy in the Florentine Republic', in *Essays Presented to Myron P. Gilmore*, ed. S. Bertelli and G. Ramakus (Florence, 1978), 317–34; Paolo Grillo, 'Cistercensi e società cittadina in età comunale: il monastero di Chiaravalle milanese fra impegno politico ed esperienze spirituali (1180–1276)', *Studi Storici*, 40 (1999), 357–94, esp. 386–391; *idem, Milano in età comunale (1183–1276). Istituzioni, società, economia* (Spoleto, 2001); and Paolo Pirillo, 'I Cistercensi e il comune di Firenze (secoli xiii–xiv)', *Studi storici*, 40 (1999), 395–405. Of these, only Trexler gave more than passing attention to the issue. See Frances Andrews, 'Monastic Observance and Communal Life: Siena and the Employment of Religious', in *Pope, Church and City. Essays in Honour of Brenda M. Bolton*, ed. Frances Andrews, Christoph Egger and Constance Rousseau (Leiden, 2004), 357–83, and most recently, Giovanna Casagrande, 'Religiosi a servizio del comune: Perugia secoli xiii–xiv', *Bollettino della deputazione di storia patria per l'Umbria*, 104/2 (2007), 253–83.

monastic behaviour in the late Middle Ages, the uses to which those expectations might be put and ways in which they could be negotiated.

Before pursuing this in detail, it is worth pausing both to underline the importance to contemporaries of such officials in the administration of public life, and to recall the growing emphasis on the separation of lay and clerical roles which the phenomenon described here would seem to defy. Both secular and ecclesiastical writers in the period point to the critical significance of government officials. Treatises on city government most often focused on the office of podestà, the chief magistrate and, at this date, still usually the head of communal government. They produced texts such as Orfino da Lodi's poem *De sapientia potestatis* (1245/6), or the anonymous *Oculus pastoralis* (c. 1222 or later), which also includes guidelines on the selection and training of officials.[6] The high expectations of men holding elected office in city governments at all levels (as in the Church) can, however, most succinctly be illustrated by reference to the widely circulated constitutions issued in November 1215 at the Fourth Lateran Council, staged in Rome by Pope Innocent III (1198–1215).[7] The third rubric, part of an attempt to engage the energies of secular authorities against heretics, placed the onus for action on 'secular powers, whatever *office* they may hold'.[8] To its recipients in the early thirteenth-century Italian cities, the generic term 'secular powers' might evoke an imperial presence (or absence), as also a podestà, elected members of an urban council or indeed a communal treasurer. The association is evident in the ensuing enumeration of penalties for those who listened to heretics or otherwise patronised them. Should they refuse to mend their ways within a year of excommunication, they were *ipso iure* rendered infamous, to be excluded from 'public offices or deliberations', and from 'the *election* of others to such offices'.[9]

The constitutions of Lateran IV thus epitomise the public, exemplary, role attributable to elected office holders by clerics. The same constitutions also include a rubric which implies that the canon lawyers drafting the text assumed that in writing about secular office they were describing laymen, or at least that clerical involvement in such offices should remain

[6] 'Oculus pastoralis pascens officia et continens radium dulcibus pomis suis', ed. Dora Franceschi, *Memorie dell'Accademia delle scienze di Torino. Classe di scienze morali, storiche e filologiche*, fourth series, 11 (1966). Also available as 'Oculus pastoralis sive libellus erudiens futurum rectorem populorum', ed. Ludovico Muratori in *Antiquitates Italicae medii aevi sive dissertationes*, IV (Milan, 1741), cols. 92–128; Orfino da Lodi, 'De regimine et sapientia potestatis', *Archivio storico lodigiano*, second series, 16 (1968), 3–115; and an earlier edition by A. Ceruti, *Miscellanea di storia italiana*, VII (Turin, 1869), 29–94.

[7] See, for example, *Constitutiones Concilii quarti Lateranensis una cum Commentariis glossatorum*, ed. Antonio Garcia y Garcia (Vatican City, 1981).

[8] 'Constitutiones Concilii Lateranensis IV', *Conciliorum oecumenicorum decreta*, ed. J. Alberigo, J. A. Dossetti, P. Joannou, C. Leonardi and P. Prodi (Bologna, 1973), 233.

[9] *Ibid.*

minimal. Reiterating and extending a provision of the Third Lateran Council (1179), which had advocated the disengagement of clergy from acting as proctors or otherwise engaging in the secular courts (quoting the Pauline epigram 'nemo militans deo implicat se negotiis secularibus', 2 Timothy 2, 4), the sixteenth constitution of Lateran IV prescribes that 'clerics shall not engage in secular offices or affairs, above all dishonest ones' ('clerici officia vel commercia saecularia non exerceant, maxime inhonesta').[10] This attempt at the 'clericalisation of the clergy' did not rule out the possibility of carrying out 'officia vel commercia honesta'.[11] But there can be little doubt about the thrust of what was intended: 'officia vel commercia saecularia' were to be the business of laymen, a clerical view of secular office also accepted by some lay legislators. It was used, for example, as a reason not to employ churchmen as royal bailiffs (*baiuli*) in the *Liber Augustalis* (1231), a book of laws issued for the kingdom of southern Italy in the name of Emperor Frederick II (and a collection which also began with anti-heretical legislation). The 1231 rubric simply asserts that the very fact of clerical status bars clergy from affairs of court and therefore from this role: 'clerici quoque quos a forensibus negotiis ipse ordo clericalis excludit'.[12]

The arguments for a separation of clerical and secular roles underlying the thinking of these lawmakers had acquired increasing currency in the aftermath of the eleventh-century reforms usually identified with Pope Gregory VII (1073–84), their most radical advocate. Both lay and ecclesiastical reformers had set out to distinguish clerical behaviour from that of the laity and to enhance clerical rather than secular authority in spiritual and political terms.[13] The nature and impact of this 'Gregorian' reform has, of course, been widely debated and, in a useful contribution to that discussion, Maureen Miller has argued that insufficient credit has

---

[10] *Ibid.*, 218, 243.

[11] See Michele Maccarrone, 'Cura animarum e parochialis sacerdos nelle costituzioni del IV concilio lateranense (1215). Applicazioni in Italia nel secolo XIII', in *Pievi e parrocchie in Italia nel basso medioevo (secc. XIII–XV). Atti del VI convegno di storia della Chiesa in Italia (Firenze 21–25 sett. 1981)* (2 vols., Rome, 1984), I, 81–195 143. Now also in *idem, Nuovi Studi su Innocenzo III*, ed. Roberto Lambertini (Rome, 1995), 271–367.

[12] *Die Konstitutionen Friedrichs II. für das Königreich Sizilien*, ed. W. Stürner, *Monumenta Germaniae Historica, Leges*, IV, *Constitutiones et acta publica imperatorum et regum*, II (Hannover, 1996), 240 (Book 1, titulus 72, rubric 1). This phrase is rendered as 'state business' in *The Liber Augustalis*, trans. James M. Powell (Syracuse, NY, 1971), 39, but the term 'forensis', linked to the market or forum, could also refer either to commercial or legal contexts. If the latter, it may be related to the problem of shedding blood, on which see below text at n. 57.

[13] For recent accounts see Colin Morris, *The Papal Monarchy: The Western Church from 1050 to 1250* (Oxford, 1991); Maureen Miller, *Power and the Holy in the Age of the Investiture Conflict: A Brief History with Documents* (Bedford, 2005); Kathleen Cushing, *Reform and the Papacy in the Eleventh Century: Spirituality and Social Change* (Manchester and New York, 2005).

been given to the redefinition of clerical mindsets and behaviour in the wake of reform. Positing that 'religion makes a difference', or, at least, more of a difference than usually acknowledged, she draws on the material culture of bishops – in particular the building and decoration of their halls – to underline the divergence.[14] The enforcement of changes such as clerical celibacy was, as she remarks, never complete, but 'institutional pressure, particularly through the training of clerics, was strong enough to inculcate different patterns of thought and behavior'.[15] At the same time, the laity expected their clergy to be different, to be held to higher standards of behaviour, not to 'live like lay people'.[16] Miller also very acutely observes that as well as race, ethnicity and gender, common subjects for the historical analysis of difference, 'religion can share the defining characteristics that Joan Scott once set out for gender as an analytical category'. In other words, religion may be a '"constitutive element of social relations based on perceived differences" and a "primary way of signifying power relations"'.[17] She concludes that the clergy were different from the laity, and that 'understanding these differences is important because power was at stake'.[18]

Miller's focus was the diocesan bishop and her primary aim was to show that clergy and laity were divided by material culture, not just a clerical mindset, but her arguments about divergence might be expected to resonate all the more powerfully if we turn to the sort of monastic figure represented by Ugo of San Galgano. Monks were committed to a rule of life centred on prayer: to state the obvious, they were regulars because they followed a rule. In their hairstyles, their celibacy, their routines, they were (or were supposed to be) the antithesis of male secular culture. This need not, despite the legislation noted above, exclude them from economic activity. By the early thirteenth century the Cistercians, for example, were already managing huge estates and had evolved into famously efficient entrepreneurs.[19] But the ideal purpose of their lives and these communities remained the praise of God. Their economic activity was, broadly conceived, directed at the well-being of their own communities: if they held offices it was as a cellarer or infirmarer, prior

[14] Maureen Miller, 'Religion Makes a Difference: Clerical and Lay Cultures in the Courts of Northern Italy, 1000–1300', *American Historical Review*, 105 (2000), 1095–130.
[15] *Ibid.*, 1099.
[16] *Ibid.*, 1098–9.
[17] Cited *ibid.*, 1097.
[18] *Ibid.*, 1096.
[19] See Constance H. Berman, *Medieval Agriculture, the Southern French Countryside and the Early Cistercians: A Study of Forty-three Monasteries* (Philadelphia, 1986); Constance B. Bouchard, *Holy Entrepreneurs. Cistercians, Knights and Economic Exchange in Twelfth-Century Burgundy* (Ithaca, NY, 1991); Reinhard Schneider, *Vom Klosterhaushalt zum Stadt- und Staatshaushalt. Der zisterziensische Beitrag* (Stuttgart, 1994).

or abbot. And, indeed, there is currently no evidence that in November 1215, when the constitutions were read out at the spectacular climax of the Lateran Council, either Cistercians or other professed religious of whatever status were assuming elected or paid offices in the Italian cities. At all levels such positions seem to have been held by laymen, elected or appointed by urban councils protective of their autonomy from imperial and ecclesiastical power, and often men of substance, since the poor were expected to be more susceptible to temptation.[20] This exclusion of the clergy is, somewhat paradoxically, both what medieval religious reformers probably desired and what modern historians, at least since the work of Jakob Burckhardt, might have expected of the political and social world that generated the Italian Renaissance: a world of growing lay confidence and emergent secularism, with churchmen gradually disappearing from positions of temporal authority or responsibility.[21] Within a few years, however, the situation began to transform.

Some of the earliest known cases of men of religion employed as salaried urban officials were lay penitents and members of the order of the Humiliati.[22] Thus for example, in the northern lakeside town of Como the two 'religiosi et honesti viri in religione comorantes' to be employed as 'massari' with oversight of the communal treasury seem to have been Humiliati tertiaries.[23] In numerous cities, however (though not Como), they were soon joined, and in several cases superseded, by Cistercians like Ugo of San Galgano, as well as, much less systematically, by other monastics bound by profession to a rule.[24]

From the end of the 1250s men of religion like Ugo were thus to be found holding a multiplicity of paid, term-bound offices in urban governments in ever-increasing numbers across central and northern Italy. Alongside tertiaries, lay penitents and *conversi* (in this case lay religious belonging to Cistercian houses), they served in positions previously reserved to the laity,

[20] For early examples of lay treasurers see Andrea Castagnetti, *Mercanti, società e politica nella Marca Veronese-Trevigiana (secoli XI–XIV)* (Verona, 1990), 49, 50, 52 and, for a man of substance, Roberta Mucciarelli, *I Tolomei Banchieri di Siena. La parabola di un casato nel xiii e xiv secolo* (Siena, 1995), 41; On the need for 'substance', see 'Oculus pastoralis', ed. Muratori, col. 102.

[21] Jakob Burckhardt, *Die Kultur der Renaissance in Italien*, first published 1860 and many times translated and reprinted. It should be noted that Burckhardt's views have long been challenged. See for example, Charles Dejob, *La foi religieuse en Italie au quatorzième siècle* (Paris, 1906).

[22] For the tri-partite structure of the Humiliati, see Frances Andrews, *The Early Humiliati* (Cambridge 1999), 99–135, 256 (Appendix 1, 7–9).

[23] 'Liber statutorum Consulum Cumanorum', ed. A. Ceruti, *Historia Patriae Monumenta*, XVI, Leges municipales II/1 (Turin, 1876), c. 103. Mistakenly dated to the 1220s in Zanoni, *Gli Umiliati*, 227.

[24] For a first analysis of the Sienese material, see Andrews, 'Monastic Observance', 357–83.

sometimes alone, sometimes sharing their tasks with those same laymen. In serving as a treasurer in Siena, for example, Ugo worked alongside a whole team of scribes and messengers and, in particular, four laymen, known as *provisores*, who acted as general overseers of the accounts and were chosen, like the treasurer, to hold office for fixed terms. And men like Ugo were to return to office again and again, in many cases over several decades, even, in a few, over centuries.[25]

As already indicated, there is abundant evidence for this practice of employing men of religion outside the Church. It survives not only in the rubrics of urban legislation like that of Como, but also in the (much less common) minutes recording the debates and decisions of urban council meetings. The men employed also left behind ever-increasing numbers of books of accounts and, in one case at least, to which we will return, their activities are recorded in a concession granted by an urban to a monastic community.[26] Although typically incomplete, when brought together this material exposes the different ways in which religious status might be envisaged and exploited in the late medieval urban Italian world. It thus allows an alternative approach to the divergence of lay and clerical behaviours and mindsets discussed by Miller. It suggests that religious status (treated as a subset of 'clerical culture') could become an important object of negotiation between city and churchmen, a tool in the repertoire of power relations and, it will be argued, more contingent and fluid than the norm-based models with which we are more usually resigned to working.

This discussion concentrates on the role of treasurers, perhaps the key administrative figures after the podestà. Their relative importance is reflected in the usual location of rubrics concerning them, in the first book or 'distinction' of statute compilations, immediately following those concerning the podestà. The focus here is also intended to highlight what is perhaps the least likely role for professed religious in the age of Francis of Assisi (d. 1226), whose horror of coins was to be profoundly influential, as well as increasingly controversial.[27] But it should be borne in mind that the figure of treasurer also stands for a still more complex reality. Men of religion could be found holding a wide range of different administrative and supervisory roles in the late medieval Italian cities. They were employed to look after the lion kept as a symbol by Florence

[25] For fifteenth-century examples: Siena, Archivio di Stato (hereafter ASSi), Concistoro 2174, 29 Dec. 1412; Florence, Archivio di Stato (hereafter ASFi), Libri Fabarum, 57, fo. 91r (17 Aug. 1436).
[26] See below text at n. 49.
[27] See Lester K. Little, *Religious Poverty and the Profit Economy in Medieval Europe* (Ithaca, NY, 1978); David Burr, *The Spiritual Franciscans. From Protest to Persecution in the Century after St Francis* (University Park, PA., 2001); Giacomo Todeschini, *Ricchezza francescana. Dalla povertà volontaria alla società di mercato* (Bologna, 2004).

and, more prosaically, they manned tolls, served as scrutineers in elections, as ambassadors and messengers on behalf of governments or overseers for public building works. In numerous cities the face of administration must often have been a religious one.

The present paper sets out a number of case studies, prioritising the evidence for communal treasurers in the thirteenth- and early fourteenth-century city of Florence and a few of her Tuscan neighbours, where the surviving sources are particularly extensive. It then briefly broadens the discussion to sample cases from other cities, before seeking to draw these different elements together to a conclusion.

Florence in the thirteenth and early fourteenth centuries

From the middle of the thirteenth century, monastic treasurers in the commune of Florence were generally recruited either from among the Humiliati of Ognissanti or from the Cistercians of San Salvatore di Settimo. The Humiliati, a daughter house of San Michele in Alessandria (Piedmont), had first settled at San Donato in September 1239, but in 1251 moved to a larger church, which became Ognissanti, within the city but outside the twelfth-century circuit of walls.[28] The monks at Settimo on the other hand, who replaced a Benedictine community, were a daughter house of San Galgano, established in June 1236 in the Arno valley ten miles down river from Florence, and were soon employed to administer the estates of the bishop, Ardingo, who had been instrumental in bringing both orders to his diocese.[29]

The first evidence of the use of these men as communal treasurers coincides with the rise of the new men of the *primo popolo* (1250–60), mostly non-noble guild members, who were at this date (but by no means always) aligned with anti-imperial, pro-papal politics ('Guelf' in Florentine politics and beyond).[30] The choice of monastics as holders of the communal purse strings may in this instance have had something to do with a relative lack of skills: at this early date in the history of the Florentine *popolo*, monks perhaps had greater administrative experience than their lay counterparts. But the *popolo* rose to power in a reaction against the

---

[28] See Anna Benvenuti Papi, 'Vangelo e tiratoi. Gli umiliati ed il loro insediamento fiorentino', in *La 'Madonna d'Ognissanti' di Giotto restaurata* (Florence, 1992), 75–84, at 78; George W. Dameron, *Episcopal Power and Florentine Society 1000–1320* (Cambridge MA, 1991), 129. Andrews, *Humiliati*, 143, 269 (Appendix I *54).

[29] Philip Jones, 'Le finanze della badia cistercense di Settimo nel secolo XIV', *Rivista di storia della chiesa in Italia*, 10 (1956), 90–122; Pirillo, 'I Cistercensi', 395; on the financial expertise of the Cistercians see Schneider, *Klosterhaushalt*, 96–138.

[30] See Daniela De Rosa, *Alle origini della repubblica fiorentina: dai consoli al 'primo popolo' (1172–1260)* (Florence, 1995), and John M. Najemy, *A History of Florence 1200–1575* (Oxford, 2006), 68. On the terminology and implications of 'Guelf' and 'Ghibelline' see now *Guelfi e Ghibellini nell'Italia del Rinascimento*, ed. Marco Gentile (Rome, 2005).

domination of elite factions, so it might be expected that a perception of monastics as detached from the manoeuvrings of those elites played an equally important role.

In the following century the Florentine chronicler Giovanni Villani (d. 1348), seems to have accepted a correlation of this arrangement with contemporary political imperatives.[31] He reports on the re-configuring of the commune and *popolo* by the elite faction of the Guelfs after the arrival in the city in 1267 of the papally appointed *servator pacis*, Charles of Anjou, and the expulsion of the 'Ghibellines' (who had in turn replaced the *primo popolo* in 1260, having defeated them in battle at Montaperti).[32] Villani's account of this realignment closes with a brief note, adding that the Guelfs appointed religious by turn from the houses of Settimo and Ognissanti as treasurers for six-month terms: 'In questo modo s'ordinò lo stato e corso del Comune e del popolo di Firenze alla tornata de' Guelfi; e camerlenghi della pecunia fecioni religiosi di Settimo e d'Ognesanti di sei in sei mesi.'[33]

Like modern historians, Villani viewed the past of his city with the troublesome benefit of retrospection, though undoubtedly with more information at his disposal than can now be obtained. It is not immediately obvious why he associated this detail about monastic treasurers with the arrival of the Angevins and the shift to government by the elite faction of the Guelfs. It may simply be that he neither knew nor cared when the practice started, or saw the changes of 1267 as a move away from political neutrality. Or perhaps Villani never saw it as a question of impartiality. Whereas the documented origins of the practice – sometime in the mid-1250s – might suggest either a lack of expertise among the laymen of the *popolo* or a link with their attempts to establish non-elite government, Villani's account tends to confirm that at least by the time he was writing, there was an accepted nexus between the faction of the Guelfs and monastic treasurers.

Whatever its origins, Villani's retrospective association of religious working in the communal treasury with Guelf political interests in Florence (and in turn with the *popolo*) can also be constructed directly from thirteenth-century evidence. From 1278, for example, in apparently unforced partnership with the *Pars Guelfa*, the Humiliati undertook a major development project in the area around their convent, which saw the construction of a new borgo and the expansion of the *Pratum*

---

[31] On Villani see F. Ragone, *Giovanni Villani e i suoi continuatori. La scrittura delle cronache a Firenze nel Trecento* (Rome, 1998).

[32] See Jean Dunbabin, *Charles I of Anjou. Power, Kingship and Statemaking in Thirteenth-Century Europe* (London and New York, 1998), 83–6, 135.

[33] Giovanni Villani, *Nuova Cronica*, ed. Giuseppe Porta (3 vols., Parma 1990–1), I, 439–40 (Book 8, cap. 16).

comunis (communal open ground), also to be known as the *Pratum Omniumsanctorum*.[34] The Cistercians too obtained land in the city which, over the following decades, they developed into a substantial residential district.[35]

These associations with the elite faction were also, inevitably, enacted in the councils of government. In May 1289, for example, twenty-two years after the return of the *popolo*, Angelo, a monk of Settimo ('honestus vir dominus dompnus Angelus de septimo cisterciensis ordinis'), treasurer of the commune, made a speech before the Council of the *popolo*. He requested authority to spend up to 1,200 gold florins on welcoming to the city the Angevin Charles II of Sicily (who had been released from Aragonese imprisonment in October of the previous year). The request was approved by a vote of 280 to 35.[36] Charles appears only to have come to Florence in the mid-1290s, but it seems unarguable that Angelo, like other monastic spokesmen in such circumstances, was hereby identified with both the government and the Angevin/Guelf faction that Charles represented.[37]

Numerous monastics had held office as treasurers in Florence by this date, but there is also continuing evidence for laymen in the role. In February 1289 for example, three months before Angelo's speech, a layman, Ghinus Davançi, *camerarius comunis florentie*, presented a petition to the government on behalf of himself and his associates in the office of the treasury.[38] The autumn of that year then witnessed a major innovation, which amounted to an increased laicisation of the role. Provisions issued in September laid down that there were now to be four men appointed as treasurers, only one of whom was to be a religious, alternating 'as is the custom, from the usual religious [houses]'. The three laymen chosen were to be experienced seculars from the guilds of Florence, of proven integrity and fairness (literally 'law worthiness').[39] The text setting out

---

34 Guido Pampaloni, *Firenze al tempo di Dante. Documenti sull'urbanistica fiorentina* (Rome, 1973), 100–4, 133, 156, 163–4; Franek Snzura, *L'espansione urbana di Firenze nel Dugento* (Florence, 1975), 80–2; Paula Spilner "'Ut civitas amplietur". Studies in Florentine Urban Development 1282–1400' (Ph.D. thesis, Columbia University, 1987), 30–2, 40.

35 Spilner, "'Ut civitas amplietur"', 275–93, 350–6, 520–63 (appendices V–VII).

36 ASFi, Provvisioni, Registri, 1, fo. 204.

37 For other examples see ASFi, Provvisioni, Registri, 1, fos. 84–5 (14 Jan 1286); *Consigli della Repubblica Fiorentina*, I, ed. Bernardino Barbadoro, Atti delle Assemblee Costituzionali Italiane dal medio evo al 1831, serie terza, Parlamenti e Consigli Maggiori dei Comuni Italiani, sezione quarta: Consigli della Repubblica Fiorentina (Bologna, 1921, reprinted 1971), part 1, 18–19 (11 July 1301); and, for Siena, William M. Bowsky, 'The Anatomy of Rebellion in Fourteenth-Century Siena: From Commune to Signory', in *Violence and Civil Disorder in Italian Cities 1200–1500*, ed. Lauro Martines (Berkeley, 1972), 229–72, at 241–4, and Andrews, 'Monastic Observance', 374. On Charles II in Florence see Villani, *Nuova Cronica*, II, 31–2 (Book 8, cap. 13).

38 ASFi, Provvisioni, Registri, 2, fo. 81.

39 ASFi, Camera del Comune, Provvisioni Canonizzate, 1, fo. 1r.

the reasoning behind this new arrangement is a devastating assessment of recent procedures. According to the rubric, there had been constant disputes and complaints against the treasurers and the government itself, caused by inadequate care shown towards the money and property of the commune and slipshod book-keeping, so that the accounts (*rationes*) of the treasury could not be reviewed unless with some confusion, because of the indiscriminate way in which income and expenditure were described, without appropriate division ('qui sine discretione aliqua speciei vel generis modo promischuo describuntur'). The situation, it was claimed, needed to be remedied so as to protect the reputation (*fama*) of the officials of the treasury.[40]

For some years the government of Florence had been engaged in dispute with the Cistercians of Settimo over a mill and weir on the river Arno, constructions which were hindering navigation to the city. The controversy was to rumble on for decades, finding resolution only in the 1330s, and it is not impossible that this influenced the decision to reduce the presence of religious in the treasury.[41] Yet, as the Humiliati appear not to have been implicated in the disagreement, it seems unlikely. The increasing complexity of the Florentine economy and attempts to improve transparency may have driven a demand for greater proficiency.[42] It is possible that this rubric alludes to a general failure on the part of the treasurers – monastic and lay – to match the growing expertise among laymen keeping personal accounts, for which there is good evidence by this date, so that lay members of the *popolo* could now do a better job than the religious.[43] As constructed here, however, it was incompetence, perhaps exposed by auditors, which was endangering the reputation of the officials themselves, their office and the government (*regimen*). It is a view of reputation which chimes with the importance attributed to office holders in the constitutions of the Fourth Lateran Council and which the canon lawyers of 1215 had sought to exploit: officials could be intimately associated with the good (and bad) name of government. We do not know why the change was made, but whether or not they were at fault, the criticisms cannot have done much for the reputation of the monastic houses

---

[40] *Ibid.*

[41] As proposed by Pirillo, 'I Cistercensi', 398, 399, and *idem*, 'Il fiume come investimento: i mulini e i porti sull'Arno della Badia a Settimo (secc. xiii–xiv)', *Storia e Arte della Abbazia Cistercense di San Salvatore a Settimo a Scandicci*, ed. Goffredo Viti (Certosa di Firenze, 1995), 63–90.

[42] As argued by Pirillo, 'I Cistercensi', 397.

[43] See Geoffrey Alan Lee, 'The Development of Italian Bookkeeping, 1211–1300', *Abacus* 9/2 (1973), 137–55; *idem*, 'The Coming of Age of Double Entry: The Giovanni Farolfi Ledger of 1299–1300', *Accounting Historians Journal*, 4/2 (1977), 79–95; and Bruce G. Carruthers and Wendy Nelson Espeland, 'Accounting for Rationality: Double-Entry Bookkeeping and the Rhetoric of Economic Rationality', *American Journal of Sociology*, 97/1 (1991), 31–69.

involved. And yet, while the decision was made to increase the numbers of laymen in the treasury, men of religion were still to be employed.

At this legislative level, professional religious appear to have become indispensable in the treasury of Florence. In practice, for several years after 1289, the only treasurers documented appear to be laymen, though the evidence is far from comprehensive.[44] With the new century, however, monks are again to be found working regularly in the treasury: in August and September 1303 for example, Ubaldo, a monk of Settimo, was serving as treasurer alongside three laymen, each appointed, as required by the provisions of 1289, from a different administrative division (*sesto*) of the city.[45] And in 1307, after the podestà had been caught taking off with the communal seal, it was retrieved and handed for safekeeping to the monks at Settimo.[46]

Evidence from the early fourteenth century provides further insight into the dynamics of this relationship between monastics and commune. In 1312, when the German emperor Henry VII, who had come south of the Alps seeking to reassert imperial rule, was besieging the city, he took the monastery of Settimo into his protection, a move undoubtedly designed to build support for his cause.[47] In April of the following year, with Henry no longer at the gates, the governing body of the city (the Priors and Standardbearer of Justice) in turn undertook to bring the rights and property of the abbot, monks, *conversi* and oblates of Settimo into their protection. According to the surviving copy of the agreement in the books of the Cistercians, this concession was made for several reasons, each of which is briefly itemised. The first was the continual disruptions of war and the inability of the religious houses in the district of Florence to defend and sustain themselves and their rights. Protection was also explicitly offered so that the abbot and monks would remain 'loyal to the commune and *popolo* of Florence and the primary advocates of its peaceful and tranquil state', and as a response to 'the alms and prayers offered to God in the monastery', again so that God would 'maintain Florence and its contado in a state of peace'. These were not uncommon grounds for promoting jurisdictional expansion.[48] But the reiteration also reads as an

---

[44] ASFi, Provvisioni, Registri, 2, c. 134, 161, 165, 171, 185 (1290); *ibid.*, Inventory V/307, 65, 142 (1294).

[45] ASFi, Camera del Comune, Camarlinghi, unnumbered document following uscita 388; *ibid.*, Provvisioni Canonizzate, 1, fo. 1r (rubrics 1 and 2). See also A. Gherardi, 'L'antica camera del comune di Firenze', *Archivio Storico Italiano*, fourth series, 16 (1885), 313–61, at 325.

[46] An oft-cited episode, but see for example Pirillo, 'I Cistercensi', 398.

[47] ASFi, Diplomatico, Cestello, 27 Oct. 1312; Villani, *Nuova Cronica*, II, 247–50 (Book 10, cap. 47); Pirillo, 'I Cistercensi', 399; William M. Bowsky, *Henry VII in Italy. The Conflict of Empire and City-State 1310–1313* (Lincoln, NB, 1960).

[48] See George W. Dameron, *Florence and its Church in the Age of Dante* (Philadelphia, 2005), 160–1.

anxious rejoinder to Henry's earlier privilege, and points to the urgency of ensuring Settimo's peaceful relations with the city. The last reason specified, however, adopts a very different tack: the city also undertook to protect the house as an acknowledgement of the labours which monks and *conversi* of the monastery had 'endured until then and daily tolerated' ('tollerant et subportant'), both in the treasury of the commune and in other communal offices (*offitia comunis*).[49] The monastery of Settimo thus acquired protection from its powerful neighbour, almost certainly in response to an immediate and urgent need on both sides. This was also presented, at least in part, as recompense for specific, long-standing endeavours by the monks and lay brothers in the administrative service of the commune. To someone involved in the preparation of this text, the employment of religious in the city appeared to be a matter for negotiation.

The link between service and reward in this document is unusually explicit. The candour may stem from the Cistercian context in which it survives, since detailed elaboration of government decisions is rare outside either chronicle accounts or the more succinct official minutes of communal assemblies and legislative bodies. Its echo is nonetheless found in near-contemporary urban legislation, which also encompasses the Humiliati, and reiterates the emphasis on the labours of both religious communities on behalf of the *popolo* and commune. Two rubrics in the statutes produced in the name of the Florentine *Capitano del popolo*, datable before 1321, connect the service rendered to the *popolo* and commune by the Cistercians and Humiliati, not with protection, but instead with tax immunities awarded to the two houses. In the case of the Humiliati of Ognissanti, the concession is also linked to their role in accommodating officials. Fiscal immunity is thus granted:

> Cum fratres humiliati Omnium Sanctorum de Florentia cotidie quasi labores tollerent et incommoda et expensas in servitium populi et communis Florentie, et maxime in retinendo offitiales ipsius Communis et populi qui ad condendum leges et statuta et fatiendum alia negotia populi et communis eiusdem deputantur, et ad egestatem devenerint.[50]

---

[49] ASFi, Compagnie religiose soppresse da Pietro Leopoldo, 481, fo. 46r. I am very grateful to Dr Paula Spilner for first drawing my attention to this document.

[50] *Statuto del Capitano del Popolo degli anni 1322–25*, Statuti della Repubblica Fiorentina, 1, ed. Romolo Caggese (Florence, 1910). New edition by Giuliano Pinto, Francesco Salvestrini and Andrea Zorzi (Florence, 1999), 270–1 (Book 5, rubrics 72–3): 'Because the Humiliati brothers of Ognissanti in Florence put up almost daily with labours and inconvenience and expense in the service of the *popolo* and commune of Florence, and in particular in housing officials of the Commune and *popolo* who are deputed to composing laws and statutes and undertaking other business on behalf of the *popolo* and commune and will be rendered destitute.' See also ASFi, Compagnie religiose soppresse da Pietro Leopoldo, 481, fos. 42r–45v. On urban attempts to limit the effects of such immunities, see A. Pertile, *Storia del diritto italiano* (6 vols., Turin, 1896–1903), IV, 386–95.

The early archives of the Humiliati of Ognissanti are not accessible (they were damaged in the disastrous flood of the river Arno in 1966), so this assertion of the house's financial vulnerability cannot be tested, but it seems unlikely. Claims of poverty were in any case a standard strategy used, for example, in petitions to the papal and episcopal authorities to justify changes in monastic affairs.[51] Yet its use here implies at least that the authors of this rubric thought sufficient numbers of Florentines would be likely to accept its logic: engagement in the service of the commune was an onerous affair and justified the mitigation of any tax burden. The location of the passage in the Statutes of the Capitano also reinforces the link with a particular political body and, of course, it is the (Guelf) *popolo*.

The Cistercians of Settimo and the Humiliati of Ognissanti had been serving regularly as treasurers in Florence for more than half a century by this date. They had also remained in office through changes of regime from 'Guelf' to 'Ghibelline' elites (and between Black and White Guelfs).[52] So, if the protection and immunity offered were new, they cannot have been the initial triggers. Both texts may simply have refreshed long-standing but undocumented arrangements, rendered critical by the actions of Henry VII. But there are other clues to suggest that there was more to this picture than protection in time of war. In 1313 the city government offered itself (its *signoria*) to King Robert of Naples, heir to Charles II and leader of the Guelf alliance against Henry VII in Tuscany and southern Italy.[53] Barely eighteen months later, in September 1314, the administrative burden in the treasury reverted from one religious and three laymen to just two religious personnel, to alternate as before between the Humiliati of Ognissanti and the Cistercians of Settimo.[54] On 25 September 1314 the change was approved in the Council of One Hundred by a vote of ninety-one to two.[55] There might of course be no necessary cause and effect in this juxtaposition of a key political alliance with increased use of religious in the treasury. The practice of using men of religion had after all already reacquired its customary quality by this date. Nonetheless, the heightened dependence on men of religion may well have had political overtones and this is confirmed by details in the new *provvisioni*. Alongside the two religious treasurers there was to be the

[51] For examples, Andrews, *Humiliati*, 260, 274, 288–9 (Appendix 1, 22, 70, 110). Robert Davidsohn, *Forschungen zur Geschichte von Florenz* (4 vols., Berlin, 1896–1908), IV, 402.

[52] The best account of these factions is Dino Compagni, *Cronica*, ed. Davide Cappi (Rome, 2000), also available in English as *Dino Compagni's Chronicle of Florence*, trans. Daniel E. Bornstein (Philadelphia, 1986).

[53] Davidsohn, *Forschungen*, IV, 544, 556.

[54] ASFi, Camera del Comune, Provvisioni Canonizzate, 1, fos. 16r–18r.

[55] ASFi, Libri Fabarum, 10, fo. 93v, 25 Sept. 1314.

usual team of laymen: notaries, judges and accountants, 'all of whom must be Guelfs' ('qui omnes sint et esse debeant Guelfi').[56]

The powers ascribed to the two religious treasurers in 1314 are explicitly equated to unspecified earlier periods when there had been just three lay treasurers (perhaps before the 1250s or at some point in the 1290s), or three laymen and one religious, as instituted in 1289. In future, according to the statutes, no laymen were to be elected as treasurers. Moreover, the men of religion appointed as treasurers were now explicitly exempted from attending council meetings and from any requirement to engage in activities which might infringe 'ecclesiastical liberty', or involve payment of an executioner.[57] This last provision accommodated both the canon law prohibition on clerical participation in the spilling of blood and the reform agenda of church leaders for whom 'liberty', understood in terms of autonomy over property and person (and of course tax exemption), remained an essential principle of action.

The explicit promise of protection for the Cistercians does not seem to have been necessary to the Humiliati, who had probably never occasioned the particular interest of Henry VII and were in any case based at the church of Ognissanti, by this date enclosed within the new circuit of walls which had been hurriedly thrown up around the western part of Florence, in the winter and spring of 1310–11.[58] On the other hand, it is significant that a further concession to both houses was now also made. The abbot of Settimo and provost of Ognissanti were assigned responsibility for distributing 2,000 florins, donated by the commune in alms each year to religious houses and hospitals in the city and contado.[59] In a diocese where, like many another, there was endemic tension between the different ecclesiastical communities, regular and secular, this must have been a delicate but perhaps also an attractive position.[60]

Analysis of this Florentine evidence points to the agency of both commune and professional religious. Each had potential needs which the other might supply: protection, fiscal immunity, resources (both influence and property), in exchange for loyalty, politically (and perhaps financially) trusted officials and, of course, prayers and alms. Each made compromises to allow this practice to continue. Whatever explanation we choose to highlight – the impartial separateness attributed to men of religion, their integrity, their particular expertise or their political

[56] ASFi, Camera del Comune, Provvisioni Canonizzate, I, fo. 17r.

[57] Ibid., fos. 16v, 17v, 18r.

[58] Villani, Nuova Cronica, II, 218–19 (Book 9, chapter 10); Bowsky, Henry VII, 115, and, on the walls more generally, Snzura, L'espansione urbana di Firenze nel Dugento.

[59] ASFi, Camera del Comune, Provvisioni Canonizzate, I, fos. 18r–19r.

[60] See in general Dameron, Episcopal Power, and idem, Florence and its Church.

affinities – this evidence suggests above all that negotiation lay at the core of the appointment of professional religious to urban office.

That negotiated agreement was a key to office holding (and not just in Florence) is further underlined by the fact that cities could and did survive without professional religious as office holders, or alternated between lay and religious officials and varying combinations of the two. Some urban authorities forbade the employment of religious altogether. In 1265 in Padua for instance, a city where, incidentally, neither Humiliati nor Cistercians were to be found, but a Benedictine congregation of *monaci albi* built close ties with the commune, it was decreed that: 'no lay brother [tertiary, penitent or *conversus*] or other person following a religious rule [may] be established in any ordinary or extraordinary office, honour or civil responsibility by the commune of Padua, nor hold such position'.[61] Elsewhere, monks, tertiaries and lay penitents could be, and often were, replaced in public office by laymen or by other religious, either because those making the rules changed their preference – as in Florence in 1289 and 1314 – or because the professional religious withdrew. Evidence from the city of Siena illustrates this last point. From the 1250s when monastics like Ugo of San Galgano were employed as treasurers in the city, the accounts reveal that the monastery was contacted to ensure that their appointment was confirmed.[62] By 1280 this had become both a matter of statute and a problem.[63] The Sienese podestà for that year, Matteo Rosso Orsini, reported to the general council of the commune on 26 December that in accordance with statute, the abbot and convent of San Galgano had been asked and required (*requisiti et rogati*) to produce a treasurer by means of letters and ambassadors from the commune. All requests had nonetheless been rejected: the monastery absolutely denied that it could provide (*concedere*) a treasurer, so they would have to look elsewhere.[64] Orsini may indeed have been describing a *fait accompli*: a Vallombrosan monk from San Michele in Poggio San Donato was already to be found as *camerarius* in January 1281 and remained until the end of 1282. By 1284 the Cistercians of San Galgano were to return.[65]

---

[61] *Statuti del Comune di Padova dal secolo XII all'anno 1285*, ed. Andrea Gloria (Padua 1873), reedited and translated in *Statuti del comune di Padova*, ed. Guido Beltrame, Guerrino Citton and Daniela Mazzon (Cittadella 2000), 114 (Book I, rubric XXIII). Antonio Rigon, 'La Chiesa nell'età comunale e carrarese', in *Diocesi di Padova, Storia Religiosa del Veneto*, VI (Padua, 1996), 117–60, at 123–7.

[62] Andrews, 'Monastic Observance', 366–7.

[63] Earlier provisions allowed for greater flexibility: See for example, ASSi, Consiglio Generale (hereafter CG), 9, c. 13v (18 Dec. 1259).

[64] ASSi, CG 24, fo. 10v. Transcribed and discussed in Andrews, 'Monastic Observance', 368–9 and n. 51.

[65] Andrews, 'Monastic Observance', 369.

We do not know what reason the abbot of San Galgano had given, if any, for his refusal, nor the wider context that led to this stalemate. But this episode underscores the negotiated nature of the choices made, and the verbs ascribed to Orsini by the communal scribe are revealing. On one hand the commune set out to ask and demand (*requirere*), on the other, the abbot refused to grant (*concedere*). Both verbs lay claim to authority, but as the holder of a resource the commune wanted (men of religion, whether monks or *conversi*), the monastery (presumably in the person of the abbot) is portrayed as the benefactor choosing and able to say no, however fleetingly.

The minutes of the communal assembly in the small town (*burgum, castrum*) of San Gimignano, between Florence and Siena, introduce a further element to this relationship of monastic superior to city office.[66] In the winter of 1264/5:

> Donnus Petrus Prior Abatie de Murchio [a Camaldolese house a mile or so from the town] electus camerarius communis Sancti Geminiani, habita licentia a donno Barthal[ome]o Priore ordinis Camaldulensium ipsum camarlingatus officium acceptauit; promittens id ipsum officium bene et legaliter facere et exercere in omnibus et per omnia secundum quod continetur in capitulo constituti communis Sancti Geminiani ipsius camarlingatus.[67]

Pietro's promise was delivered to Rosselmino, judge of the commune, in the choir of the *pieve* (the main urban church), before the principal assembly of the city, the Council of the Bell. The parallels and dissonances with a monastic profession of vows are manifest. He performed a predetermined ritual promise (not an oath, which was forbidden to professed religious), according to a normative text or set of rules. He delivered this promise to an individual who, together with the witnesses, personified the commune of San Gimignano. He did so as the result, however, not of a noviciate but of some sort of election, and it was to be a temporary arrangement, for six months (though in practice he was reelected for the following semester).[68] Far from being broken, the monastic vow of obedience was publicly endorsed by reference to the permission of the superior.[69]

[66] See D. Waley, 'Introduction', in *Il libro bianco di San Gimignano. I documenti più antichi del comune (secolo xii–xiv)*, I, ed. Donatella Ciampoli (Siena, 1996).
[67] ASFi, Comune di San Gimignano, 99, fo. 3r (15 Jan. 1265): 'Dom Pietro, prior of the abbey of Murchio, elected treasurer of the commune of San Gimignano, having permission from dom Bartal[ome]o, prior of the order of Camaldoli, accepted the office of treasurer, promising to carry out this office well and fairly (lawfully) and in everything according to what is contained in the chapter of the constitution of the commune of San Gimignano on the treasury.' I am very grateful to Professor Oretta Muzzi who first allowed me to consult her own lists of *camerlenghi* in San Gimignano.
[68] ASFi, Comune di San Gimignano, 100, fo. 58r (1 July 1265).
[69] The importance of the vow was underlined by Trexler, 'Honor', 319.

Pietro is unusual because he was himself a monastic superior and took office explicitly with the licence of his own superior, Bartolomeo, the prior general of his order (1263–5). Bartolomeo was frequently active in Florence, where he had been prior of San Salvatore di Camaldoli, so obtaining this authorisation was perhaps relatively straightforward.[70] It is remarkable, nonetheless, because it never seems to be matched for religious from other orders. Reference to local abbots allowing, even encouraging, individuals to take office can be traced, both implicitly (as above) and explicitly.[71] The approval or disapproval of the wider Cistercian order is, however, never alluded to in these sources, despite substantial evidence in their General Chapter statutes for discussions of loans of monks and *conversi* to various secular and episcopal lords (loans which were generally, though not always, refused, reflecting an undoubted ambivalence).[72] Nor is there evidence for the approval of the Master General of the Humiliati. Papal bulls reacting to petitions from both Humiliati and lay penitents point instead to their opposition to this sort of employment for the fully professed, though in the case of the Humiliati, for example, they are restricted to the middle of the thirteenth century and never touch upon either Florence or Siena.[73]

Just as statute drafters like those in Florence in 1289 insisted on the need to appoint men who were honest, prudent and law-abiding or an analogous combination of qualities (*honestus, bonus, prudens, legalis*), so – like the monk Angelo encountered above – in the records of office themselves the individuals chosen were usually given soubriquets in the same terms, all related to 'integrity'.[74] These were of course frequently used epithets, applied in a formulaic, office-driven manner comparable to the *magnificus vir* habitual for innumerable podestà, whether or not such men were ever truly superb.[75] Nor were such terms exclusive to the clergy, either regular or secular.[76] The insistence of communal councils on the uprightness and

---

[70] ASFi, Diplomatico Camaldoli, eremo, 1 Nov. 1263, 25 Jan. 1266 and ad datam. I am particularly grateful to Dr Cécile Caby for this information.

[71] Andrews, 'Monastic Observance', 366.

[72] Schneider, *Klosterhaushalt*, 29–85.

[73] Andrews, *Humiliati*, 273–4, 276, 280–5 (Appendix 1, 65–6 (1247), 70 (1249), 88–91, 95 (1251), 97a–c (1250–1) 98, (1252), 102–3 (1253)). *Bullarium Franciscanum pontificum constitutiones, epistolas, ac diplomata continens tribus ordinibus minorum, clarissarum et poenitentium*, ed. J. Sbaralea, I–II (Rome, 1759–60), I, 30 (25 June 1227), 39–40 (30 Mar. 1228), 65–6 (7 June 1230), 71 (5 Apr. 1231), 99 (15 Mar. 1233), 532 (4 Nov. 1249), II, 42 (27 Apr. 1255).

[74] See, for example, epithets for the treasurers in Siena: ASSi, Biccherna, 107, fo. 140r: 'religioso et honesto dompno Guidone', 113, fo. 145r: 'a Religioso et honesto viro frater Thomasino de humiliatis camerario Communis', 123 fo. 1r: 'religiosi et honesti viri fratris Bartholomei de humiliatis camerarii'. *Statuti del comune di San Gimignano compilati nel 1255*, ed. L. Pecori (Florence, 1853), Book 1, rubric 9, 668, refers to the election of 'unus bonus et probus camerarius, seu religiosus'.

[75] For example, ASSi, Biccherna, 107 fo. 138 (1291).

[76] The statutes of Florence of 1289 applied to both lay and clerical appointees. See also, for example, the reference to appointing 'decem bonos, prudentes et legales homines de

suitability of *all* office holders does nonetheless tend to support the thesis that men of religion may have been sought because they could be deemed less likely to engage in fraud. Monks like Ugo were also, theoretically at least, less able to use money than their lay counterparts, as they had no personal property and so, it might be argued, no reason to embezzle.[77]

Extending the evidence beyond Tuscany also allows us further to demonstrate the flexibility of lay attitudes towards the status of men of religion. As we have seen, in Siena a Vallombrosan could replace a Cistercian, despite rubrics requiring exclusive appointment of Cistercians. This is unremarkable, but in Perugia in the 1340s, the statutes suggest that another kind of equation of religious was also possible. The statutes of 1342 underline that in future the treasurer (*masaio del comuno*): 'essere degga per lo tenpo che verrà relegioso e de relegione e eleggase la religione overo el capitolo de la relegione tanto e non alcuno nomenatamente secondo co' de la relegione piacerà al conselglo del popolo ordenare'.[78] The frequent repetition of *relegione*, even allowing for its distinct uses to indicate both a religious order in general and a particular house, points to the magnitude of the issue. The following rubric again reiterates that the treasurer may not be a secular, thereby demonstrating a different kind of duplication, typical of urban statutes which are, of course, documents generated by continuous redrafting. It does not tell us *why* Perugia wanted a man of religion, but it is, nonetheless, a renewed indication of the particular importance assigned at this moment to avoiding the engagement of laymen. The definition of *religioso* supplied at the end of the first rubric is particularly revealing. As a gloss to the previous passage, it asserts that for the purposes of the office of treasurer the friars of penance are also to be understood to be religious: 'E che ei frate de la Penetentia se entendano essere, quanto a l'offitio del masariato, relegiose e de relegione.'[79] There are questions of jurisdiction at play here: the friars of penance are not being defined as fully professed religious on a par with those who live within a monastic community (the usual meaning of *de relegione*). Nor are they being exempted from taxes and military service. They are being equated to such fully professed religious for a single, contingent purpose – holding office in the treasury.

vero populo civitatis Mutine', in Emilio Vicini, *Respublica Mutinensis (1306–7)*, I (Milan, 1929), 12–13.

[77] These sort of arguments were made by Zanoni, *Gli Umiliati*, 219; Bowsky, *Finance*, 7; Trexler, 'Honor', 319–22. Discussed in Andrews 'Monastic Observance', 359.

[78] *Statuto del comune e del popolo di Perugia del 1342 in volgare*, ed. Mahmoud Salem Elsheikh (4 vols., Perugia, 2000), I, 180 (Book I, cap. 48): 'must in future be [a] religious and from a religious house (*ordo*) and let the order be chosen, or rather the chapter of the order alone and not an individual by name, according to the monastic house that it shall please the Council of the *Popolo* to determine'.

[79] *Ibid.*

The Perugia legislators' gloss serves as a reminder that *vir religiosus* was a flexible term, which in some contexts simply indicated a pious individual. It need not apply only to those dedicated to a rule. In the texts discussed here it is titles and labels such as *dompnus*, *monachus* or *frater* which confirm specific, religious status. These are also the distinctions upon which canon lawyers would insist. But the city legislators thought nothing of redefining lay penitents in monastic terms to meet a presumably pressing need: lay expectations and demands of religious status could and did change.

Broadening the range of examples still further beyond central Italy allows us to explore yet other ways in which this issue might be approached. The rubric from Como mentioned above asserts that the podestà should use coercion to compel the men of religion to perform the task: 'Religiosi et honesti viri in professione religionis comorantes quos fratres potestas teneatur modis omnibus habere et eos cohercere ad ipsum officium faciendum.'[80] In a similar tone, a rubric of 1288 from the statutes of the north-eastern city of Verona requires ministers and brothers of the religious houses involved to give of their 'most useful and best' men to take office ('de utilioribus et melioribus'). If they fail to do so and if for that reason the commune is defrauded in any way, the podestà is to compel the religious community to refund the loss.[81] Like the Como statute, the language of compulsion used here fits well with a financial line of reasoning: the unpleasant prospect of exposure to risk might well explain the coercive tenor.[82] Yet this very tone points equally to the rhetorical and discursive purpose of these rubrics: they voice an aspiration, which may or may not have been capable of practical enactment. After all, while the tertiary Humiliati may have been relatively vulnerable, it cannot have been easy to force a monastic community to pay any monies due. Lay patrons invested substantially in the wealth and beauty of religious houses. Although little now survives of Humiliati buildings in Como or Verona, for example, the order enjoyed generous patronage of its churches in these cities, as it did in Florence, Siena and in numerous centres all over central and northern Italy. Other regular orders benefited from similar or still greater lay generosity. To what purpose would they, or their patrons, allow this prosperity to be put at risk or turned to other purposes? And, indeed, there is very little, if any, evidence for such payments. Luigi Zanoni, the historian of the Humiliati, noted a sum demanded in Parma,

---

[80] Ceruti, 'Liber statutorum Cumanorum', c. 105: 'Religious and honest men living as professed religious, brothers whom the podestà is required to have by any means and to force to do this office.'

[81] *Gli Statuti Veronesi del 1276 colle correzioni e le aggiunte fino al 1323 (Cod. Campostrini, Bibl. Civica di Verona)*, ed. Gino Sandri, Deputazione di Storia Patria per le Venezie, n.s. 3 (Venezia 1940), 72–3 (Book I, rubric LXXV).

[82] For the economic/financial angle, see Zanoni, *Gli Umiliati*, 219.

but it is recorded because the money was to be returned.[83] It might be objected that there must have been unrecorded transactions, but if this practice were widespread, we might equally expect to find these payments entered in the many extant books of communal accounts. There can be little doubt that strapped-for-cash communes were keen to tap into ecclesiastical wealth: evidence abounds of communes instituting taxes on ecclesiastics, not without success.[84] What little corroboration there is for office holding as a way to access or exploit the wealth of religious houses implies, instead, that it was not effective.

A further reason which may have guided the employment of religious is their relative expertise. The statutes of Bologna of 1288 for example refer frequently to tasks which would entail the ability to count (*numerari*), and not just in the treasury. A rubric requiring the appointment of two friars of penance as supervisors of bridge-building works and other construction projects paid for with communal monies further specifies that one of the two must know how to write: *litteratus qui scribere sciat*.[85] A comparable insistence on using *litterati* (most appropriately translated in this context as 'experts') is found in a description of Dominican and Franciscan friars to be appointed to supervise elections in Brescia in 1313.[86] That the drafters of these statutes highlighted such expertise is, naturally, an acknowledgement of the potential lack of such abilities within Mendicant ranks, as among the laity. Any equation of cleric with *litteratus*, in the case of friars of penance and even of monks or Mendicants, could never be inevitable at the level of the individual. Choir monks and Mendicant friars were very likely to be highly literate and numerate by contemporary standards, but the monopoly of the Friars over such skills centred on the new universities and the production of more sophisticated tools for theological study and preaching, not book-keeping.[87] Monks and *conversi* did keep the books to enable them to administer large estates – as we have seen, in the early days of the *primo popolo* in Florence this may have been a key consideration in their appointment – but, if literacy or numeracy

---

[83] *Ibid.* See *Statuta communis Parmae digesta anno mcclv*, Monumenta historica ad provincias Parmensem et Placentinam pertinentia, ed. A. Ronchini (Parma, 1855), I, 462 (1264).

[84] See, for example, G. Biscaro, 'Gli estimi del comune di Milano nel secolo XIII', *Archivio Storico Lombardo*, 55 (1928), 343–495. Andrews, *Humiliati*, 210.

[85] *Statuti di Bologna dell'anno 1288*, ed. Gina Fasoli and Pietro Sella (Vatican City, 1937), I, 48 (Book II, rubric III).

[86] 'Statuti di Brescia dell'anno mcccxiii', *Historia Patriae Monumenta*, XVI, Leges municipales II/1 (Turin, 1876), col. 1632 (rubric clix): 'De sortibus generalibus bis in anno dandis . . . habeantur duo fratres Praedicatores, et duo Minores, litterati, foresterii.' On uses of *litteratus* see M. T. Clanchy, *From Memory to Written Record, England 1066–1307*, 2nd edn (Oxford and Cambridge, MA, 1993).

[87] See, for example, Michael T. Clanchy, 'Parchment and Paper: Manuscript Culture 1100–1500', in *A Companion to the History of the Book*, ed. Simon Eliot and Jonathan Rose (Oxford and Cambridge, MA, 2007), 194–206, at 194.

were really the main issue behind urban office holding, within a very few years such skills were widely available among the mercantile laity, without resort to men like Ugo of San Galgano.[88] Accounting was not taught with the abacus at school but was learned on the job.[89] This was the period when laymen in Florence and other Italian cities were developing the financial acumen which would eventually result in the emergence of techniques such as double-entry book-keeping. It seems equally likely that laymen could also have been found who had substantial administrative experience. Italian merchants and bankers were, after all, developing extensive and sophisticated parchment and paper trails to support their international trade networks.

A final concern is that of detachment: that those appointed could be considered to be distant from any direct relations with others holding office.[90] As we have seen, it might be argued that this is what drove the choice of monastics in the Florence of the *primo popolo*. Yet in many other cases, the assumption on which hypotheses of detachment are based may in practice be an illusion resulting in part from ignorance about the social status of individuals. Family names based on lineage or location emerged in the thirteenth century as a way for elites to denote their status.[91] At the same time detachment from family was encouraged in monastic rules. As a mark of their new life, therefore, on entering a monastic house, monks of all types usually abandoned any family name, so that in the written record they do indeed appear 'family-less', detached from kin in a way comparable to outsider-appointees such as a podestà. This makes it difficult to identify the social background of many of the professional religious involved in holding office. There seem, for example, to be just two exceptions to this rule in the thirteenth-century Sienese treasury, one of whom, a man named Bartolomeo de Alexis, monk of San Galgano, served as communal treasurer in the 1270s and became abbot of his house in the early fourteenth century – an unlikely candidate for detached status.[92] His case implies, incidentally, that being an urban treasurer need not damage an ecclesiastical career, though one case hardly substantiates the

[88] Robert D. Black, *Education and Society in Florentine Tuscany: Teachers, Pupils and Schools, c. 1250 to 1500* (Leiden, 2007), and *idem, Humanism and Education in Medieval and Renaissance Italy: Tradition and Innovation in Latin Schools, 1200–1500* (Cambridge, 2001).

[89] As observed by Richard A. Goldthwaite, *The Economy of Renaissance Florence* (Baltimore, 2009), 91.

[90] As argued by Zanoni, *Gli Umiliati*, 219; Manselli, 'Gli Umiliati', 231–6. See also Kamp, *Istituzioni comunali*, 24; Bowsky, *Finance*, 7, and more recently, Grillo, 'Cistercensi', esp. 386–91, and *idem, Milano*, 586.

[91] See *L'anthroponymie, document de l'histoire sociale des mondes méditerranéens médiévaux: actes du colloque international*, ed. Monique Bourin, Jean-Marie Martin and François Menant (Rome, 1996).

[92] ASSi, Conventi, 162, Caleffo di San Galgano (copied 1319–21), c. 285r–v. Andrews, 'Monastic Observance', 378.

broader argument. Other examples have been unearthed in Milan and will be discussed below, but in practice, in most cases we cannot know whether the individual Cistercians chosen as treasurers in Siena, as in Florence, came from low- or high-status families, from the politically engaged or from the politically and socially disenfranchised. Similar uncertainties surface if we try to pin down the social status of individuals from the other orders typically involved, including the Humiliati, who encompassed men of varying social status, dominated perhaps by the 'middle class'.[93] Nonetheless, it is very probable that many of the monks of San Galgano were originally Sienese and that the majority of the Humiliati in Florence or Siena were also indigenous.[94] If so, whatever their original social status, any detachment would have depended on the construction of difference, on Miller's 'different patterns of thought and behavior', since client–patron relations certainly crossed social groups.

On the other hand, whether it was practicable or not, there is evidence that the *degree* of 'detachment' was indeed sometimes a factor in the thinking of legislators about urban appointments. In Como, alongside the *religiosi viri* in the treasury, the statute makers explicitly sought *homines religiosi* without wife or family to serve as assessors against fraudulent weights and measures and to check the quality of the salt.[95] In San Gimignano, the statutes assigned different rates of pay for appointees to the treasury, allowing foreigners to be paid more than their domestic counterparts.[96] In other cases, *outsiders* were explicitly preferred: thus the Dominican and Franciscan friars chosen to scrutinise elections in the Lombard city of Brescia in 1313 were also required to be *foresterii*.[97] Such thinking of course tends to confirm that their opposites – local, indigenous religious – need not be detached from politics, nor expected to be. Like the men of the Florentine treasury in 1314, in Bologna in 1288 the link is once again made clear. A rubric in one copy of the city statutes specifies that the penitents appointed to supervise communal works must be aligned with the faction of the Church, the *Geremie*.[98]

93 Andrews, *Humiliati*, 31–2.

94 As observed, with reference to the Cistercians, by Bowsky, *Finance*, 7.

95 Ceruti, 'Liber statutorum Cumanorum', c. 235 (rubric 398).

96 *Statuti del comune di San Gimignano compilati nel 1255*, ed. L. Pecori (Florence, 1853), 668 (Book 1, rubric 9).

97 See above nn. 85 and 86. See also Dejob, *La foi religieuse*, 92, with reference to Florence in 1328.

98 *Statuti di Bologna dell'anno 1288*, ed. Fasoli and Sella, I, 48, Book II, rubric III: 'Item elligantur duo fratres penitentie partis Ecclesie, qui debeant superesse ad faciendum fieri pontes et alia laboreria facienda expensis comunis Bononie de parte ecclesie seu Ieremiensium civitatis Bononie'; see also *ibid.*, II, 161–2n. Elsewhere, the same statutes explicitly exempted their opponents' penitents from this restriction: I, 59, Book II, rubric VIII: '*De Lambertaciis qui non possunt habere offitium nec esse consiliarii* . . . Salvo quod predicta non

The examples could be multiplied, but the point would remain the same: status as a man of religion need not mean either exemption from factional interests or inevitably being deemed to be detached. Whether a monk from San Galgano or Settimo, a Vallombrosan or Camaldolese brother, or a Humiliati *frater* from the Sienese or Florentine houses could (or would wish to) remain sufficiently aloof to act as a check on the activities of their lay associates in the communal treasuries remains at best uncertain. It is, on the other hand, clear that contemporaries, at least those generating and drafting statutes, did sometimes think of religious office holders in terms of detachment (*qua* outsiders) or attachment (to a *pars*).

This last point in particular is verifiable in further evidence from other cities. A detailed study of the Humiliati in the northern city of Bergamo demonstrates, for example, that their employment by the commune was 'more substantial in periods of city life characterised by a Guelf tendency'.[99] Evidence from Milan gives added weight to this factional perspective. Details about the brothers from the Cistercian abbey of Chiaravalle Milanese, some three miles south-east of the city, make it possible to identify the kin groups of some of the men chosen as urban treasurers. This reveals that they came from the same families of the *popolo* who, after the middle of the thirteenth century, dominated the commune.[100] As in Florence, this may have had something to do with their relatively high proficiency as administrators when compared to the men of the *popolo*. But clerical separateness is here subsumed into political or factional affiliation. And here the effect this might have on a religious community when the politics changed is also apparent: like the Cistercians, the Humiliati held offices in Milan in the third quarter of the thirteenth century. After 1277, when the della Torre faction was ousted by Ottone Visconti, who initiated his family's domination of the city, the *popolo* lost its position and with it Humiliati engagement in office holding declined. The role of exactors of the ecclesiastical *fodrum* (hearth tax), for example, passed from Humiliati to brothers of the Hospital of the Brolo.[101] Perhaps the Humiliati had become politically untrustworthy because they were identified with the della Torre faction, while the Brolo was close to the Visconti. It should be noted, nonetheless, that the replacements were still *fratres*, still men of religion: the choice being made was between groups of professional religious, not between religious and laymen. As in Florence, the principle of employing men of religion survived the change of regime.[102]

habeant locum in fratribus penitentie de parte Lambertaciorum, qui possint habere offitia ad voluntatem consilii populi.'

[99] Maria Teresa Brolis, *Gli Umiliati a Bergamo nei secoli xiii e xiv* (Milan, 1991), 186.
[100] See Grillo, 'Cistercensi', 386–91, and *idem*, *Milano*, 586.
[101] Grillo, *Milano*, 587.
[102] For an exception to this in Siena, see Andrews, 'Monastic Observance', 365–6.

It is not difficult – and, indeed, not an unreasonable activity for historians – to use the evidence presented here to set out a list of possible explanations for the employment of men such as Ugo of San Galgano, or his Humiliati, Camaldolese and other regular and penitent associates. I have outlined some of the arguments in the cases considered above. They remain useful ways to approach lay constructions of clerical mindsets and behaviours. The regular clergy might indeed be thought to be impartial, men of integrity, trustworthy. These factors, given different emphases by previous historians, might be used to construct an account of normative clerical behaviour in the period. The common thread to the urban sources here is, however, their contingent, conditional nature. Fragmentary as they are, they tell us more about how men of government responded to and manipulated the possibilities than they do about the realities of difference or any fundamental motivation driving their decisions. Even in the disconnected form in which they have inevitably been presented here, they reveal a great deal about the fluidity of expectations of men of religion. City governments might depend on men of religion in office, curb their dependence, or decide not to use them at all. Churchmen like the abbot of San Galgano might allow his monks to participate in city office, encourage them or refuse outright. The men of religion holding urban office in this period, like their lay counterparts, might be considered detached and impartial or required to be attached (and partial). Whatever their origins, the practice of using them in government offices acquired the weight of custom, and was embodied in statute; but custom could, of course, be changed. The sort of negotiation found in these texts draws attention to the conditional implications of religious status. Its separateness was a tool used in the engagement between city authorities and monastic communities. Like gender, the expectations of professional religious could be socially or politically determined and contingent. Power was at stake and like gender, religious status, often narrowly defined as membership of a particular house, determined the activities allowed to particular individuals or communities, and, at times, access to resources. The distinction between laymen and clergy might be underlined by the insistence on employing one to the exclusion of the other. Yet it might also be obscured by the requirement that, once in office, they undertake (almost) the same tasks.

As we have seen, laymen and men of religion, as in Florence in the thirteenth and early fourteenth centuries, often worked alongside each other. There are some key differences: laymen were usually elected by scrutiny, whilst men of religion were generally selected by the superior of their house (in turn identified by the communal authorities). A rubric might also explicitly safeguard *libertas ecclesie*. Otherwise, the duties required of the men appointed were, inevitably, more or less

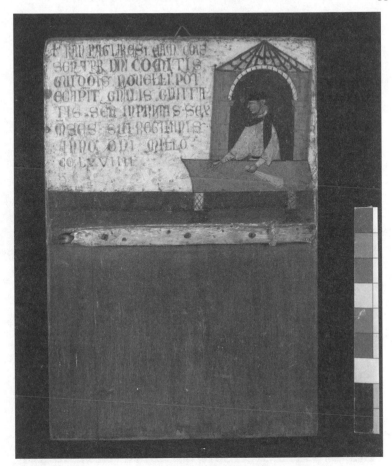

Figure 2 Attributed to Diotisalvi di Speme, Ranieri Pagliaresi. Tavola di Biccherna, Siena, Archivio di Stato, 4 (January–June 1270). Reproduced by permission of the Archive.

identical.[103] At different junctures city legislators might determine a preference for lay or religious officials, but the rubrics guiding their activities suggest that the two were to some degree interchangeable and might be viewed in closely comparable ways. Such overlapping perceptions can be seen in two slightly later covers of the books of the

[103] See for example ASFi, Camera del Comune, Provvisioni Canonizzate, 1 fo. 2v (rubric 6).

Figure 3 Anonymous, Bartolomeo, monk of San Galgano. Tavola di Biccherna, Siena, Archivio di Stato, 6 (January–June 1276). Reproduced by permission of the Archive.

Sienese Biccherna with which we began. One portrays a lay treasurer, Ranieri Pagliaresi, who held office in 1270 (Figure 2), the other shows Bartolomeo, a monk of San Galgano, in the same role six years later (Figure 3). Bartolomeo's pose is notably similar to the depiction of Ranieri: both stand in a booth behind a trestle table.[104] Both are shown with a

---

[104] This iconography is also close to other covers: ASSi, Biccherna, 2 (1264); Berlin, Gemäldegalerie M 580 (1278), which shows Bartolomeo de Alexis, monk of San Galgano and future abbot, and ASSi, Biccherna 7 (1280). See *Le Biccherne*, ed. Tomei, 114–15, 124–7.

moneybag, indicating or counting coins. Bartolomeo is in three-quarter view, leaning forward in his hooded white habit with his head bent towards the piles of coins he is counting into the bag. Ranieri is in profile, wearing a black skullcap, cloak and belt over a white tunic with elegant buttoned sleeves, a delicate red ribbon at his neck. His fingers too are counting coins, though his face looks to the distance. The special status of Bartolomeo as monk-treasurer is restricted to his clothing and tonsure: in this instance the habit did indeed make the monk.

The iconography of these two images of course depends as much on artistic convention and the painters employed as it does on the office portrayed. Yet it suggests that it was unobjectionable not just to employ a monk in the treasury, but to depict him in an explicitly financial position, his eyes focused on coins. Like the drafters of urban statutes, the painters apparently found nothing strange in allotting the two men such similar roles. Miller has observed that the laity demanded different moral standards of their religious leaders, the clergy.[105] What the evidence presented here suggests is that the regular clergy and lay penitents were indeed expected to be different, but that this difference might be exploited in ways which sometimes involved blurring the distinction, if not (quite) living like the laity.

[105] Miller, 'Religion', 1098.

Transactions of the RHS 20 (2010), pp. 57–83 © Royal Historical Society 2010
doi:10.1017/S0080440110000058

OLIVER CROMWELL AND THE PROTECTORATE
By Blair Worden

READ 8 MAY 2009

ABSTRACT. It is often said that if Oliver Cromwell had lived longer the Puritan Revolution could have survived. The monarchical component of protectoral rule, and the protector's endeavours to broaden the base of his regime, are taken to have signalled a return towards normality and thus towards stability. That mood has been contrasted with the self-destruction of the revolution in the two years after Cromwell's death, a period of twilit anarchy which only the restoration of the Stuarts could end. That interpretation has its points but is misleadingly one-sided. The protectorate had frailties which it never overcame. It failed to live down its origins in the military coups of 1653. Those episodes affronted principles of civilian rule and parliamentary supremacy which commanded widespread support but which have been obscured by the 'revisionist' trend of parliamentary history. Though he aimed at 'healing and settling', the protector healed little and settled nothing. His attempts to woo mainstream opinion were unsuccessful. In so far as he won its compliance or tolerance, the achievement was conditional upon his readiness to submit to the principles of rule which his seizure of power had broken. It was a condition he could not or would not meet. By the end of his life, military obstruction to civilian and parliamentary rule had reduced his regime to paralysis, and had deepened the divisions between civilian and military aspirations that would soon bring down his successor and would destroy each of the fleeting regimes that followed.

On 24 February 1657 John Thurloe, whom observers agreed to be the 'intimus' and 'right-hand man' of the lord protector,[1] wrote to George Monck, commander-in-chief of the occupying English forces in Scotland, to report the presentation to parliament, on the previous day, of the Remonstrance that offered to make Oliver Cromwell king. This was the document that, after modification by the Commons, would become the Humble Petition and Advice. Thurloe, that inveterate spinner of news, remembered the disaffection among the forces in Scotland that had followed Cromwell's elevation to the protectorate in December 1653, and he feared the renewal of discontent now. So he gave Monck information about the Remonstrance that would enable the general, on whose cooperation Thurloe could rely, to 'satisfie any ... who may have scruples about this bussines'. One point Thurloe particularly wished to

---

[1] *Swedish Diplomats at Cromwell's Court, 1655–1656*, ed. Michael Roberts (Camden Society, fourth series, 36, 1988), 114, 127, 289; Blair Worden, 'Oliver Cromwell and the Council', in *The Cromwellian Protectorate*, ed. Patrick Little (Woodbridge, 2007), 97.

get across: that the move to crown Cromwell owed nothing to the personal ambition of which the protector was widely suspected. Thurloe 'assured' Monck that the Remonstrance 'arises from the parliament only; His Highness knew nothinge of the particulars untill they were brought into the house'.[2]

Thurloe's claim is supported by a report of the Dutch ambassador in London, who was well informed about the Remonstrance: 'the whole business is so managed, that the protector is left out of it'.[3] The management must have been adroit. Four days before the presentation of the Remonstrance, a copy of it had been seen in the hands of Oliver's son and heir Richard.[4] Those who also saw the document in advance included that 'discontented and dangerous person', as Monck called him,[5] William Packer, the commander of the protector's own regiment of horse, whose hostility to the Humble Petition would result in his own dismissal a year later.[6]

Cromwell was practised at not knowing. He had achieved a larger feat of ignorance in December 1648. Having stayed in the north of England, in ruminative mood, while the revolution of which he had become the leading spirit neared its climax of Pride's Purge and the regicide, he travelled south so slowly as to reach the capital only on the evening of the day that Colonel Pride had had the army's leading opponents in the Commons arrested.[7] On his arrival he was able to declare – according to the admittedly garbled but, on such a point, essentially reliable source in which the statement has come down to us – 'that he had not been acquainted with this design'.[8] Five years after the purge there was a feat of ignorance more impressive still. On 12 December 1653 he succeeded, even as lord general of the army, in being unaware of the military coup that terminated the rule of Barebone's Parliament, the body which he had summoned – on his authority as lord general – five months earlier. In September 1654 he assured another parliament, 'in the presence of divers persons here, who do know whether I lie in that, that I did not know one tittle of' the resignation of Barebone's,[9] even though the event was managed by his close advisers, who persuaded the assembly to return its power to him. Four days after its expiry he was installed as lord protector under the new constitution, the Instrument of Government. In the same speech of 1654 he told parliament that he had not been 'privy' to the

[2] *The Clarke Papers*, ed. C. H. Firth (Camden Society, 4 vols., 1891–1901), III, 89–90.
[3] *A Collection of the State Papers of John Thurloe*, ed. Thomas Birch (7 vols., 1742), VI, 85.
[4] C. H. Firth, *The Last Years of the Protectorate* (2 vols., 1909), I, 129n.
[5] *Collection*, ed. Birch, VI, 807.
[6] Firth, *Last Years of the Protectorate*, I, 129n.
[7] David Underdown, *Pride's Purge* (Oxford, 1971), 148–50.
[8] *Memoirs of Edmund Ludlow*, ed. C. H. Firth (2 vols., Oxford, 1894), I, 211.
[9] *Speeches of Oliver Cromwell*, ed. Ivan Roots (1989), 45.

'counsels' that led to the drawing up of the Instrument, and appealed to 'the gentlemen that undertook to frame' the constitution as witnesses.[10]

There is no more dextrous a political art than knowing how not to know. Equally there is none likelier to arouse mistrust. Cromwell was universally mistrusted. His elevation in 1653 had long been predicted, not only by royalists but by critics on his own side. Levellers, commonwealthmen and sectaries whom he courted or sounded were left to reflect, in rueful retrospect, on the duplicitous purpose they had come to detect in the advances of friendship he had made to them. The supposition that his avowals of godliness, and his commitment to liberty of conscience, were masks for his own advancement, or were means to it, was not only made by observers in whose minds we might suppose Puritan religious experience to have been a blind spot: Clarendon, Hobbes, foreign rulers and ambassadors. It was held by men who had been bound to him in spiritual exertion, among them Sir Henry Vane[11] and Cromwell's brother-in-law Valentine Walton,[12] he whose son's death by a cannon-shot at Marston Moor had prompted that memorable letter of consolation from Oliver.[13] Even people sympathetic to Cromwell remarked on the 'temptations' to which he had been vulnerable[14] (a weakness, admittedly, that Puritans commonly detected in each other). The sympathisers were outnumbered by the haters, and the hatred was most intense not among royalists but among his former allies.

The mistrust of Cromwell was largely inspired by his deployment of the beliefs and language of Puritanism to political ends. Over the past generation or so, historians have become more interested in the intensity or the content of his religion than most scholars were during the debates about the civil war that caught the headlines in the middle third of the twentieth century. In that earlier time a common assumption informed perspectives, Tory, Whig and Marxist, that clashed on other fronts: the assumption that religion was the seventeenth century's way of talking about something else – about economic or political aspiration or disappointment, the subjects where the real historical interest was taken to lie. Nowadays, when more effort goes into the recovery than into the explanation of the Puritan movement, we are readier to study Cromwell's religion on the terms on which he himself professed it. That religion,

[10] *Ibid.*, 46.

[11] Blair Worden, 'Oliver Cromwell and the Sin of Achan', reprinted in *Cromwell and the Interregnum*, ed. David L. Smith (Oxford, 2003), 52.

[12] *Collection*, ed. Birch, VII, 795.

[13] *Writings and Speeches of Oliver Cromwell*, ed. W. C. Abbott (4 vols., Cambridge, MA, 1937–47), I, 287.

[14] *Collection*, ed. Birch, II, 620, III, 294; *Diary of Thomas Burton*, ed. J. T. Rutt (4 vols., 1828), III, 211; *Writings and Speeches*, ed. Abbott, IV, 879; Peter Toon, *God's Statesman. The Life and Work of John Owen* (Exeter, 1971), 100.

however, never turned away from the world it sought to transform, or shunned the manoeuvres and contrivances of power.

Puritan initiatives in public life tended to be accompanied by exercises in collective soul-searching. They always had a political dimension. Thus the prayer-meeting at Putney on 29 October 1647 that turned into the famous debate on the franchise was about a good deal other than prayer. The admonitions against betrayals of the divine spirit that were made during it, and in countless other prayer meetings or fasts held by soldiers or politicians during the revolution,[15] were instruments of political pressure. So was the monitoring of souls in Cromwell's own correspondence, as such recipients of his letters as Robert Hammond[16] and Lord Wharton[17] and Charles Fleetwood[18] could have testified. There is no mistaking Cromwell's sensitivity to imputations that he cloaked 'carnal' or 'politic' designs in providentialist rhetoric,[19] an interpretation which to his mind merely confirmed the blindness of his accusers to God's purposes.[20] Yet how congruent divine impulsion and political calculation could be. Who can doubt the place in Cromwell's heart of the cause of European Protestantism? A few hours before his death he 'was distracted and in those fits he would cry out, "What will they do with the poor Protestants in Piedmont, in Poland and other places?", and such kinds of discourses.'[21] Yet his Protestant diplomacy was also calculated, as Thurloe acknowledged, 'for the support of things at home'.[22] The termination of the Dutch war at the outset of the protectorate, and the decision to fight Spain instead, were challenges to Antichrist – and were simultaneously intended to widen the support for the government through a return to the traditional diplomatic objectives of Puritanism. Cromwell's programme of religious and moral reform at home was meant to create a commonwealth fit for God's eyes and to avert the divine wrath – and simultaneously to reconstruct, as the basis of his own rule, the Puritan consensus of 1640. It would be a mistake to suppose that the practitioners of ideologies which aspire to transcend the laws of political life are less likely to be animated or constrained by them than politicians of more mundane outlook. Today I shall look, from selected angles, at the terrestrial rather than the cosmic predicaments of the protectorate.[23]

---

[15] Worden, 'Oliver Cromwell and the Sin of Achan', 42–6, 50–1.

[16] *Writings and Speeches*, ed. Abbott, I, 577, 676–8, 696–9.

[17] *Ibid.*, I, 646, II, 189–90, 328–9, 453, 560–1.

[18] *Ibid.*, III, 88–9, 756.

[19] *Speeches of Oliver Cromwell*, ed. Roots, 7, 75.

[20] *Ibid.*, 74.

[21] *The Clarke Papers V*, ed. Frances Henderson (Camden Society, fifth series, 27, 2005), 272.

[22] *Swedish Diplomats at Cromwell's Court*, ed. Roberts, 28n.

[23] I have said something of the latter in my 'Oliver Cromwell and the Sin of Achan', and in my 'Providence and Politics in Cromwellian England', *Past and Present*, 109 (1985), 55–99.

At some point between the parliament of 1654 and that of 1656, an anonymous polemicist alleged that the protector had told the Scottish politician John Hay, second earl of Tweeddale,

> that there was something amiss in the church and state, . . . and as for those things that were amiss in the church, [he] hoped to rectify by degrees, as opportunity presented itself; but before [he] could do this work, the anabaptists must be taken out of the army, and this [he] could not do with sharp corrosive measures, but it must be done by degrees.[24]

We cannot tell whether Cromwell said such a thing. Yet in Tweeddale's country, as Thurloe appreciatively observed, Monck successfully undertook the 'weeding out of the army troublesome and discontented spirits'.[25] Henry Cromwell confronted the anabaptists in Ireland and strove to 'keep them from power' there.[26] He and his followers were urged to be 'patient', 'for a while', until the protector's approval of his policies could be displayed.[27] Henry himself hoped that his father would 'at length' 'distinguish . . . true freinds from others', and that 'by degrees' he would 'wind out power and armes out of the hands of' Henry's own enemies in England, to whom anabaptists looked for protection.

Over the course of the protectorate, most of the people who had rejoiced in the regicide or in the abolition of monarchy, or who wanted structural change in the church or the law or the universities, saw their cause in retreat. Leading figures – Fleetwood in Ireland, Robert Lilburne in Scotland, John Lawson in the fleet, John Owen at Oxford University – who, even though they had come on board the protectorate, retained sympathy for commonwealthmen who had not, lost their places or their influence. Presbyterian divines were welcomed to court, among them John Howe, a scourge of heresy who became chaplain to the protector;[28] and Thomas Manton, who had sided with the presbyterian majority in parliament against the new model army in 1647, but who conducted the prayers at Cromwell's installation under the Humble Petition,[29] and who prayed with him on the last day of the protector's life.[30] On the council the alliance of Thurloe and Philip Jones,[31] men eager for Cromwell to be king, gradually outreached the influence of civilian colleagues dismayed by that prospect. Among the regime's administrators and diplomats, such pragmatic figures as George Downing and William Lockhart, too young

[24] *Collection*, ed. Birch, III, 150.
[25] *Ibid.*, VI, 873.
[26] *Ibid.*, II, 149–50, 162–4; T. C. Barnard, *Cromwellian Ireland* (Oxford, 1975), 107.
[27] *The Correspondence of Henry Cromwell 1655–1659*, ed. Peter Gaunt (Camden Society, fifth series, 31, 2007), 168, 178.
[28] *Oxford Dictionary of National Biography* (*ODNB*): 'Howe, John'; and see Lee Prosser, 'Writings and Sources XXII: The Palace of the Republic', *Cromwelliana* (2009), 82.
[29] *ODNB*: 'Manton, Thomas'.
[30] *Clarke Papers V*, ed. Henderson, 272.
[31] Worden, 'Oliver Cromwell and the Council', 103.

to have been shaped by those experiences of the 1620s which had forged
the political Puritanism that destroyed Charles I, replaced superannuated
ideologues.

And yet how slow was the shift, and how incomplete. Always Cromwell
had one eye on the resistance it encountered. The opposition, like so
much else in protectoral politics, turned on perceptions of his character.
Had he not, it was asked, succumbed to allurements of the will or
the self, or to the slipperiness of high places? Had he not, like King
Jehu in the Second Book of Kings,[32] used a programme of godly
reformation as the engine of his own advancement, and abandoned or
fatally compromised it once the advancement had been achieved? Was
it true, it was suspiciously asked early in the protectorate, that he was
'serv'd upon the knee' at table?[33] And if, as he sometimes indicated, he
wanted to preserve the spirit of a commonwealth even as he suspended
its forms – or if, as he liked to insist, he did not intend the government
to pass to members of his own family[34] – then why did he not, as proof
of his 'sincerity', make provision for the exclusion of his sons from the
succession?[35] Not only was there hostility outside the regime, among
saints and commonwealthmen whom he would have carried with him if
he could. There was unease, and often more than unease, within it. Army
officers who had been bound to Cromwell from dark and humble days –
John Desborough, Edward Whalley, William Goffe, James Berry – were
accustomed to a blunt egalitarianism in their dealings with him that the
deferences of the new court seem to have done nothing to soften.[36] Those
officers had close allies among the civilians on the council in William
Sydenham (himself a former soldier), Walter Strickland, and Sir Gilbert
Pickering,[37] who monitored no less closely the protector's contentions with
temptation.

[32] *A Collection of Scarce and Valuable Tracts*, ed. Walter Scott (13 vols., 1809–15), VI, 474; Blair
Worden, *Roundhead Reputations. The English Civil Wars and the Passions of Posterity* (2001), 58; and
see W[illia]m S[heppard], *Sincerity and Hypocricy* (1658), 24.

[33] *Collection*, ed. Birch, II, 163.

[34] *Correspondence of Henry Cromwell*, ed. Gaunt, 76; *Writings and Speeches*, ed. Abbott, III, 756.

[35] 'Johannes Cornubiensis', *The Grand Catastrophe* (1654), 13. As well as the familiar sources
for the public roles given to Richard and Henry Cromwell, see the eminence accorded to
Henry by the secretariat of the council of state in minutes of council meetings in the month
before Oliver's assumption of the protectorate: The National Archives (TNA), SP25/4–6,
25/72.

[36] Desborough: Blair Worden, *Literature and Politics in Cromwellian England* (Oxford, 2007),
328; Whalley: 'The Correspondence of Henry Cromwell, 1655–1659', ed. Clyve Jones
(M.Litt. thesis, University of Lancaster, 1969), 213; Goffe: *Writings and Speeches*, ed. Abbott,
I, 541; *Conscience-Oppression* (1657), 52; Berry: *Collection*, ed. Birch, IV, 498 (cf. *ibid.*, VII, 365). I
am most grateful to Mr Jones for enabling me to use a copy of his invaluable dissertation.
On the officers see too *Correspondence of Henry Cromwell*, ed. Gaunt, 277.

[37] Worden, 'Oliver Cromwell and the Council', 101–2.

Historians may never agree whether it was from choice or necessity – whether from conscience and conviction or from a recognition of facts of power – that the protector restrained the counter-revolutionary trend which he simultaneously encouraged, and positioned himself midway between the two pressures. Either way, a pervasive and persistent ambiguity was worn on the face of power. Was the protector, or was he not, a kind of king? Earlier protectors had been, not kings, but temporary substitutes for them. The title was familiar to the nation as an interim expedient, suited to the rule of a minor or of a disqualified monarch. Cromwell told parliament in 1657 that he had expected his own tenure of the office to be 'temporary, to supply the present emergency'. He had undertaken it 'not so much out of hope of doing any good, as out of a desire to prevent mischief and evil, which I did see was imminent upon the nation'.[38] Unrelenting government propaganda justified the coup of December 1653 as the nation's escape from the anarchy to which Barebone's had almost reduced it, an argument which did give the regime initial appeal, though it became less effectual with time. Yet, whereas a time-limit had been set on the rule of Barebone's,[39] the new constitution was apparently designed for posterity. The regime's conduct in its early stages did nothing to discourage that perception. The Instrument entitled the government, during the first nine months of its existence, to pass ordinances 'for the peace and welfare of these nations where it shall be necessary', which would be subject to confirmation by parliament.[40] One might suppose that they, too, would have been emergency measures. Yet some of the ordinances went far beyond the immediate claims of 'necessity' and aimed to secure lasting changes in the church, in the law, in the universities.[41] There was nothing temporary, either, about the repair and refurbishment, on a regal scale, of the protector's palaces from early in 1654.[42]

During Oliver's rule there ran frequent rumours that the great offices of state that had accompanied the rule of kings would be revived, and that a lord chancellor or lord treasurer or lord high admiral or lord privy seal was about to be appointed.[43] Instead, his councillors preserved a collective anonymity. Thurloe, it is true, became *de facto* secretary of state. Visiting

---

[38] *Speeches of Oliver Cromwell*, ed. Roots, 132–3, 140.

[39] *Writings and Speeches*, ed. Abbott, III, 67.

[40] *Constitutional Documents of the Puritan Revolution*, ed. S. R. Gardiner (Oxford, 1899), 414.

[41] On them see Peter Gaunt, '"To Create a Little World out of Chaos": The Protectoral Ordinances of 1653–1654 Reconsidered', in *Cromwellian Protectorate*, ed. Little, 105–26.

[42] On it see Paul Hunneyball, 'Cromwellian Style: The Architectural Trappings of the Protectorate Regime', in *Cromwellian Protectorate*, ed. Little, 53–81.

[43] *Clarke Papers*, ed. Firth, III, 42, 43; *Certain Passages of Every Dayes Intelligence*, 17–24 Aug. 1655, 52; *Collection*, ed. Birch, I, 645, III, 538; Ruth Spalding, *Contemporaries of Bulstrode Whitelocke 1605–1675: Biographies, Illustrated by Letters and Other Documents* (Oxford, 1990), 52; and the

ambassadors, and sometimes Englishmen, were invited to know him by that title, or even as 'principal secretary of state'.[44] Yet he seems never to have been formally appointed. He was secretary of state and he wasn't. In the status of Cromwell's 'intimus', indeed, ambiguity approached an art form. Until 1657, when he was made a member of the council, the only post Thurloe officially held was as its 'secretary'. Yet in December 1653 an ambiguously worded order of that body implied that he was a councillor in all but name.[45] Ambiguity extended, too, to Sir Gilbert Pickering. From August 1655, when he was informally reported to have been given the post of lord chamberlain,[46] until the winter of 1657-8, when he seems, through some protracted and to us invisible process, to have formally assumed it,[47] Pickering held the office and he didn't. Semantic uncertainty preserved ambiguity on other fronts. Sometimes Cromwell employed the royal 'we'; sometimes he eschewed it; sometimes he got muddled between the two. In official communications he referred to the government's executive body sometimes as 'his' or 'our' council, in the way that a monarch might do; sometimes as 'the council', a term more appropriate to the independent body of state envisaged by the Instrument; and sometimes as 'the council of state', which had been the official term for the executive bodies of the Rump and Barebone's, but which, while it was often used colloquially to describe the council of the protectorate, had no official meaning under it.[48] In 1657 the introduction of the Humble Petition brought some formalisation of nomenclature. Yet ambiguity had not lost its scope. It seems safe to infer, from Cromwell's complaisant silence on the subject during the negotiations over the new constitution, that its designers knew that he would find acceptable its original and ingeniously ambiguous solution to the dilemma over the succession: the office of

numerous reports in the newsbooks in May and June 1655. See too *Constitutional Documents*, ed. Gardiner, 413, 416.

[44] TNA, SP 18/67, no. 56, 25/75: 6 Aug. 1657, item 6; *Writings and Speeches*, ed. Abbott, III, 774, 784; *Calendar of State Papers Domestic (CSPD) 1655*, 128, *1656-7*, 82; *Severall Proceedings of State Affaires*, 30 Mar. – 6 Apr. 1654, 3749; *Swedish Diplomats at Cromwell's Court*, ed. Roberts, 74; *Collection*, ed. Birch, II, 106, 245, VI, 428, VII, 64; F. P. G. Guizot, *History of Oliver Cromwell and the English Commonwealth*, trans. A. R. Scoble (2 vols., 1854), II, 436 (though cf. *ibid.*, II, 446-9). In the minutes of the protectoral council he was often called 'Mr. Secretary', the courtesy title that had customarily been given to secretaries of state.

[45] TNA, SP25/75, 10 (*CSPD 1653-4*, 309).

[46] *Clarke Papers*, ed. Firth, III, 47.

[47] *Ibid.*, III, 141; Bodleian Library, Carte MS 73, fo. 187v; *CSPD 1657-8*, 344.

[48] These inconsistencies and confusions can be glimpsed in *Collection*, ed. Birch, II, 285; *Writings and Speeches*, ed. Abbott, III, 296-7, 507, 809; and the references of petitions to the council by Cromwell (e.g. TNA, SP 18/69, no. 71, 18/76, no. 7, 18/99, no. 58). The suggestion in Peter Gaunt's admirable article, '"The Single Person's Confidants and Dependants"? Oliver Cromwell and his Protectoral Councillors', *Historical Journal*, 32 (1991), 553, that Cromwell used the word 'we' to refer to decisions taken by him together with the council could explain only some of the cases.

protector was to be neither hereditary nor elective but nominative. He sustained the ambiguity unto his deathbed: he nominated Richard to succeed him, and he didn't.[49]

Ambiguity was the instrument of balance. In Ireland, even when, in 1657, two years of ambiguous, not to say contradictory command were ended by Henry Cromwell's appointment as lord deputy, his rival and counterweight Fleetwood retained his capacity to undermine him at Whitehall, while the membership of the Irish council, as Henry complained, was 'looked upon as a mere balance of three against three'.[50] In June 1658 the protector appointed a body of nine to decide on the next political move. On it the rival parties were so carefully poised that agreement was unattainable.[51] There was, urged Henry Cromwell and his allies, an answer to the paralysis that afflicted the regime in its later stages: an end to the 'bare balance or aequilibrium', which 'will not serve',[52] and a reconfiguration both of the English council and, more important, of the military high command.[53] Thus could the protector subdue the 'depraved appetites' of the 'sick minds'[54] – Fleetwood, Desborough and their friends – who obstructed the desire for a monarchical settlement, and by whom, as Henry's new brother-in-law Lord Fauconberg told him, Henry himself was 'so very much feared and hated'.[55] Instead, the shift towards monarchy halted; as Oliver's end approached, there were expectations within the regime of 'civill warres after his death';[56] and in that 'miserable posture' of affairs Fauconberg prepared to confront his and Henry Cromwell's enemies over control of the army.[57] Nine months after Richard's succession a regime that had awed Europe was destroyed from within when Oliver's son-in-law Fleetwood and his brother-in-law Desborough toppled his son.

Royalists, who had looked to Cromwell's death for a revival of their fortunes, were disappointed. Clarendon, perceiving only the external power of the government and unaware of its internal contentions, remembered that, 'contrary to all expectation at home and abroad', Richard succeeded with a smoothness that an established dynasty might

[49] Historians consequently cannot agree whether he did: *Complete Prose Works of John Milton*, ed. D. M. Wolfe *et al.* (8 vols., New Haven, 1953–82), VII, 4–5.
[50] *Collection*, ed. Birch, VI, 506.
[51] *Ibid.*, VII, 193, 269.
[52] *Ibid.*, VI, 858.
[53] Worden, 'Oliver Cromwell and the Council', 103.
[54] *Collection*, ed. Birch, VI, 93.
[55] *Ibid.*, VII, 451.
[56] *Ibid.*, VII, 348; cf. *ibid.*, VII, 269.
[57] *Ibid.*, VII, 365, 366.

have envied.[58] Sir Charles Firth, the master-historian of the protectorate, was likewise impressed by its standing in the last phase of Oliver's life. He noted the protector's continuing decisiveness and stressed the humbling of royalist conspiracy. He saw the protector's panic-stricken dissolution of parliament in February 1658, when Cromwell had to hail a hackney-carriage to get him to Westminster to forestall the presentation of a mass petition demanding the restoration of the 'supreme power' of the Commons, as a response to a merely temporary problem posed by the creation of the Other House. Firth regarded the feats of Blake's navy and the acquisition of Mardyke and Dunkirk as vindications of Oliver's diplomatic ambitions – even if the means had not been found to pay for them or sustain the army at home.[59]

I shall present a different view of the protectorate, and emphasise what seem to me the narrowness and shallowness of its base. Because the regime brought a return to government by a single ruler, and because it crushed the alien plant of republican rule, it has become customary to think of it as, in David Underdown's words, 'a half-way house on the road to 1660'.[60] From that perspective the restoration of the Rump in 1659 looks like a moment of twilit resistance to the tide. The protectorate, wrote Underdown, was 'a government closer to the hearts of the gentry than any since the Civil War',[61] though he emphasised that it was not as close as all that, and he anyway made a large exception for the period of the rule of the major-generals. Certainly the government strove from the outset to widen its support. It immediately withdrew the 'engagement' of loyalty to kingless rule that the Rump had divisively imposed.[62] It distanced itself from the memory of the regicide.[63] Parliamentary elections brought political presbyterians – men who, or whose allies or members of whose families, had been driven from parliament in 1648 – back to Westminster, first in 1654, then in 1656, then, under Richard Cromwell, in 1659. There were intermittent initiatives to conciliate royalists and Anglicans, and there was a frequent readiness to connive at their dissent, provided it was peaceable – though those concessions were unlikely to impress victims of the major-generals and the decimation tax. In some counties established families returned to the agencies of local government – though, if a single pattern emerges from the diversity of regional experience that

[58] Edward Hyde, earl of Clarendon, *The History of the Rebellion*, ed. W. D. Macray (6 vols., Oxford, repr. 1958), VI, 98.

[59] C. H. Firth, *Oliver Cromwell and the Rule of the Puritans in England* (1900), 425–6, 428; Firth, *Last Years of the Protectorate*, II, ch. 12.

[60] David Underdown, *Somerset in the Civil War and Interregnum* (Newton Abbot, 1973), 175.

[61] *Idem*, 'Settlement in the Counties', in *The Interregnum. The Quest for Settlement*, ed. G. E. Aylmer (1972), 174.

[62] *Acts and Ordinances of the Interregnum*, ed. C. H. Firth and R. S. Rait (3 vols., 1911), II, 830–1.

[63] Worden, *Literature and Politics in Cromwellian England*, 142.

modern studies of the shires in the 1650s have uncovered, it is that the more the leading families involved themselves in the running of the localities, the more the counties were able to put local priorities ahead of Whitehall's.

Yet there is, and was at the time, an alternative perspective. Within it, it is the protectorate, not the parliamentary rule on either side of it, that is the most fundamental aberration. Recent advances in the study of seventeenth-century parliaments are indebted to the challenge levelled by Conrad Russell and others at 'Whig' interpretations. Yet something has been lost by Russell's insistence that parliament was 'an event' rather than 'an institution'. It was both. The event mattered because the institution mattered. The politically inspired exploration of medieval parliamentary history by seventeenth-century lawyers and antiquaries involved the recovery not merely of tactically useful precedents but of a vision of parliament as the great council of the realm, where ultimate authority, and where emergency powers, lay: a council, that is, entitled in the last resort not merely to give advice to kings but to make decisions without them. How else can we explain the confidence of the Long Parliament in 1640–2, when it claimed to control the militia; by-passed the royal veto; asserted that, as the repository of the community's will, it was entitled to place necessity above the law; and in effect took over the executive? Whatever the theoretical or legal objections which those initiatives encountered, the breadth and depth of national sentiment behind them enabled them to prevail. Edward Hyde, earl of Clarendon, would time and again remember the king's difficulty, even after the Long Parliament had appropriated executive powers, in constructing a royalist case that would overcome the 'reverence' and 'veneration' and 'superstition' that were 'generally . . . entertained for parliament', that 'fatal disease' by which 'the whole kingdom was misled', and which, Hyde judged, gave Westminster an unassailable advantage in the recruitment and maintenance of armies.[64] At least Hyde managed to persuade the king, in royal declarations of 1642, implicitly to renounce his earlier non-parliamentary rule, and to explain that his own actions were directed not against 'the dignity, privilege and freedom of parliaments', 'whose freedom distinguishes the condition of his majesty's subjects from those of any monarchy in Europe',[65] but only against the 'seditious' ringleaders who had perverted the institution.[66] At his trial and on the scaffold, the king remembered to insist on his respect for the 'privileges' of parliament.[67]

[64] Clarendon, *History of the Rebellion*, I, 476–7, II, 82, 461, 479 (cf. II, 25), III, 117, 181, 259.
[65] *Ibid.*, II, 202, 279.
[66] *Ibid.*, II, 66, 149.
[67] *The Trial of Charles I*, ed. David Iagomarsino and Charles J. Wood (Dartmouth, NH, 1989), 81, 140.

Of course, no one among Charles's opponents in the Long Parliament aimed at what they inadvertently achieved: a parliament in permanent session, allegedly exercising a tyranny of its own. Parliaments were regarded as supreme in the sense that they were the source and sanction of legitimate rule. They were not meant, in normal circumstances, to administer it. Most of the time, it was universally assumed, there should not be a parliament in being. The one basic constitutional point about which the parliament of 1654–5 found it easy to agree with the protector was that parliaments should not be 'perpetual'.[68] Equally, MPs did not want new parliaments to be too frequent. When medieval precedents suggested to them that parliaments ought to be summoned annually, they shrank from the logic of their own antiquarianism. The supremacy attained by the Long Parliament was full of contradictions. The more the assembly claimed to be acting as the representative of the people, the less representative it became. The trial of the king was carried out on the authority of a House of Commons which invoked its own supremacy in vindication, but which had had to be forcibly purged of its majority for that purpose. The new regime struggled to justify not only the end of monarchy but the abolition of the House of Lords, a subject that, in the decade that followed the event, few people seem to have known how to tackle head-on, unless by resort to the sociology of James Harrington. MPs on the parliamentarian side responded in varying ways to the dilemmas about constitutional authority with which the developments that followed the civil wars of the 1640s unexpectedly presented them. Some pronounced all the regimes of 1648 to 1659 to be illegal. Others aimed to steer Puritan rule back to constitutional legality. Some became republicans. Others converted to royalism. Some held to their positions obdurately: others altered or compromised them in the light of events. What in most cases cut across those positions was an assumption that without parliamentary consent there was no legitimate basis of law or government – even if disagreement often flared about how consent could or should be identified and achieved.

More than 200 MPs were willing to sit in the Rump.[69] The majority of them had been opposed to Pride's Purge and the execution of the king, the events that brought the Commonwealth to power. Yet in the circumstances of 1649 they accepted the unicameral rule of the House of Commons. In February a number of peers and commoners who refused to give retrospective endorsement to the regicide, but who now joined the council of state, declared themselves ready to 'live and die' with the

[68] *Speeches of Oliver Cromwell*, ed. Roots, 51; *Diary of Thomas Burton*, ed. Burton, I, xxxii, xl; *Journal of the House of Commons*, 14, 15 Nov. 1654.
[69] The conduct and motives of its members, and the composition of its membership, are described in my *The Rump Parliament 1648–1653* (Cambridge, 1974).

Commons as 'the supreme power of the nation', 'in whom the liberty and freedom of the people is so involved'.[70] They might prefer the ancient constitution to a republic, but they also knew that God permits mankind to alter forms of rule for reasons of prudence and circumstance; and in 1649 no less than in 1642 necessity pressed. They knew too that the army was irresistibly bent on the destruction of the ancient constitution. The Rump made clear its view of Pride's Purge by omitting Henry Ireton and Thomas Harrison, the MPs who as army officers bore most responsibility for it, from the council of state.[71] In December 1648 Ireton had wanted to go further and dissolve the Long Parliament.[72] MPs hoped that by prolonging it, even in a purged form, even under the shadow of military intervention, and even after the overthrow of the ancient constitution, they could preserve the principle of parliamentary supremacy. A decade after the regicide the prominent former rumper Sir Arthur Hesilrige would recall that in early 1649 'two of the three estates were . . . gone. Then, for the third estate, that, God knows!, had been much shattered and broken. Force was much upon us. What should we do? We turned ourselves into the Commonwealth.'[73] Another prominent rumper, Bulstrode Whitelocke, thus explained his readiness, even as he repudiated the regicide, to accept the supremacy of the Commons after it: 'Unavoidable necessity hath put us upon those courses, which otherwise perhaps we should not have taken.'[74]

During the Rump's rule Cromwell strove, in the face of opposition within the regime, to secure the return to active politics of MPs who had been excluded in December 1648 or had absented themselves thereafter.[75] We might think that as protector, eager as he remained to reconstruct the parliamentarian party of the 1640s, he had his chance. Yet the permanently vacant seats, about a third of the whole, on the protectoral council, to which he hoped to appoint parliamentarian grandees, signal his failure.[76] Scarcely any members of the Long Parliament who had ceased to sit in the Long Parliament in 1648, and only one of them who had achieved political stature in the 1640s, Cromwell's councillor Nathaniel Fiennes, can be found anywhere near the centre of his regime. Fiennes had belonged to the moderate or constitutionalist wing of the Independent party. Presbyterian survivors of the Long Parliament, who were to be

---

[70] TNA, SP25/62: 19 Feb. 1649, 3; Ann Hughes, *Politics and Civil War in Warwickshire*, 1620–1660 (Cambridge, 1987), 223.

[71] Worden, *The Rump Parliament*, 180.

[72] Underdown, *Pride's Purge*, 140–1.

[73] *Diary of Thomas Burton*, ed. Burton, III, 97.

[74] Bulstrode Whitelocke, *Memorials of the English Affairs* (4 vols., Oxford, 1853), II, 526.

[75] Worden, *Rump Parliament*, 277.

[76] *Idem*, 'Oliver Cromwell and the Council', 85.

found in significant numbers at Westminster under the protectorate, were rarely glimpsed in Whitehall.

What, then, of the former members of the Rump? If, in 1649, its rule was a parliamentary alternative to military government, in December 1653 the protectorate replaced parliamentary rule by a military usurpation. In that sense the termination of Barebone's was a more profound alteration of the revolution's course than the expulsion of the Rump eight months earlier. Cromwell's instructions to Barebone's in July 1653 had honoured the principle of parliamentary supremacy. They pointed towards a return to the rule of a sovereign parliament by 1655.[77] In 1654, by contrast, Cromwell refused to honour the principle. Having submitted the Instrument of Government to parliament for approval, he would not take its refusal for an answer. If presbyterian MPs purged by Colonel Pride were absent from the centre of protectoral power, few former rumpers were to be found there either. It might be answered that a high number of rumpers, perhaps even a majority of them, had played little part in the executive machinery of the republic, and were the kind of country gentlemen whom we would sooner expect to find running their estates than occupying posts in Whitehall. Yet around a third of the Rump's members had been more often at Westminster than not,[78] and had played active parts in the government of the country. In 1653 most of them vanished from the political scene. That year was one of those occasions in politics when a generation leaves the stage (though in this case the generation would return, in 1659–60). It was not the Long Parliament but Barebone's, which in retrospect can be seen as the auditions for the protectorate, that supplied a large proportion of the officials – members of the army committee; admiralty commissioners; excise commissioners; and so on – at the centre of Cromwell's government.[79]

There were exceptions to the rule. Seven former rumpers served on the council of the protectorate: Philip Jones, Francis Rous, Philip Skippon, Walter Strickland, Sir Gilbert Pickering, William Sydenham, and Charles Fleetwood. Only the first of them, however, visibly supported the monarchical trend of the protectorate, and the last four opposed it. There were eleven professional lawyers who seem to have made the transition from parliamentary to protectoral service easily enough, and to whose identity and behaviour I shall come. But only three other rumpers seem to have held office in the central administration of the protectorate: Luke Hodges of Gloucestershire, who became an excise commissioner;[80]

[77] *Writings and Speeches*, ed. Abbott, III, 67.
[78] Worden, *Rump Parliament*, 26.
[79] Austin Woolrych, *Commonwealth to Protectorate* (Oxford, 1982), 384–5.
[80] *CSPD 1653–4*, 309.

William Masham of Essex, who was made a treasury commissioner;[81] and John Lowry, formerly Cromwell's fellow-MP for Cambridge, who was given a post in the customs.[82] For all we know there may have been a number who, like Robert Bennett of Cornwall,[83] would have been glad to be invited to serve in similar ways. In the provinces there was a handful of rumpers, beside Bennett, whom the protectorate may have thought of as friends. Perhaps John Bingham, the governor of the Isle of Wight,[84] Sir William Strickland of Yorkshire,[85] and Dennis Bond and John Trenchard of Dorset,[86] belonged to such a category. If so, however, the friendships are unlikely to have run deep.[87] Occasionally former members of the Rump can be seen addressing the regime with prudent politeness when they had petitions or private concerns to press in Whitehall.[88] Yet outward civility to rulers has never, on its own, been evidence of support for their rule.

Even rumpers who were drawn into public service do not always look like enthusiasts for the protectorate. Two of them served the regime abroad: Robert Blake, the great admiral of the fleet, and Richard Salwey, who was appointed ambassador to Constantinople. Yet it is probable that both men thought of themselves as acting for their country rather than for its present government. Blake showed no commitment to the regime, and Salwey's loyalty to it was doubtful.[89] The slippery John Jones became brother-in-law to the protector and gave practical support to the government in his native Wales,[90] but the favour bestowed on him was keenly opposed by Henry Cromwell, who remembered his republican past and thought him still 'dissatisfied'.[91] Some rumpers, though not many, were appointed as commissioners for the public faith, and a larger quantity, alongside a great number of other parliamentarians or Puritans, as commissioners for the ejection of ungodly ministers. At least six were named to

---

[81] *CSPD 1654*, 284; *Memoirs of Edmund Ludlow*, ed. Firth, I, 372.

[82] Andrew Barclay, 'The Lord Protector and his Court', in *Oliver Cromwell: New Perspectives*, ed. Patrick Little (Basingstoke, 2009), 205.

[83] Woolrych, *Commonwealth to Protectorate*, 389–90.

[84] TNA, SP25/77, 311–12.

[85] *Collection*, ed. Birch, IV, 593.

[86] *CSPD 1655–6*, 354.

[87] Sir John Trevor of Surrey is another candidate (*CSPD 1655–6*, 354; see too SP25/153: 1 Jan. 1657, item 1), but the evidence does not always allow us to distinguish him from his son, John.

[88] *Collection*, ed. Birch, IV, 644 (William Masham's father and fellow-rumper Sir William Masham), V, 711 (Thomas Scot), VI, 624 (Dennis Bond); Bodleian Library, Rawlinson MS A24, 74 (James Ashe).

[89] *Collection*, ed. Birch, IV, 589.

[90] *Ibid.*, IV, 413.

[91] *Ibid.*, IV, 606.

the council of trade.[92] Yet it seems unlikely, at least in most cases, that the rumpers appointed to those bodies were consulted before their appointments or that they ever took them up. A number of rumpers did retain their customary involvement in local government. In the absence of other evidence, however, their willingness cannot be taken to betoken more than a determination to preserve the workings of local communities or their own places in them. Some, among them five MPs from Buckinghamshire who acted as militia commissioners in the county under the major-generals,[93] were willing to assist the government against the Cavaliers, the 'common enemy' as parliamentarians of various hues liked to call them.[94] Yet that attitude, too, is no indication of a liking for Cromwell's rule. It was shared by Matthew Alured, one of the 'three colonels' who mounted a conspiracy against the protectorate during the first of its parliaments.[95] Thomas Scot, a prominent rumper and zealous opponent of the protectorate, who had run the Commonwealth's intelligence system, was ready to pass information about royalist conspiracy to Thurloe, his successor in that post.[96] In Sussex another MP who had exerted great influence in the Rump, Herbert Morley, agreed to assist the major-general in the county 'to the utmost' as a JP, but not otherwise.[97] He was ready – readier than he wanted it to be known – to aid the government in the raising of seamen and in combating royalist conspiracy or piracy on the county's coast.[98] Nonetheless the council, which knew his underlying antipathy to the government, excluded him, as it did Scot, from the parliament of 1656.[99]

It is no surprise to find men whom, at least by 1653, it may be legitimate to think of as committed republicans – Scot, Hesilrige, Vane, Ludlow, John Weaver – in conflict with the protectorate. But the hostility of former rumpers was more widespread. At its heart was not republican

[92] *Writings and Speeches*, ed. Abbott, IV, 64 (Godfrey Bosvile and William Purefoy), 97 (John Jones); *CSPD 1655*, 240 (Oliver St John, Dennis Bond and the republican Thomas Chaloner).

[93] *Collection*, ed. Birch, IV, 583: George Fleetwood, Richard Ingoldsby, Edmund West, Cornelius Holland and Simon Maine.

[94] The rumper John Dove, the sheriff of Wiltshire who was captured by the royalist insurrectionaries of March 1655, subsequently assisted the government in their suppression: *Collection*, ed. Birch, III, 318–19.

[95] *Ibid.*, IV, 359. An opponent of the protectorate in Cheshire, Robert Duckenfield (who like Alured was not an MP, but who like him had been happy to serve the Rump), offered to accept from Cromwell a 'handsome military command' to fight on the Continent, but was unwilling to accept a commission 'within this nation' (*ibid.*, III, 294).

[96] *Ibid.*, III, 350, V, 711.

[97] *Ibid.*, III, 161.

[98] *Ibid.*, III, 369, IV, 549, 573–4. On Morley, and the conduct of Sussex MPs associated with him, see Anthony Fletcher, *A County Community in Peace and War: Sussex 1600–1660* (1975).

[99] *Collection*, ed. Birch, V, 490.

but parliamentarian sentiment, of which commitment to kingless rule was an extreme or eccentric form. The protectorate knew of the dislike of its own existence among prominent rumpers who as far as we can see had no principled objection to kingship: Valentine Walton,[100] Sir William Brereton of Cheshire,[101] Thomas Fell of Lancashire,[102] Robert Wallop, Nicholas Love and Robert Reynolds of Hampshire.[103] Opposition broadened from the time of the dissolution of the first protectorate parliament in January 1655. Until that point there was a chance that the regime could acquire parliamentary sanction. After it the government was cast back on the naked military power that had brought it into being. One rumper who now took his stand was the judge Francis Thorpe, who had opposed the regicide but had delighted the Rump, in March 1649, by declaring on its behalf that the people were 'the original of all just power'.[104] Now he broke ranks with most of the other rumpers who were professional lawyers and was dismissed after refusing to implement Cromwell's treason ordinance.[105] Another was Cromwell's former friend[106] Sir Peter Wentworth, who had collectors of non-parliamentary taxation arrested in his native Warwickshire, and who was summoned to Whitehall for his pains. There – according to our garbled but here again essentially reliable source, Ludlow's *Memoirs* – he told Cromwell to his face that 'by the law of England no money ought to be levied upon the people without their consent in parliament'.[107] How could John Hampden, had he still been alive, not have concurred? The rumper Lord Grey of Groby, who had stood at Colonel Pride's side during the purge of 1648, was now arrested for conspiring against the protectorate.[108] There was a more substantial figure – not a rumper – among the politicians disaffected under the protectorate. Sir Thomas Fairfax, who had viewed the revolution of 1648–9 with impotent unease, and who had resigned the leadership of the army in 1650, would nonetheless collude with the commonwealthmen in Richard Cromwell's parliament, where he conspicuously sat at the side of Sir Arthur Hesilrige.[109] In December

---

[100] Peter Gaunt, 'The Councils of the Protectorate' (Ph.D. thesis, Exeter University, 1983), 129; cf. *Collection*, ed. Birch, VII, 587.

[101] *Collection*, ed. Birch, V, 313.

[102] *Ibid.*, IV, 423.

[103] Andrew Coleby, *Central Government and the Localities: Hampshire 1649–1689* (Cambridge, 1987), 72, 78. In Coleby's account (p. 61) the rumper John Dunch was a supporter of the regime in Hampshire.

[104] *ODNB*: 'Thorpe, Francis'.

[105] S. R. Gardiner, *History of the Commonwealth and Protectorate* (4 vols., repr, New York, 1965), III, 298–9.

[106] *Writings and Speeches*, ed. Abbott, I, 346.

[107] *Memoirs of Edmund Ludlow*, ed. Firth, I, 414.

[108] *Ibid.*, I, 414; Gardiner, *History of the Commonwealth and Protectorate*, III, 226–7, 229, 269.

[109] *Diary of Thomas Burton*, ed. Burton, III, 48.

1657 Fairfax was reported to have declared that 'since the dissolving' of the Long Parliament in 1653, 'which was broke up wrongfully, there was nothing but shifting and a kind of confusion'.[110]

The military origins of the protectorate plagued its quest for settlement. On the ninth day of its first parliament, 12 September 1654, the protector, dismayed by the assembly's opposition to the Instrument of Government, forcibly purged it. Members who wished to resume their seats were required to subscribe to a loosely worded 'Recognition' that engaged them to fidelity to the protector and to acceptance of the government 'as it is settled in a single person and a Parliament'. In one sense the purge was successful. In the opening days of the parliament, Cromwell had been opposed by two formidable sets of politicians. There were the leading presbyterians, John Birch, John Bulkeley, and Sir Richard Onslow at their head, all of whom had been imprisoned at Pride's Purge. And there were the commonwealthmen, Hesilrige and Scot at *their* head, who had been forcibly expelled in 1653. In the initial sessions of the parliament the two groups joined forces against the Instrument. The purge of 12 September removed most of the commonwealthmen.[111] The event was the opposite of Pride's Purge, for this time it was the presbyterians who survived. The presbyterians were ready to negotiate with Cromwell, as in 1648 they had been willing to negotiate with Charles I.

Yet no more than the rumpers who had decided to return to parliament in February 1649 were they enthusiasts for their course. After the purge of September 1654 a number of them withdrew for a time and hesitated before resuming their seats. It was the presbyterians' turn to face the argument from necessity. Some of them, including John Birch and probably John Bulkeley, returned only after several weeks and after extensive debate among themselves, during which they at last resolved to 'give way to the present necessity'. The 'sin' of the pledge that was now required of them, decided one of the presbyterian MPs, lay with its 'imposers', not its 'subscribers'.[112] There was much in the Instrument of Government that the presbyterians would have wanted to revise even if it had been introduced through some constitutional and civilian mechanism. They contended strongly against the provisions of the document for liberty of conscience and concerning the control and pay of the armed forces. Yet their basic objection was not to the content

---

[110] *Collection*, ed. Birch, VI, 706, VII, 84. When parliamentary rule was restored in May 1659 Fairfax was appointed to the council of state, though he did not take his seat (*CSPD 1658–9*, xxiv, 349; *1659–60*, xxiii–xxv), and we cannot tell whether he agreed to the appointment.

[111] This can be deduced from the names of members which appear or do not appear in the *Journal of the House of Commons*. The only significant exception, if we count him as a commonwealthman, was Herbert Morley.

[112] 'Three Letters Illustrative of English History', ed. Henry Ellis, *Archaeologia*, 25 (1832), 139–40; and see *Diary of Thomas Burton*, ed. Burton, I, xxxv–xxxvi.

of the Instrument. It was to its genesis in armed force. The MPs were willing to sanction the general outline of the Instrument, but on one condition: that the authority of the constitution, and of the protector himself, be acknowledged to derive from parliament itself, not from the soldiers who had introduced it. On that premise his rule from December 1653 to September 1654 had been a usurpation. Only now, through the consent of parliament, would Cromwell's rule acquire legitimacy. No one in the assembly other than the court party seems to have been impressed by Cromwell's flimsy claim that since December 1653 the readiness of judges or justices to sit, or electors to vote, or political organisers in towns or counties to send him addresses, indicated that the nation had consented to his rule.[113] To make its point the parliament of 1654–5 adopted a fiction. Even as it went through the Instrument, revising its clauses, it affected to be drafting instead a bill entirely of its own devising. Only a month before the dissolution did the assembly give itself leave 'to consider of the printed document, intituled The Government of the Commonwealth' – the name under which the Instrument had been published.[114] Five years later John Bulkeley told the Commons that, 'in the bowels of it', the Instrument 'took away your rights'. That he had in mind the genesis rather than the content of the Instrument is indicated by his acknowledgement that the constitution itself 'had much good in it'. If only Cromwell and parliament could have agreed on its revision, he intimated, England would have acquired 'a happy government and foundation for posterity'.[115]

Uncompromising assertions of the sovereign rights of parliament were made in the debates of 1654–5. We might expect them to have been voiced solely by commonwealthmen. It is likely to have been commonwealthmen who, on the day before the purge of September 1654, described 'the former government, by King and Parliament,' as 'but an usurpation upon the common right'.[116] Perhaps it was they who, in the same debate, insisted that 'the supreme power was originally in the people'.[117] Yet when 'the more moderate men on both sides' turned the debate towards a search for common ground, 'the sense and opinion of the House ran generally' in favour of the principle of parliamentary supremacy. 'The Government', it was agreed, 'should be in the Parliament and a single person, limited and restrained as the Parliament should think fit.'[118] That view prevailed in the Commons after the withdrawal of the commonwealthmen, when the right of parliament to 'limit and restrict'

[113] *Speeches of Oliver Cromwell*, ed. Roots, 48–9; *Diary of Thomas Burton*, ed. Burton, I, xxix, xxx.
[114] *Journal of the House of Commons*, 19 Dec. 1654.
[115] *Diary of Thomas Burton*, ed. Burton, III, 107.
[116] *Ibid.*, I, xxx.
[117] *Ibid.*, I, xxix.
[118] *Ibid.*, I, xxxii.

the protector's powers continued to be asserted.[119] When the question arose whether Cromwell's successor should be chosen by parliament or by the executive council of the protectorate, it was 'agreed on all sides, that it was an original fundamental right, inherent in the Parliament, to choose their supreme officers'.[120] 'There is no Englishman', it was argued, 'but will rather part with his life, his liberty, his estate . . . than with the just rights and freedoms of the people'; and 'the legislature was ever in the people'.[121] The Commons decided that any power which the protector might hold to veto legislation would be bestowed as the 'gift' of parliament, though under pressure from the court 'the more moderate' members did persuade the Commons to 'change the word "give" into "declare"'.[122]

Between the parliament of 1654–5 and that of 1656–8 there are significant contrasts.[123] In 1654–5 court and council were more or less united in defence of the Instrument. In 1656–7, the time of the first session of the second protectorate parliament, court and council were split, and the rival parties took the battle to parliament. A number of courtiers and councillors joined the MPs who brought the Remonstrance into the house, and who commanded a strong majority for it. They commanded it because presbyterians who had opposed the Instrument in 1654 supported the new constitution of 1657, as they would support it again in 1659. Why that contrast? There were differences of content between the Humble Petition and the Instrument of Government, the constitution which the Humble Petition was meant to replace. Yet, like the differences in 1654 between the Instrument and the bill into which the parliament converted it, they were not the nub of the matter. In 1654 and 1657 alike, parliament adopted its own constitution. The contrast lay in the attitude not of MPs but of Cromwell, who was hostile to the first constitution but welcomed the second. In 1657 the negotiations between parliament and protector were consequently as courtly as in 1654 they had been confrontational. Yet the principle on which the presbyterians had taken their stand three years earlier was preserved. If, in 1654, MPs denied Cromwell's right to impose his rule on them, in 1657 they questioned, in their discussions with him over parliament's offer of kingship, his right to refuse a constitution which the people's representatives were pressing on him: pressing, moreover, not as a basis for negotiation, but to be accepted or rejected in its entirety – though he characteristically contrived to wriggle out of that stipulation.

[119] *Ibid.*, I, lvi.
[120] *Ibid.*, I, liii.
[121] *Ibid.*, I, lxv; cf. *ibid.*, I, xxx–xxxi.
[122] *Ibid.*, I, lxvi–vii; *Journal of the House of Commons*, 10, 11 Nov. 1654.
[123] The two assemblies are penetratingly analysed in Patrick Little and David L. Smith, *Parliaments and Politics during the Cromwellian Protectorate* (Cambridge, 2007).

During the talks between Cromwell and the parliamentary delegates, Nathaniel Fiennes, in his capacity as an MP, told Cromwell that the new constitution, while it was modestly called a 'petition', was 'in some sort a petition of right', which Cromwell had an 'obligation' to accept.[124] Sir Charles Wolseley concurred: the protector should 'give the people leave to choose their own servant; that is a due you cannot, you will not certainly deny them.'[125] There was, it is true, a tactical aspect to the suave wording of Fiennes and Wolseley, councillors of Cromwell who wanted him to accept the title. Their master, who in 1657 was as concerned not to alienate parliament as in 1654 he had been ready to take it on, was himself careful to endorse the notion that the house was entitled to do as it wanted with him[126] – though when it came to it he wriggled again. But the appropriateness of the tactic arose from the Commons' perception of its supreme role in the resolution of the nation's constitutional crisis.

Wide as the parliamentary backing for the Humble Petition was, it cannot properly be interpreted as support for the government. It was support for the party within the government that wanted not to entrench the protectorate but to change it: to turn it into a parliamentary, and civilian, monarchy. The presbyterians who had opposed the Instrument in 1654, and who backed the Humble Petition in 1657–9, had not, or mostly had not, become courtiers. Sir Richard Onslow, the veteran presbyterian MP who urged Cromwell to accept kingship, was fairly described by Henry Cromwell's agent Anthony Morgan as 'head of the country party for' the Humble Petition.[127] With presbyterian or country party support – for the two had become hard to distinguish – the Humble Petition secured parliament's consent, even after Cromwell had procured amendments to it. Yet his refusal of the crown, at the army's behest, showed how little security for civilian and parliamentary rule the new constitution gave. The group that had been behind the offer was broken by his decision.[128] In the months before his refusal, the opposing faction, led by Fleetwood and Desborough, had seemed in decline. Cromwell's rejection of the crown revived its fortunes and thus erected what proved to be a permanent block to the civilianisation of the regime. Two years later the two generals would bring down Richard Cromwell. Admittedly Richard, being, as MPs said, 'without guile or gall',[129] and being unlikely to lead military coups against parliament as his father had done, had much to be said for him

---

[124] *Collection of Scarce and Valuable Tracts*, ed. Scott, VI, 380.

[125] *Ibid.*, VI, 360.

[126] *Speeches of Oliver Cromwell*, ed. Roots, 116–17; cf. *ibid.*, 118, 130.

[127] *Correspondence of Henry Cromwell*, ed. Gaunt, 205. Cf. *Collection*, ed. Birch, III, 161, and John Bulkeley's speech in *Diary of Thomas Burton*, ed. Burton, IV, 347.

[128] Firth, *Last Years of the Protectorate*, I, 193–8; Fletcher, *County Community in Peace and War*, 315; cf. Little and Smith, *Parliaments and Politics*, 107–8.

[129] *Diary of Thomas Burton*, ed. Burton, III, 132; Little and Smith, *Parliaments and Politics*, 160.

as a potential parliamentary monarch, if only – but it proved too big an 'if' – he could control the generals. The rumper John Stephens, who had no love for the protectorate,[130] nonetheless saw in the Humble Petition and Advice, when it was debated in the parliament called by Richard Cromwell, a means to return to the ancient constitution.[131] He had found the 'little fingers of the Major-generals . . . heavier than the loins of the greatest tyrant kings that went before'. Now he was 'glad to find one in possession' – Richard – 'who will rule according to the law, and not the sword'.[132] It was because of such sentiments that support for the Humble Petition commanded a majority in Richard's parliament. It was because the constitution commanded that support that the army destroyed the regime.[133]

Yet when the protectorate fell, who lamented its passing? In 1660, as the revolution disintegrated, there were stray, despairing thoughts of restoring Richard, but there is no sign that those who made the suggestion supposed that the Humble Petition, let alone the Instrument of Government, was recoverable. Thus the only two written constitutions to have been implemented in English history, the first created by the new model, the second aborted by it, fell to dust. On Richard's fall and the restoration of the Rump, large numbers of rumpers who had boycotted the protectorate returned, bringing their portion of the displaced generation back with them. William Purefoy of Warwickshire, apparently aged nearly eighty, who had disliked the protectorate and had retreated into semi-retirement under it, returned 'rejuvenated' to Westminster.[134] The lawyer Oliver St John, Oliver's Cromwell's cousin and close friend, who had been Hampden's counsel and then a parliamentary grandee of the 1640s and early 1650s, had subsequently given backstairs advice to both protectors. Yet, while he had hesitantly continued to sit as chief justice of the Common Pleas, he had evaded the exercise of political office. Cromwell got him appointed as a treasury commissioner,[135] but there is no sign that he took up the post. After the restoration of the Rump in May 1659, by contrast, he served on its council of state.[136]

Other professional lawyers had responded differently to Cromwell's elevation. The MPs who had served as the Rump's attorney-general and solicitor-general, Edmund Prideaux and William Ellys, remained in their posts. The rewards of office made Prideaux a rich man in the 1650s. He and Ellys were made baronets by Cromwell three weeks

[130] Andrew Warmington, *Civil War, Interregnum and Restoration in Gloucestershire 1640–1672* (Woodbridge, 1997), 118, 120.
[131] *Diary of Thomas Burton*, ed. Burton, III, 158, 357–8.
[132] *Ibid.*, IV, 11.
[133] The point is astutely conveyed by Little and Smith, *Parliaments and Politics*, esp. ch. 7.
[134] Hughes, *Politics and Civil War in Warwickshire*, 292.
[135] *CSPD 1654*, 284, 411; *CSPD 1655*, 173; *Journal of the House of Commons*, 24 Oct. 1654.
[136] *CSPD 1658–9*, xxiv, 349; *CSPD 1659–60*, xxiii–xxv.

before the protector's death.[137] Other rumpers in the profession proved equally pliable on Cromwell's elevation. Bulstrode Whitelocke and John Lisle remained commissioners of the Great Seal; Nicholas Lechmere of Worcestershire acquired a new legal office; William Lenthall, the former speaker of the Long Parliament, remained master of the rolls and would accept membership of Cromwell's 'other house', the protectorate's substitute for the House of Lords; his son John retained his post as one of the six clerks of Chancery and would be knighted by the protector. Lislibone Long and the brothers Nathaniel and Francis Bacon became the protectorate's masters of requests. Roger Hill served the protectoral judiciary. The compliance of all those lawyers might prompt us to cynical reflections on the careerist priorities of their profession in illegal times. Their adaptability was doubtless enhanced by the panic in the legal profession when Barebone's voted to abolish the Court of Chancery, and by the relief when Cromwell's elevation removed that threat. William Lenthall reflected after the protector's installation that on the eve of it the nation had stood 'upon the brincke . . . of Confusuon and desolation'.

Yet if the legal profession and public order were preserved by the coup, there was another question for the lawyers. Would the rule of the protector be the rule of law? Lenthall hoped so. With others he saw Cromwell's elevation as a necessary military means towards the demilitarisation of politics. He told himself that the new government, under which 'Our Laws have ther freedom and countenance and property challenges her own without interruption', would 'produce much happinesse and safety to all . . . and as much settlement to our Lawes and Liberties'.[138] Thurloe hoped the same. He proclaimed at the outset of the protectorate that the regime would bring an end to 'arbitrariness' in government.[139] The claim was echoed by Cromwell,[140] and perhaps would have been vindicated had he reached agreement with the parliament of 1654 or taken the crown in 1657. There proved, however, to be narrow limits to the constitutionalism of the protectorate. Even before the parliament of 1654–5 had met, William Ellys, the solicitor-general, had to remonstrate against the council's readiness to bypass the legislative processes of parliament.[141] In Richard Cromwell's parliament he would urge the Commons to adhere to the Humble Petition, for 'If we lose this foundation we must go to Major-generals, and the Instrument of Government, that had no foundation in Parliament.'[142]

Then there is the Suffolk lawyer Nathaniel Bacon, who in the 1640s had been a prominent administrator in the Eastern Association. Bacon's *An*

[137] *Writings and Speeches*, ed. Abbott, IV, 866.
[138] Spalding, *Contemporaries of Bulstrode Whitelocke*, 166.
[139] *Ibid.*, 374.
[140] *Speeches of Oliver Cromwell*, ed. Roots, 30, 48; cf. *ibid.*, 44.
[141] Gaunt, '"To Create a Little World"', 121–2.
[142] *Diary of Thomas Burton*, ed. Burton, III, 567.

Historicall Discourse of the Uniformity of the Government of England, published in 1647 and continued in 1651, has been called 'the English *Franco-Gallia*'.[143] It claimed that Saxon and medieval history showed the English monarchy to be elective and contractual and to be subject to parliamentary supervision. Richard Baxter declared the book one of the four most influential works to have been written on the parliamentarian side. It influenced posterity, too, being frequently reprinted, and invoked by politicians, in the later seventeenth century and the eighteenth.[144] Bacon had sat only fleetingly in the Rump and had evidently been uneasy about the republic.[145] After the protector's purge of the parliament of 1654 he waited for a month before resuming his seat.[146] So it seems a surprise to find him acting, by July 1655, as a master of requests, though characteristically it is not clear whether he had been formally appointed. Except for those on the council, he became the only rumper to play a bigger part in the government of the protectorate than of the Commonwealth before it. But we can sense what he was up to: he was trying to help change the government from within. Through the crowning of Cromwell, he evidently thought, politics could be freed of military intervention, and a return to medievalist, civilian, constitutional principles of rule be achieved. From early 1656 we can watch him seeking to nudge the regime in a monarchical direction. When Cromwell referred petitions to the council which the Masters of Requests had brought before him, Bacon and his brother Francis, with surreptitious impropriety, directed the documents to 'the', or 'his', 'privy council',[147] the term that would be reintroduced to the constitution only in 1657, when the Humble Petition adopted it in order to give the body a regal flavour. Bacon supported the Humble Petition, which, he explained, was 'not so much a new Constitution, as a reviving of the Old with taking off exorbitances'. It deserved acceptance because 'the people of England have a right to the single person and two Houses of Parliament, and it cannot be taken away without their consent'.[148]

Or there is Bulstrode Whitelocke. Never have a politician's autobiographical vindications backfired more disastrously. His readers might have more sympathy with his criticisms of the protectorate had he not disclosed to posterity how tickled he was by the attention and favour

[143] Glenn Burgess, *The Politics of the Ancient Constitution. An Introduction to English Political Thought 1603–1642* (1992), 96.
[144] *ODNB*: 'Bacon, Nathaniel'.
[145] Worden, *Rump Parliament*, 73, 127.
[146] 'Three Letters Illustrative of English History', ed. Ellis, 140; *Journal of the House of Commons*, 10 Oct. 1654.
[147] TNA, SP18/126, no. 123, 125, 18/127, no. 19, 18/128, nos. 5–6, 56, 78–9, 82, 18/129, nos. 25, 57, 69–70, 110, 18/130, nos. 77–8.
[148] *Diary of Thomas Burton*, ed. Burton, III, 357.

Cromwell bestowed on him, and how resentful that he did not bestow more of them.[149] After the dissolution of parliament in 1655, Whitelocke was among the defectors. He resigned, with Sir Thomas Widdrington, as a commissioner of the Great Seal sooner than implement Cromwell's extra-parliamentary ordinance for the reform of the Court of Chancery. For 'to execute that as a law upon mens estates & rights which he knew to be no law, but an exorbitant power', 'when I knew that those who made it had no legal power to make a law, ... would be a betraying of the rights of the people of England, and too much countenancing of an illegal authority'.[150] A month later he accepted a lucrative post as a treasury commissioner instead. There is an unmistakable dimension of self-serving retrospect in his accounts of his pleas to Cromwell to revert to parliamentary and legal courses, as in much else in his recollections of his conduct in the Interregnum. Even so, his dismay at the 'wholly illegall' rule of the major-generals, and at other breaches of constitutional methods by the protector, is plain enough.[151]

Like Nathaniel Bacon, Whitelocke studied medieval history in a book that would be put to Whiggish use in the eighteenth century.[152] He visited the subject again in a 'Historie of the Parlement of England', of 'our great, publique, supreame Generall Counsell of the Nation'.[153] Like Bacon he believed the English monarchy to have been elective and to have rested on consent. Like Bacon he preferred mixed forms of government, and regarded England's ancient constitution as one. He supported the Humble Petition, albeit with reservations, and urged Cromwell to become king. Yet in other circumstances his commitment to parliamentary supremacy, and to the principle of political consent, could assume non-monarchical forms. It could also lead him into anti-protectoral company, most strikingly that of the Leveller John Wildman, with whom he formed a devoted friendship. In 1655, after Cromwell's failure to win parliamentary sanction for the Instrument, Whitelocke received and transcribed a copy of the vituperative declaration in which Wildman sought to incite an armed rising against 'the tyrant Oliver Cromwell' in defence of 'native rights and freedoms': a document, remarked Whitelocke, wherein 'there was too much of truth'.[154] In late 1659 he and Wildman came together to draft 'the form of a free state', a document which proscribed the rule of a single person and adopted the

[149] Bulstrode Whitelocke, *A Journal of the Swedish Embassy* (2 vols., 1855), I, 5, 322; Whitelocke, *Memorials*, IV, 188; *The Diary of Bulstrode Whitelocke*, ed. Ruth Spalding (Oxford, 1990), 401–2, 414, 438, 464, 476, 477, 478.

[150] *Diary of Bulstrode Whitelocke*, ed. Spalding, 407; Whitelocke, *Memorials*, IV, 204.

[151] *Diary of Bulstrode Whitelocke*, ed. Spalding, 415, 417, 477, 485, 488, 489 (cf. *ibid.*, 400).

[152] *Whitelockes Notes upon the Kings Writt*, ed. Charles Morton (2 vols., 1766), I, xxii.

[153] British Library, Stowe MS. 333.

[154] Whitelocke, *Memorials*, IV, 187; *Diary of Bulstrode Whitelocke*, ed. Spalding, 401.

Leveller principle that the people may impose restraints on their delegates in parliament.[155]

Whitelocke was outraged by Cromwell's expulsion of the Rump in 1653, when 'this great parliament, which had done so great things', 'famous through the world for its undertakings, actions, and successes', was 'routed' by its 'servants'. He remembered that 'all honest and prudent indifferent men were highly distasted at' the coup,[156] and that in 1659 'many others' joined him in welcoming the return of the Rump 'for setling the peace and liberty of the nation, and the more because they were uppon the first right and foundation of that long Parliament, which had done so great things'.[157] Yet the army, the creator and destroyer of every regime of the Interregnum, soon expelled the Rump for the second time. If ever in the Puritan Revolution two bodies ought to have been able to find common ground of policy, it was the restored Rump and the army which had restored it. Yet they quarrelled irreparably over the issue of civilian command of the forces. For the principle of parliamentary supremacy, which in the civil war had been defended against the king, had since 1647 faced an alternative enemy in the new model, ironically a body that in its programme of political reform had done so much to champion it. In 1659–60 the conflict destroyed the revolution. A mortal blow was the second dismissal of the Rump in October 1659. The Sussex grandee Herbert Morley, the prominent rumper who had kept his distance from the protectorate, was moved to an outrage that no opponent of Charles I could have surpassed. The army, he and others who challenged its authority alleged, had revived an 'old court design, to affright Englishmen out of their ... love to a parliament', and out of 'their hereditary and birthright privilege of making their own laws, by which they shall be governed'. In the present crisis there were 'many thousands of our mind who know no help, under God, like that of a parliament', a hope towards which 'the spirit of the free-born Englishmen' was aspiring.[158]

In 1659–60 accusations of 'sword-government', of rule by 'muskets' and 'red-coats', were hurled at the army by victims of its various purges of parliaments.[159] Now as in 1640–2, opponents of arbitrary rule looked to parliament as the nation's only saviour. In 1642 the cry thrown in Charles I's face in the streets of London, 'Privileges of parliament!', had announced the collapse of his authority in the capital: in 1659–60 it was the cry for 'a free parliament' that set the avalanche of the Restoration

[155] Longleat House, Whitelocke Papers, XXIV, 399–400; Spalding, *Contemporaries of Bulstrode Whitelocke*, 459–60.

[156] Whitelocke, *Memorials*, IV, 6.

[157] *Diary of Bulstrode Whitelocke*, ed. Spalding, 514.

[158] *Collection*, ed. Birch, VII, 772; cf. *ibid.*, VII, 794.

[159] See e.g. *ibid.*, VII, 772–3, 797.

in motion. When, in February 1660, George Monck resisted pressure to restore the members who had been purged in 1648, on the ground that if they were readmitted they would restore the king, among those who protested was the rumper Richard Norton of Hampshire, once a close friend of Oliver Cromwell. Under the protectorate he had been willing to 'keepe Portsmouth', where he was made governor of the garrison in 1655, 'safe' against a royalist invasion or insurrection,[160] but that was all. To Cromwell's dismay he refused to cooperate with the rule of the major-generals,[161] which permanently alienated him from Puritan rule. Now, in 1660, he told Monck that 'freedome of parliament was the just right and interest of the nation, and if they [parliament] thought it fitt to bring in the Turke they ought not to be imposed on to the contrary'.[162]

Everyone knew what a 'free parliament' would do. The term was often used as code for the return, in some form, of the monarchy, a goal which could not be openly proclaimed until shortly before the event. Yet the choice of code indicates the place of parliament in national esteem. The Restoration was the restoration of parliament before it was the restoration of the monarchy, which was restored through parliament's choice. Even the most entrenched republicans conceded that in 1660 the nation, however foolishly or wickedly, had consented to the king's return. Rumpers who had opposed the protectorate or distanced themselves from it – Norton, Morley, Alexander Popham – became at least half-royalists in the late stages of the revolution: parliamentary royalists, that is, who looked to parliament to reestablish the monarchy. The success of Monck, during the early months of 1660, in moving from apparent support for the commonwealthmen to insistence on the Restoration becomes the more explicable when we remember the common commitment to parliamentary authority that underlay those otherwise opposing positions.

The Restoration was the closest England had come to a unified political will since the first six months of the Long Parliament. In spite of it, both parliamentarian and Puritan ideals survived. In some quarters even republicanism, and even admiration for the regicide, clung on. Cromwell's name, and the memory of his deeds, endured too. What went mostly unlamented were the coup which had made him protector; the military basis of his rule; and the constitutions under which he had sought to cloak it.

---

[160] *Correspondence of Henry Cromwell*, ed. Gaunt, 202.
[161] *Collection*, ed. Birch, IV, 238.
[162] Coleby, *Central Government and the Localities*, 81; cf. *ibid.*, 21, 33, 71 (though also 79); *Collection*, ed. Birch, IV, 452; Jason Peacey, 'The Upbringing of Richard Cromwell', in *Oliver Cromwell. New Perspectives*, ed. Patrick Little (Basingstoke, 2009), 250–1.

Transactions of the RHS 20 (2010), pp. 85–112 © Royal Historical Society 2010
doi:10.1017/S008044011000006X

REFASHIONING PURITAN NEW ENGLAND: THE CHURCH OF ENGLAND IN BRITISH NORTH AMERICA, *c.* 1680–*c.* 1770

By Jeremy Gregory

READ 6 FEBRUARY 2009

ABSTRACT. The position of the Church of England in colonial New England has usually been seen through the lens of the 'bishop controversy' of the 1760s and early 1770s, where Congregational fears of the introduction of a Laudian style bishop to British North America have been viewed as one of the key factors leading to the American Revolution. By contrast, this paper explores some of the successes enjoyed by the Church of England in New England, particularly in the period from the 1730s to the early 1760s, and examines some of the reasons for the Church's growth in these years. It argues that in some respects the Church in New England was in fact becoming rather more popular, more indigenous and more integrated into New England life than both eighteenth-century Congregationalists or modern historians have wanted to believe, and that the Church was making headway both in the Puritan heartlands, and in the newer centres of population growth. Up until the early 1760s, the progress of the Church of England in New England was beginning to look like a success story rather than one with in-built failure.

In 1744 the churchwardens of Christ Church, Boston, New England (which was built in 1723 as the second Church of England place of worship in the town), having recently had a spire added to the tower of their church, and having now raised a subscription for a ring of bells, were in protracted negotiations with Abel Rudhall, bell-founder of Gloucester, Old England. The vestry were concerned that the tower would not be strong enough to hold bells which weighed 80 hundredweight or more, and Rudhall, one of the leading British bell-founders of his generation, had tried, unsuccessfully, to convince them not to have smaller ones cast. Having settled, for safety reasons, on a lighter set of bells, the vestry then urged Rudhall, through their intermediary, Thomas Gunter, to 'use his utmost endeavour to have them as musical and compleat as he can, which will no doubt encourage people here as well as the neighbouring governments to send for one, this being the first ring in English America'.[1]

---

[1] Massachusetts Historical Society (hereafter MHS), Records of Christ Church, Boston, MS N-2249, Box 21, folder 2, Vestry to Gunter, 12 Mar. 1744. On the establishment of the Rudhall firm, see L. M. Middleton, 'Rudhall, Abraham, the Elder

The vestry had panicked that no one in New England would know how to install the bells, and Rudhall initially persuaded John Baker, a local Gloucester man, to go over to set them up, but at the last minute Baker bottled out when his wife fainted on hearing that the ship taking him and the bells to Boston had docked at Bristol.[2] The eight bells cost Christ Church vestry £560, with an additional £93 for some special apparatus and wheels sent over by Rudhall to help put them in position, with a detailed set of instructions explaining how this should be done.[3] Once the bells had arrived in 1745, the vestry had an inscription engraved on each of them. On the tenor bell, the inscription read: 'this peal of eight bells is the gift of a number of generous patrons to Christ Church'; on the third bell: 'we are the first ring of bells cast for the British Empire in North America'; on the fourth: 'God preserve the Church of England'; on the fifth: 'William Shirley, Esq, Governor of Massachusetts Bay'; and on the eighth: 'Abel Rudhall of Gloucester cast us all'.[4]

The story of how Christ Church obtained its bells can, in many ways, be taken as representing in miniature the position of the Church of England in eighteenth-century New England.[5] Just as its bells had to be manufactured in Old England, so Christ Church, and other Church of England churches, both in the heart of Puritan North America, and on the Continent more generally, were largely dependent for the essentials and the trappings of the Church's functioning on exports from England, which are graphic reminders of the reliance of the New World on some English goods and services in the 1740s and beyond.[6] Above all, the churches required Books of Common Prayer to be sent over in large

(1657–1736)', rev. Giles Hudson, *Oxford Dictionary of National Biography* (Oxford, 2004) (www.oxforddnb.com/view/article/24254, accessed 10 Dec. 2009). Bells made by the Rudhalls also reached South Carolina, and the West and East Indies: George Worrall Counsel, *The History and Description of the City of Gloucester: From the Earliest Times to the Present* (Gloucester, 1829), 218. Information relating to the bells has been collected in Arthur H. Nicols, 'Christ Church Bells, Boston, Mass.', *New England Historical and Genealogical and Register* (1904), 63–71.

[2] MHS, MS N-2249, Box, 21, folder 2, Rudhall to Gunter, 9 Mar. 1744.

[3] It is not easy to be precise about this from the extant records, but this is the surmise of Asa Eaton, *Historical Account of Christ Church, Boston. A Discourse, 29 December 1823* (Boston, MA, 1824), 24; MHS, MS N-2249, Box, 21, folder 2, Rudhall to Gunter, 9 Mar. 1744.

[4] Eaton, *Historical Account*, 24–25.

[5] See John Frederick Woolverton, *Colonial Anglicanism in North America* (Detroit, 1984); James B. Bell, *The Imperial Origins of the King's Church in Early America, 1607–1783* (Basingstoke, 2004).

[6] Richard R. Johnson, 'Growth and Mastery: British North America, 1690–1748', in *The Oxford History of the British Empire*, II: *The Eighteenth Century*, ed. P. J. Marshall (Oxford, 1998), 289–91; John J. McCusker, 'The Current Value of English Exports, 1697 to 1800', *William and Mary Quarterly*, 28 (1971), 623–7; R. L. Bushman, *The Refinement of America: Persons, Houses, Cities* (New York, 1992), chs. 3–5; John E. Crowley, *The Invention of Comfort: Sensibilities and Design in Early Modern Britain and Early America* (Baltimore, 2001).

quantities, for this was the Church's liturgical manual and without it the Church could not operate, but since 1651 it had been unlawful to use it in worship in much of New England.[7] The churches were also recipients from Old England of clergy, via the Society for the Propagation of the Gospel in Foreign Parts (SPG), founded in 1701 and the main conduit for sending Anglican goods to New England, such as bibles, books, pamphlets, catechisms, sermons and tracts.[8] New England Anglicans also received from across the Atlantic church plate (often the treasured gifts of monarchs from William and Mary to George III), vestments, furnishings, including altars, and altar pieces, and boards with the ten commandments, creed and Lord's Prayer painted on them, and, in one instance, an altar painting.[9] On occasion they even had to send certain

[7] On the centrality of the Book of Common Prayer to the Church, see Judith Maltby, 'The Prayer Book and the Parish Church: From the Elizabethan Settlement to the Restoration', Jeremy Gregory, 'The Prayer Book and the Parish Church: From the Restoration to the Oxford Movement', and William L. Sachs, 'Plantations, Missions and Colonies', in *The Oxford Guide to the Book of Common Prayer Worldwide*, ed. C. Hefling and C. Shattuck (Oxford, 2006), 80–93, 93–105, 153–65. For its proscription in New England, see Carla Pestana, *The English Atlantic in an Age of Revolution, 1640–1661* (Cambridge, MA, 2004), 123ff.

[8] Standard histories of the SPG are H. P. Thompson, *Into All Lands: The History of the Society for the Propagation of the Gospel in Foreign Parts* (1951), and Daniel O'Connor *et al.*, *Three Centuries of Mission. The United Society for the Propagation of the Gospel, 1701–2000* (2000). See also Rowan Strong, *Anglicanism and the British Empire, c. 1700–1850* (Oxford, 2006), and Andrew Porter, *Religion Versus Empire? Protestant Missionaries and Overseas Expansion, 1700–1914* (Manchester, 2004), 16–28. The SPG's export of suitable books for the New England mission needs to be seen as part of the broader book trade between Britain and the colonies: see *A History of the Book in America*, 1: *The Colonial Book in the Atlantic World*, ed. Hugh Amory and David D. Hall (Cambridge, 2000). See also Irving Henry King, 'The S.P.G. in New England, 1701–1784' (Ph.D. thesis, University of Maine, 1968), and John Kendall Nelson, 'Anglican Missions in America, 1701–1725. A Study of the Society for the Propagation of the Gospel in Foreign Parts' (Ph.D. thesis, Northwestern University, 1962).

[9] For such gifts to Christ Church, Boston, see MHS, MS N-2249 (XT) Old North Church, Vestry Book, 1724–1802, 45, 7 Sept. 1733; Henry Wilder Foote, *Annals of the King's Chapel. From the Puritan Age of New England to the Present Day* (2 vols., Boston, MA, 1882), I, 122. The altar painting (depicting 'The Last Supper') was for the King's Chapel, although, in deference to Puritan sensibilities, it was never put up in the chapel: Kenneth Walter Cameron, *Letter-Book of the Rev. Henry Caner, SPG Missionary in Colonial Connecticut and Massachusetts until the Revolution. A Review of his Correspondence from 1728 through 1778* (Hartford, 1972), 55. On Church of England attitudes to art in this period, see Jeremy Gregory, 'Anglicanism and the Arts: Religion, Culture and Politics in the Eighteenth Century', in *Culture, Politics and Society in Britain, 1660–1800*, ed. Jeremy Black and Jeremy Gregory (Manchester, 1991), 81–109, and Claire Haynes, *Pictures and Popery: Art and Religion in England, 1660–1760* (Ashgate, 2006). For 'Puritan' suspicion of religious art in churches, see Patrick Collinson, *From Iconoclasm to Iconophobia: The Cultural Impact of the Second English Reformation* (Reading, 1998); Margaret Aston, 'Puritans and Iconoclasm, 1560–1660', in *The Culture of English Puritanism, 1560–1700*, ed. C. Durston and J. Eales (Basingstoke, 1996), 91–121; Julie Spraggon, *Puritan Iconoclasm in the English Civil War* (Woodbridge, 2003).

books, such as large bibles, back to London to have them re-bound,[10] and at times they were forced to inquire in London for organists, since Church of England churches in New England had the first church organs, as well as the first peal of bells, in British North America, and those able to play them were thin on the ground.[11] The inscription on the bell memorialising Governor William Shirley, a churchman and English-born,[12] who held a number of high-level posts within the empire, can be taken as emblematic of the sometimes wished-for alliance of the Church of England and the state (even in New England), in a setting where Congregationalism was the *de facto* established church, but where it was frequently hoped that the Church of England would prosper. As such, Shirley can be taken as a representative of the English settlers and government officials who brought over and sustained the Church in what was an alien and hostile religious environment. In the inscriptions on Christ Church's bells, the bells themselves were highlighted as aural accompaniments to the tune of empire, and the role of the subscribers (virtually all members of the laity) in providing funding was also emphasised, indicating the massive dependency of the Episcopal Church in New England, and in British North America more broadly, on lay backing.[13]

  This reading of the place of the Church of England in New England in particular (and in other parts of British North America) as an agent of imperialism and reliant on external support has much to commend it.[14] As well as Bostonians, many of the subscribers for the bells were men and women living in England, naval and army officers, who were only stationed in Boston sporadically, and merchants from far-flung parts of the empire,[15] demonstrating the town's prominent position as one of the imperial hubs. Indicative of this was King's chapel, Boston, the first Church of England building erected in New England, built in October 1689 by a congregation which had been meeting since 1686 at the instigation of representatives of James II's government.[16] John Dunton, the Presbyterian London book-seller who was in Boston in May 1686 when the Anglican clergyman Robert Ratcliffe sailed into the harbour as part of the retinue of Edward Randolph, councillor in

[10] MHS, MS N-2249 (XT) Old North Church, Vestry Book, 1724–1802, 111, 1 Sept. 1746: sending the large bible belonging to Christ Church, Boston to London to be rebound.
  [11] *Ibid.*, 136.
  [12] J. A. Schutz, *William Shirley: King's Governor of Massachusetts* (1961). See also Paul David Nelson, 'Shirley, William (1694–1771)', *Oxford Dictionary of National Biography* (www.oxforddnb.com/view/article/25442, accessed 18 Jan 2010).
  [13] Woolverton, *Colonial Anglicanism*, 235–8.
  [14] See Boyd Stanley Schlenther, 'Religious Faith and Commercial Empire', in *The Oxford History of the British Empire*, II, ed. Marshall, 128–50.
  [15] For the list of subscribers, see Nicols, 'Christ Church Bells'.
  [16] Foote, *King's Chapel*, 41–89.

the new Dominion of New England (a political entity which overrode the original Massachusetts charter, and was thus detested by many New Englanders), noted the strangeness of the situation:

> on Lord's Days [he] read the Common Prayer in His Surplice, and preach'd in the Town-House. Mr Ratcliffe was an Eminent Preacher, and his Sermons were useful and well dress'd; I was once or twice to hear him, and 'twas noise'd about that Dr Annesly's son-in law was turn'd Apostate. But I cou'd easily forgive 'em., in Regard, the Common Prayer, and the Surplice were Religious Novelties in New England.[17]

But two years later, Randolph informed Archbishop Sancroft that Ratcliffe was attracting opprobrium: 'some calling our minister Baal's priest and some of their ministers from the pulpit calling our prayers leeks, garlic and trash'.[18] Ratcliffe's congregation soon included Edmund Andros, a crony of James II and the loathed president of the Dominion, who was imprisoned during Boston's own version of the Glorious Revolution in April 1689.[19] The chapel was used, and financially supported, by naval officers, who among other things had pews installed in the new building in 1694 (where up until then seating had been on low wooden benches used in Congregational meetings),[20] and until the early 1770s was the favoured place of worship for the military stationed in the town. Henry Caner, the rector of King's chapel from 1747 until he fled Boston in 1775, baptised a large number of children of officers serving under General Gage in the chapel, and funeral services were held here for some of the British officers killed in and around Boston during the onset of Revolution.[21]

This interpretation of the Church as largely sustained by, and catering for, people who were in some senses 'external' to New England and who should not be regarded as 'real New Englanders' also meshes with contemporary Congregationalist discourse in which the Church of England was seen as not only as being corrupt, and little more than Popery in disguise, but as being intruded on New England. Increase Mather's voluminous publications included *A Brief Discourse concerning the Unlawfulness of the Common Prayer Worship* (1686), provoked by the use of the liturgy in Boston by Ratcliffe and his congregation, which made conventional 'Puritan' criticisms of the Prayer Book as being no better than the popish mass, likening the formulaic responses to 'tennis balls' tossed between the priest and the congregation, and decrying the hopeful prayers in the burial service, the use of the ring in marriage, making the sign of

---

[17] [John Dunton], *The Life and Errors of John Dunton Late Citizen of London; Written by Himself in Solitude* (1705), 152.

[18] Bodleian Library, Oxford, MS Tanner MS 30, fo. 257, Randolph to Sancroft, 7 July 1688.

[19] Philip Haffenden, *New England in the English Nation, 1689–1713* (Oxford, 1974).

[20] Foote, *King's Chapel*, 116

[21] *Ibid.*, 438.

the cross at baptism, and kneeling when taking the sacrament.[22] His *A Testimony against Several Prophane and Superstitious New Customs now Practised by Some in New England* (published in London in 1687), which railed against the performance of stage-plays, putting-up maypoles, drinking healths, playing cards, dice or the lottery, giving new-year's presents, observing saints' days, candle-mass and Shrove Tuesday, watching cock-fighting and the keeping of Christmas, which he was appalled to find were now being talked about in New England of all places (and where 'promiscuous dancing' had been practised the previous year),[23] urged New Englanders to stay away from these wicked pastimes. Cotton Mather in 1723 accused the Anglican clergy who came to New England of being 'tippling sots', but consoled himself that 'by a strange Infatuation from Heaven' they 'have been generally men of such a Behaviour, that it was impossible to take a more effectual Course for the prejudicing of this religious countrey against that sort of men, or the begetting an Horror for the Church of England in the New England colonies'.[24] Noah Hobart in the late 1740s and early 1750s denounced what he called the 'episcopal separation', claiming that those Bostonians who had been attracted to the Church in the 1680s quickly became shame-faced and embarrassed after the Revolution of April 1689 by what they had done,[25] and Jonathan Mayhew in the early 1760s spear-headed the attack on the SPG's activities in New England as a misuse of funds (in large measure following Hobart's arguments), and broadcast the idea that Britain was about to send over a bishop.[26] From the 1680s to the 1770s, then, leading New England Congregational spokesmen portrayed the Church of England in New England as unscriptural and unloved. Nathaniel Appleton, Congregational minister at Cambridge, summed up the Congregational view, recalling the fact that early settlers had come to New England precisely to escape from the Church of

[22] Increase Mather, *A Brief Discourse concerning the Unlawfulness of the Common Prayer Worship* (Boston, MA, 1686), 2–8, 12, 14, 17, 19–20, 21.

[23] Increase Mather, *A Testimony against Several Prophane and Superstitious New Customs now Practised by Some in New England* (1687), A.2.

[24] *Diary of Cotton Mather* (2 vols., Massachusetts Historical Society *Collections*, seventh series, VII, VIII, Boston, MA, 1911–12), II, 413–14; 'Some Original Papers respecting the Episcopal Controversy in 1723' (Massachusetts Historical Society *Collections*, second series, II, Boston, MA, 1814), 39.

[25] Noah Hobart, *A Second Address to the Members of the Episcopal Separation in New-England. Occasioned by the Exceptions Made to the Former, by Dr. Johnson, Mr Wetmore, Mr Beach and Mr Caner* (Boston, MA, 1751), 26. See also Noah Hobart, *A Serious Address to the Members of the Episcopal Separation in New-England. Occasioned by Mr. Wetmore's Vindication of the Professors of the Church of England in Connecticut* (Boston, MA, 1748).

[26] Jonathan Mayhew, *Observations on the Charter and Conduct of the Society for the Propagation of the Gospel in Foreign Parts; Designed to Shew their Non-Conformity to Each Other* (1763); idem, *A Defence of the Observations on the Charter and Conduct of the Society for the Propagation of the Gospel in Foreign Parts, against an Anonymous Pamphlet Falsly Intitled, A Candid Examination of Dr. Mayhew's Observations, &c.* (Boston, MA, 1763).

England in the 1620s and 1630s, when he moaned in 1760: 'it is grievous to think that when our Pious Ancestors came over into this Land, when an howling wilderness, to enjoy ye Gospel in ye purity & simplicity of it, yt the Chh of England should thrust it self in among us'.[27]

Modern historians have, both wittingly and unwittingly, by and large accepted and reinforced this view of a Church which was either an unwanted alien in, or a feared predator on, New England. One early twentieth-century commentator, anticipating later high-profile studies by Carl Bridenbaugh in 1962,[28] J. C. D. Clark in 1994 (who has called the War of Independence a 'war of religion'),[29] and more recently James Bell,[30] referred to 'a fiercely-waged conflict' between Congregationalists and Episcopalians that 'prevailed almost unceasingly from 15 May 1686 [when Ratcliffe arrived in Boston] . . . to the Revolution [in 1776]'.[31] This echoes the view, which has seldom been properly questioned by historians, of a linear trajectory of New England suspicion and dislike of the Church from the 1680s which led inevitably to the 'bishop controversy' of the 1760s and early 1770s, where New Englanders feared that England was about to send a bishop or bishops to impose an eighteenth-century version of Laudianism on the colonies. In some interpretations this has been seen as the crucial trigger moving New Englanders, and others, to throw off the British government, and as part of that process to take revenge on clergy and members of the Church of England. This seemingly demonstrated that not only was the Church of England violently unpopular, but also that the very idea that an Anglican bishop might be sent to America was enough to stir Americans into revolt.[32] This paper does not focus on this particular issue, not only because this is well-trodden ground,[33] but more pertinently because I am more concerned with what the Church

[27] *The Literary Diary of Ezra Stiles*, ed. Franklin B. Dexter (3 vols., New York, 1901), I, 125: Appleton to Stiles, 19 July 1760. On Stiles, see Edmund S. Morgan, *The Gentle Puritan: A Life of Ezra Stiles, 1727–1795* (New Haven, 1962).

[28] Carl Bridenbaugh, *Mitre and Sceptre. Transatlantic Faiths, Ideas, Personalities and Politics, 1689–1775* (1962).

[29] J. C. D. Clark, *The Language of Liberty, 1660–1832: Political Discourse and Social Dynamics in the Anglo-American World* (Cambridge, 1994).

[30] James B. Bell, *A War of Religion. Dissenters, Anglicans and the American Revolution* (Basingstoke, 2008).

[31] MHS, MS N-1153: 'Life and Letters of Revd Mather Byles, Jr', notes by Arthur Wentworth Hamilton Eaton, 96.

[32] Bridenbaugh, *Mitre and Sceptre*.

[33] Robert G. Ingram, *Religion, Reform and Modernity in the Eighteenth Century. Thomas Secker and the Church of England* (Woodbridge, 2007); Bell, *War of Religion*; Peter M. Doll, *Revolution, Religion and National Identity: Imperial Anglicanism in British North America, 1745–1795* (Madison, 2000), esp. 155–239; Nancy Rhoden, *Revolutionary Anglicans: The Colonial Church of England Clergy during the American Revolution* (New York, 1999), 37–63; Donald F. M. Gerardi, 'The Episcopate Controversy Reconsidered: Religious Vocation and Anglican Perceptions of Authority in Mid-Eighteenth Century America', *Perspectives in American History*, 3 (1987),

was actually doing in New England, rather than with its aspirations, or with the fears of its rivals. This is not because I think that such matters are unimportant (if suspicions about an Anglican bishopric in North America did contribute to the American Revolution how could they be?) but rather because concentration on the 'bishop controversy' has obscured the actual role and place of the Church in eighteenth-century New England. Bridenbaugh came close to accepting Congregationalist angst at face value, assuming that the powers that be in London were really contemplating sending over a bishop with Laudian pretensions to enforce religious absolutism in America, when this is patently not the case (indeed what is more striking is the refusal of the English authorities to take the matter further).[34] Clark's *The Language of Liberty* to a large extent continues Bridenbaugh's analysis, and it fits neatly into his wider programme (with which I concur) of stressing the importance of religion in eighteenth-century events, in contradistinction to the secular (and economic) explanations for eighteenth-century political change which had prevailed during much of the twentieth century.[35] But Clark was largely dependent on printed pamphlet controversies for his view of the bitter denominational rivalry between religious groups in New England, and British North America more generally, and there is a danger of using controversial literature to reflect day-to-day relations. He, Bridenbaugh and Bell are no doubt right to stress the ways in which Congregational discourse from the mid-1760s was able to mesh with, and inflame, other forms of discontent (economic and political) but, I argue, there is the risk of reading back from this that the Church of England necessarily had no place and no support within eighteenth-century New England. In any case denominational rivalry and competition (of which there was plenty) are not the same as religious conflict or war.

    There have also been some other valuable studies – less geared around explaining the causes of the American Revolution – which have added immensely to our understanding of the Church of England in British North America, but which have not taken as their central concern the progress made by the Church in New England, and these have tended to concentrate, perhaps understandably, on the prosopography of the clergy and on clerical pamphlets.[36] Much less attention, however, has been paid to the actual pastoral work of the Church of England clergy in

81–114; Bridenbaugh, *Mitre and Sceptre*; Arthur Lyon Cross, *The Anglican Episcopate and the American Colonies* (New York, 1902).

    [34] Stephen Taylor, 'Whigs, Bishops and America: The Politics of Church Reform in Mid-Eighteenth-Century England', *Historical Journal*, 36 (1993), 3331–56. See also Ingram, *Religion, Reform and Modernity*, 234–59.

    [35] Clark, *Language of Liberty*. See also his *English society, 1660–1832: Religion, Ideology and Politics during the Ancien Regime* (revised edn, Cambridge, 2000).

    [36] Bell, *King's Church*.

New England, to the New England lay men and women who supported Anglicanism,[37] or to the successes in winning over adherents from other denominations. In examining the Church of England in New England, this paper explores something of the Church on the ground. I will argue that in some respects the Church in New England was in fact becoming rather more popular, and more indigenous, and more integrated into New England life, than both eighteenth-century Congregationalists or modern historians have wanted to believe, and this is particularly true of the period from the 1730s to the early 1760s, where the Church was making headway both in the Puritan heartlands, and in the newer centres of population growth. Up until the early 1760s, the progress of the Church of England in New England was beginning to look like a success story rather than one with in-built failure.

In what ways did the Church of England attempt to 'refashion' Puritan New England in the ninety years after 1680? Refashioning might imply a wholesale remaking and reordering; indeed the transformation or alteration of 'Puritan New England' into an 'Anglican New England' was advocated by a number of commentators (both clerical and lay) such as Lewis Morris, an active churchman, member of the SPG and later governor of New Jersey, who wrote to the English high churchman William Beveridge from Boston in 1702: 'If the Church can be settled in New England, it pulls up schism in America by the roots, that being the fountain that supplys with infectious streams the rest of America'.[38] Certainly, those leading Congregational spokesmen already referred to seemed to fear that the Church of England was bent on a wholesale recreation of Puritan New England along Anglican lines. Rather more modestly (and more successfully), refashioning could entail more minor modifications to Puritan New England which gave concessions to other religious bodies, and allowed some kind of religious free market, enabling other religious groups to make headway, and this by and large was the attitude favoured in practice by New England Anglicans and the SPG. Hence the protracted struggle by the Church of England, and other 'dissenting' groups such as Baptists and Quakers, to gain the right to support their own ministers and teachers, using concepts of 'liberty of conscience', and 'toleration', as arguments for not having to contribute towards the maintenance of Congregationalist ministers, a battle which had largely, if grudgingly, been won by the late 1730s.[39]

---

[37] But see Bruce E. Steiner, 'New England Anglicanism: A Genteel Faith?', *William and Mary Quarterly*, 27 (1970), 122–35.

[38] *Historical Collections relating to the American Colonial Church*, ed. William Stevens Perry (5 vols. in 4, Hartford, 1870–8), III, 72: Lewis Morris to Archdeacon Beveridge, 27 July 1702.

[39] The story can be traced in Susan M. Reed, *Church and State in Massachusetts, 1691–1740* (Urbana, 1914).

'Puritan New England' can be also regarded as refashioning itself. In part this was the product of generational differences, and one of the themes within New England historiography has been the thesis of declension after the glory days of the first two generations,[40] but there were several developments within Congregational circles in the late seventeenth and early eighteenth centuries which made it more receptive to Anglicanism. A number of leading Congregationalists by that time had considered it important to participate in the early European Enlightenment and were taken with the publications of those who might be deemed 'moderate' Anglicans, making the works of Archbishop Tillotson, at least according to one historian, the most widely read books in North America by the early eighteenth century.[41] One result of the greater acquaintance with the Anglican tradition (and this increasingly included a wider spectrum than 'latitudinarian' writers, as 'orthodox', and even what might be termed high church books, were studied)[42] were the sometimes spectacular changes of religious allegiance as Congregationalists, including some Congregational ministers, took Anglican orders, most famously in 1722 Timothy Cutler, president of Yale, who became the first rector of Christ Church (and memorialised on the second of the bells mentioned at the start of this paper).[43] In addition, there were broader political, social, economic, cultural and intellectual developments, particularly from the 1690s, and related to the wider changes in the transatlantic role of New England within the empire, which during the late seventeenth and eighteenth centuries were also reshaping New England. For example, Thomas Kidd's *The Protestant Interest: New England after Puritanism* has paid attention to the ways in which from the 1690s to the 1740s New England was brought into the wider Protestant world, backing the British government as the leading

---

[40] Perry Miller, *The New England Mind: The Seventeenth Century* (New York, 1939); but as a counter to this see Harry S. Stout, *The New England Soul: Preaching and Religious Culture in Colonial New England* (New York, 1986), and Mark A. Peterson, *The Price of Redemption: The Spiritual Economy of Puritan New England* (Stanford, 1997).

[41] Norman Fiering, 'The First American Enlightenment: Tillotson, Leverett, and Philosophical Enlightenment', *New England Quarterly*, 54 (1981), 307–44, at 309, and John Corrigan, *The Prism of Piety: Catholick Congregational Clergy at the Beginning of the Enlightenment* (New York, 1991). See also Bruce Tucker, 'The Reinvention of New England, 1691–1770', *New England Quarterly*, 63 (1985), 315–40, and Michael P. Winship, *Seers of God: Puritan Providentialism in the Restoration and Early Enlightenment* (Baltimore, 1996).

[42] Joseph J. Ellis, *The Puritan Mind in Transition. Samuel Johnson of Connecticut, 1696–1772* (New Haven, 1973), 62–7, 72–4. See also *Samuel Johnson, President of King's College: His Career and Writings*, ed. Herbert and Carol Schneider (New York, 1929).

[43] On the Yale apostasy, see Robert E. Daggy, 'Education, Church and State: Timothy Cutler and the Yale Apostasy of 1722', *Journal of Church and State*, 13 (1971), 43–67, and D. F. M. Geradi, 'Samuel Johnson and the Yale "Apostasy" of 1722: The Challenge of Anglican Sacramentalism to the New England Way', *Historical Magazine of the Protestant Episcopal Church*, 47 (1978), 153–75.

bulwark against Popery in America and Europe.[44] Puritan New England was also changing demographically, with new areas of settlement in the back country.[45] The refashioning of Puritan New England in the ways explored below was thus part of a larger story. It has become an axiom of recent writing on the relation between Britain and North America in general, and perhaps New England in particular, that there was an 'Anglicisation' during the eighteenth century that made New England by the 1760s culturally, economically, socially and even politically increasingly connected to the wider British world.[46] How far was there also an Anglicanisation of New England which was part of this broader trajectory?

Using some of Increase Mather's indicators for threats to Puritan New England, he would have been gratified to know that the stage-plays he so feared hardly encroached on colonial New England life, although in 1750 a performance of Thomas Otway's Restoration tragedy, *The Orphan* (1680), in a coffee house in State Street, Boston, caused a riot with so many Bostonians trying to see the play that the General Court enacted a law not only forbidding acting within the Commonwealth of Massachusetts, but even rendering spectators liable to a fine.[47] By contrast, two of Mather's other indices of a threat to the Puritan way – the

[44] Thomas S. Kidd, *The Protestant Interest: New England after Puritanism* (New Haven, 2004). See also Haffenden, *New England in the English Nation*, and Richard Johnson, *Adjustment to Empire: The New England Colonies, 1675–1715* (New Brunswick, 1981). See more recently Carla Pestana, *Protestant Empire: Religion and the Making of the British Atlantic World* (Philadelphia, 2009).

[45] See David Jaffee, *People of the Wachusett. Greater New England in History and Memory* (Ithaca, 1999); Charles E. Clark, *The Eastern Frontier: The Settlement of Northern New England, 1610–1763* (New York, 1970); Bruce C. Daniels, *The Connecticut Town: Growth and Development, 1635–1790* (Middletown, CT, 1979); and Lynne Withey, *Urban Growth in Colonial Rhode Island: Newport and Providence in the Eighteenth Century* (Albany, 1984).

[46] The pioneering study of 'Anglicisation' was John M. Murrin, 'Anglicising an American Colony: The Transformation of Provincial Massachusetts' (Ph.D. thesis, Yale University, 1966), summarised in 'A Roof without Walls: The Dilemma of American National Identity', in *Beyond Confederation: Origins of the Constitution and American National Identity*, ed. Richard Beeman, Stephen Botein and Edward C. Carter (Chapel Hill, 1987), 333–48. See Christopher Grasso, *A Speaking Aristocracy. Transforming Public Discourse in Eighteenth-Century Connecticut* (Chapel Hill, 1999); Ned C. Landsman, *From Colonials to Provincials: American Thought and Culture, 1680–1760* (Ithaca, 2000); Elizabeth Mancke and Carol Shammas, *The Creation of the British Atlantic World* (Baltimore, 2005); *The British Atlantic World, 1500–1800*, ed. David Armitage and Michael J. Braddick (Basingstoke, 2002); Peter Marshall, *The Making and Unmaking of Empires: Britain, India and America, 1750–1783* (Oxford, 2006); Brendan McConville, *The Rise and Fall of Royal America, 1688–1776* (Chapel Hill, 2007); and Maya Jasanoff, 'The Other Side of Revolution: Loyalists in the British Empire', *William and Mary Quarterly*, 65 (2008), 205–32.

[47] W. W. Clap, *A History of the Boston Stage* (Boston, MA, 1853), 2. However, Samuel Drake suggested that there were clandestine theatrical performances before this, *History and Antiquities of Boston* (Boston, MA, 1856), 631. See Sherwood Collins, 'Boston's Political Street

existence of the Book of Common Prayer, and celebrations of Christmas – not only became more visible in the eighteenth century, but made some impact on Puritan New England, as well as among the settler communities. The essential step in establishing a viable Anglican community in New England was to ensure that copies of the Prayer Book were available, for without these efforts to carry out the Anglican liturgy would come to nothing. This was particularly crucial since it was virtually impossible to procure copies of the Prayer Book there (although in 1705 William Bradford, a New York printer who had recently conformed to the Church, was in negotiation with the SPG about publishing an American imprint).[48] Time and again New England clergy wrote to the SPG for more copies of the Prayer Book, believing that access to it would play a key role in weaning Congregationalists away from their anti-liturgical bias, and to some extent this seems to have worked. John Troutbeck, writing from Hopkinton, Massachusetts, noted in 1757 that 'the people formerly thought that our Liturgy was a remnant of Popery, but upon Acquaintance with it, have corrected their false Prejudices',[49] and similar statements can be found from other parts of New England, so much so that in 1764 Ebenezer Thompson reported that at Scituate, Massachusetts, 'the Dissenting Congregation . . . have voted that a New Folio Bible be bought, and that their Teacher reads Lessons out of it every Sunday morning and evening, in imitation of the method of reading the Scriptures in the Church of England',[50] which is an extraordinary suggestion of the ways in which, at least in this instance, some acquaintance with the Church of England way affected Congregational practice. By 1770, the SPG had sent over more than 150,000 bibles and Books of Common Prayer to North America (in addition to other books of instruction and 'innumerable quantity of pious small tracts'),[51] and, as far as it can be calculated, a majority of these were sent to New England.

Theatre: The Eighteenth-Century Pope Day Pageants', *Educational Theatre Journal*, 25 (1973), 401–9, for a wider definition of Boston's theatre.

[48] Lambeth Palace Library, SPG Minutes 1, fo. 48v, 18 May 1705. Bradford did publish an edition of the Prayer Book in 1706, with a reissue in 1710, which was the only edition printed in North America during the colonial period: James N. Green, 'The English Book Trade in the Middle Colonies, 1680–1720', in *Colonial Book in the Atlantic World*, ed. Amory and Hall, 199–223, at 213–14. The venture was a publishing failure since, as Bradford informed the SPG, the Prayer Books were not subsidised and therefore were too expensive for people to buy.

[49] Reported in the 'Abstract of Proceedings' appended to James Johnson, *A Sermon Preached before the Incorporated Society for the Propagation of the Gospel in Foreign Parts; at their Anniversary Meeting in the Parish Church of St. Mary-le-Bow, on Friday February 24, 1758* (1758), 38.

[50] Lambeth Palace Library, MS 1124/2, fo. 257v, Thompson to SPG, 26 Mar. 1764.

[51] Frederick Keppel, *A Sermon Preached before the Incorporated Society for the Propagation of the Gospel in Foreign Parts; at their Anniversary Meeting in the Parish Church of St. Mary-le-Bow, on Friday February 16, 1770* (1770), 'Abstract of Proceedings', 2.

Besides bombarding New England with Books of Common Prayer, celebrating Christmas was another indicator of the ways in which the Church was able to make some impact on New England life. Alongside Increase Mather, Samuel Sewall, the redoubtable Puritan judge, was from the mid-1680s to the late 1720s on the look-out for Anglican encroachments, and his diary annually reported, with regret and dismay, the Christmas Day services at the King's chapel (as well as Shrove Tuesday festivities and sports), and he noted with displeasure those Bostonians who either declined to work on 25 December (pouring scorn on this as just a popish holyday) and even more disturbingly for him, those who attended Christmas Day services, including on occasion some of his extended family.[52] On 25 December 1697 Sewall recorded: 'I took occasion to dehort mine from Christmas-keeping and charged them to forbear', but evidently without much success, as he went on to lament: 'most of ye Boys went to Church'.[53] By the 1730s and 1740s, both Boston's three Church of England places of worship, and those elsewhere in New England, were able to attract larger numbers than usual for their Christmas celebrations, and these included not a small number of Congregationalists. Timothy Cutler, for example, maintained that on Christmas Day 1744, Christ Church, Boston, was 'thronged among others by some Hundreds of Dissenters'.[54] Five years previously, Ebenezer Punderson had observed that 'the Temper and spirit of many of the dissenting brethren seems much altered for the better in so much that many of them on Christmas Day last resorted to the church and behaved soberly and decently'.[55] For Noah Hobart, writing in 1748 (and having read Punderson's report to the SPG), Christmas day services were just an excuse to take time off work and this fitted into his portrayal of New England Anglicans as lax and fun-loving, and any increase there may have been in attendances, he claimed, were purely because some New Englanders wanted to enjoy a day off, and hardly represented a success for the Church. 'I hope the People of Groton, and in all other parts of the country, when they see what an improvement these Missionaries make of their keeping Christmas', he observed, 'will reform that bad Practice, and discover that they value the Religion of their

---

[52] *The Diary of Samuel Sewall, 1674–1729*, ed. M. Halsey Thomas (2 vols., New York, 1973), see I, 406, 4 Jan. 1699, II, 779, 25 Dec. 1714.

[53] *Ibid.*, I, 385, 25 Dec. 1697.

[54] Reported in the 'Abstract of Proceedings' appended to Matthew Hutton, *A Sermon Preached before the Incorporated Society for the Propagation of the Gospel in Foreign Parts; at their Anniversary Meeting in the Parish Church of St. Mary-le-Bow, on Friday February 21, 1745* (1745/6), 40.

[55] Quoted in Martin Benson, *A Sermon Preached before the Incorporated Society for the Propagation of the Gospel in Foreign Parts; at their Anniversary Meeting in the Parish-Church of St. Mary-le-Bow, on Friday, February 15, 1739–40* (1740), 55.

Country and the Morals of their Posterity above a Feast or a Frolick.'[56] Hobart may no doubt have been right to suggest that this can hardly be seen as anything more than a superficial triumph for the Church, but it hardly speaks for thorough-going Congregationalism on the part of the New England laity either.[57] Indeed, one of the reasons for Congregational ministerial rancour against New England Anglicans from the 1740s was not only out of concern that the Church was making inroads into non-Anglican territory but also because this indicated that lay understandings of Congregationalism were sometimes rather different from – and did not always lead up to the expectations of – their teachers. What is also clear is the significance placed on the Christmas Day services by the New England Anglican churches, as if both to show-case the liturgy, and to emphasise the importance of the day in the Anglican calendar. Vestry books show the care put into preparing the interior of the churches for the day; they were decorated with greenery, and candlesticks were polished.[58] By the 1760s, Christ Church, Boston, was paying to have music printed for use at the Christmas service, and in 1769 the churchwardens were trying to find some 'proper person' to sing an anthem in the church on Christmas Day.[59]

But not only were numbers of Books of Common Prayer in New England increasing, and Christmas Day services being attended by a growing number of Congregationalists, even more worrying for the Congregationalist critics of the Church of England, the number of Anglican congregations was also on the rise. Although the impetus for these often came from new English settlers, or exiled Huguenots who conformed to the Church,[60] they also attracted Congregational conformists. In their efforts to view Anglicanism as an intrusion, the Mathers and Mayhew downplayed the indigenous supporters of the Church, as well as those who conformed, dismissing those who signed petitions to the SPG requesting clergy as a very small number of ignorant, disaffected people, joining the Church because of private grudges and not out of religious reasons. Mayhew argued that the requests were usually trumped up, citing the case of Roger Price, the rector of King's chapel,

[56] Hobart, *A Serious Address*, 56.

[57] It has been suggested that many people were unchurched in the eighteenth century: Patricia U. Bonomi and Peter R. Eisenstadt, 'Church adherence in the eighteenth-century British American Colonies', *William and Mary Quarterly*, 39 (1982), 245–86. For some of the failings of the Congregationalist churches in attracting the laity, see Peter S. Onuf, 'New Lights in New London: A Group Portrait of the Separatists', *William and Mary Quarterly*, 37 (1980), 626–43.

[58] For example, MHS, MS N-2249, folder 33, 18 Feb. 1770.

[59] MHS, MS N-2249 (XT) Old North Church, Vestry Book, 1724–1802, 170.

[60] On Huguenot settlers, see Jon Butler, *The Huguenots in America. A Refugee People in New World Society* (Cambridge, MA, 1984).

Boston, who had wanted to become a missionary at Hopkinton, where he owned a farm, and who had allegedly brow-beaten his tenants to sign a petition.[61] Ezra Stiles later remarked:

> I find the Church of England, especially in New England, inspired with a secular principle, unanimated with the love of Jesus as with the love of dignities and pre-eminence, making the Church an asylum for polite vice and irreligion . . . The greater part of the converts in New England had fled from other communions for Drunkenness, whoring, swearing & other moral scandal – I say the greater part, & I say it from a very particular examination of the history of Church proselytism there for fifty years past.[62]

Nevertheless, despite Stiles's disparaging remarks, the growth of New England Anglicanism, and the inroads it was making in eighteenth-century New England deserves some attention. In 1702, it was estimated that there were fewer than 1,000 adherents of the Church of England in New England,[63] and at that date most of these were either found in Boston (the Puritan heartland), associated with the King's chapel, where it was reported that on occasion there were over 400 present at services,[64] or in communities such as Newport or South Kingston in Rhode Island, which was not part of Puritan New England proper, and where other groups who had opposed Congregationalists – such as Quakers and Baptists – had made early headway.[65] By 1760, Anglicans could be found throughout New England. The number, according to Stiles, who may have been likely to undersell his rivals, was about 12,600 Anglicans out of a total New England population of just over half a million,[66] and by 1774 he calculated that the Church had just over 24,000 adherents out of a total New England population of just under 750,000.[67] This growth is significant given that it has been estimated that Anglicans in North America as a whole quadrupled in the century, while in New England growth was at least twenty times, which made it the fastest-growing denomination there (and which in part accounts for the Congregational concern). This made Episcopalians 3 per cent of the New England population by the 1760s, and nearer 4 per cent by the mid-1770s. In some ways, this may look like a rather trivial figure, and certainly makes Mayhew's invective look rather misplaced, if not hysterical. But the small number does not mean they are not worth studying. For instance it has been reckoned that fewer than 2 per cent of the British population were Methodists in the 1790s, and yet an enormous historiography has been placed around them,

---

[61] Mayhew, *Defence of the Observations*, 16–130.
[62] *Literary Diary of Stiles*, ed. Dexter, II, 113.
[63] King, 'S.P.G. in New England', 29.
[64] Foote, *King's Chapel*, I, 53.
[65] Carla Pestana, *Quakers and Baptists in Colonial Massachusetts* (New York, 1991).
[66] Ezra Stiles, *A Discourse on the Christian Union* (Boston, MA, 1761), 142–4.
[67] *Literary Diary of Stiles*, ed. Dexter, I, 294–5, 488. Steiner, 'New England Anglicanism', puts the figure at 25,000 persons at that date (122).

including crediting them for the avoidance of a French-style Revolution in England.[68] And the figure of 4 per cent is for the whole of New England, and hides a large amount of variation. By 1774 the figure for Connecticut was over 8 per cent,[69] and individual townships, such as Reading and Newtown, had over 50 per cent Anglicans (with more attending the Church of England places of worship than the dissenting ones).[70]

We do not have a full analysis of all those who made up the New England Anglican congregations (the published records of baptisms, marriages and burials from Trinity Church, Boston, the third Anglican church founded in the town in 1733, can give us some sense of the milieu),[71] but what we do know indicates that Anglicans could come from a wide social strata ranging from the fashionable Newport smart set to much more humble groups (including some slaves and Native Americans, particularly those living *within* New England families). In some cases congregations could be fairly numerous (Christ Church, Boston, regularly had over 600 people by the 1730s),[72] which frequently led to extending churches or building galleries. James Honeyman, the rector of Newport (itself a growing congregation which necessitated that the original church of 1699 was rebuilt in 1726, and extended in 1762), noted in 1722

> that he had been to preach lately at Providence . . . to the greatest number of People he ever had together since he came to America, that no House being able to hold them, he was obliged to preach in the Fields; and that they are getting Subscriptions for Building a Church.[73]

This report is suggestive of the economic commitment congregations might give in financing the Anglican mission (if they were able), paying for the building of a church, a glebe and a house for the missionary, and contributing towards his salary. The norm was that before even approaching the SPG, as evidence of their commitment, New England

---

[68] Alan. D. Gilbert, *Religion and Society in Industrial England. Church, Chapel and Social Change, 1740–1914* (London and New York, 1976), 31–2.

[69] King, 'S.P.G. in New England', 225–6.

[70] This was according to John Beach, the missionary there, in letters to the SPG in 1762, quoted in the 'Abstract of Proceedings' appended to John Egerton, *A Sermon Preached before the Incorporated Society for the Propagation of the Gospel in Foreign Parts; at their Anniversary Meeting in the Parish Church of St. Mary-le-Bow, on Friday February 18, 1763* (1763), 51. For the original, see Lambeth Palace Library, MS 1124/2, fo. 55, Beach to SPG, 6 Apr. 1762.

[71] *The Records of Trinity Church, Boston, 1728–1830*, ed. Andrew Oliver and James Bishop Peabody, Publications of the Colonial Society of Massachusetts, LV and LVI (Boston, MA, 1980). See also Dudley Tyng, *Massachusetts Episcopalians, 1607–1957* (Pascoag, RI, 1960).

[72] For example, Cutler to SPG, 5 Feb. 1738 in *Historical Collections relating to the American Colonial Church*, ed. Perry, III, 321.

[73] Quoted in the 'Abstract of Proceedings' appended to John Waugh, *A Sermon Preached before the Incorporated Society for the Propagation of the Gospel in Foreign Parts; at their Anniversary Meeting in the Parish-Church of St. Mary-le-Bow; on Friday, February 15, 1722* (1723), 51.

Anglicans might have already built a church. To this extent New England Anglicanism was a market-driven phenomenon.

What is also clear is that if New England Anglican missions were more a response to an indigenous request than an invasion, once established they could act as a stimulus for others to join the Church of England. Why did some New Englanders want to become Anglicans in the eighteenth century? As early as 1733, George Berkeley (the clerical philosopher and future bishop), who had lived in Rhode Island for over two years (preaching regularly both at St Paul's, Kingston, and Trinity, Newport), maintained that the general population had shaken off their prejudice against the Church, and that some were conforming to Anglicanism.[74] Mayhew thought this was nonsense and informed his readers that Berkeley knew nothing about real New England, having lived as an academic recluse in Rhode Island.[75] But what we do know of eighteenth-century New England congregations suggests that those from other denominations could, as surprising as it might seem, find Anglicanism attractive. There may have been a variety of religious reasons for becoming an Anglican, and not just the secular ones highlighted by Stiles. Unlike Congregationalism, Anglican membership was open to all; whereas the sacraments of baptism and Holy Communion were denied to many New Englanders.[76] In 1732 Matthias Plant thought that the Church had increased at Newburyport because of the 'love and unity which is among them, while their dissenting neighbours are in great confusion and disorder'.[77] It is also clear that Anglicans in New England were also attempting to market the Church as being best for society as a whole. In this they argued that the Anglican Church was nearer to the primitive church; they stressed the attraction of Church of England worship (the beauty of holiness); their theology of benevolence and reason; and they made much of the connections with the Crown.[78] Congregationalists also benefited from Anglican pastoral work, with clergy visiting the sick of all denominations.[79] It also seems that the presence of an Anglican missionary might have dispelled some of the myths about the Church. There is even evidence of other denominations helping to build or improve Anglican churches, and tellingly a few

[74] George Berkeley, *A Sermon Preached before the Incorporated Society for the Propagation of the Gospel in Foreign Parts; at their Anniversary Meeting in the Parish-Church of St Mary-le-Bow, on Friday, February 18, 1731* (1732), 17, 22.

[75] Mayhew, *Observations on the Charter*, 43.

[76] Erik R. Seeman, *Pious Persuasions: Laity and Clergy in Eighteenth-Century New England* (Baltimore, 1999).

[77] Mathias Plant to SPG, 24 Sept. 1732, in *Historical Collections relating to the American Colonial Church*, ed. Perry, III, 288.

[78] Nelson, 'Anglican Missions', 449–51.

[79] Lambeth Palace Library, MS 1124/2, fo. 200, Matthew Graves to SPG, 20 Feb. 1763.

Congregationalists subscribed for the bells for Christ Church, Boston, mentioned at the start of this paper.[80] Such evidence of cooperation, slight though it is, is marginalised by Bridenbaugh and Clark.

In an unexpected way, the Church of England in New England also benefited from the religious revival of the 1740s which has been labelled 'the Great Awakening'.[81] While it is often asserted that the growth of Methodism in Old England was a threat to the Church of England (although recent research would certainly modify such a statement),[82] the Great Awakening in New England had the unforeseen consequence of attracting those Congregationalists who were unhappy with the ways in which the revival seemed to spiral out of control, and the wild enthusiasms of those associated with the revival played straight into the Church of England clergy's hands. This allowed Anglicans to claim that not only were Congregationalists in mid-eighteenth-century America potentially the same as those in mid-seventeenth-century England, but also that the mayhem associated with revivalist meetings was contemporary proof of their proclivity to 'enthusiasm'. Henry Caner, writing from Fairfield, Connecticut, in November 1743, reported that at Norwalk, Ridgefield, and Stanford there 'have been large accessions of persons who appear to have a serious sense of Religion; where the late Spirit of Enthusiasm hath most abounded the Church hath received the largest accessions, many of the deluded People as their Passions subside, seeking for Rest in the Bosom and Communion of the Church'.[83] Of course, the Great Awakening was not all gain for the Church (how could it have been with George

---

[80] For example, dissenters contributed to the refurbishment of the interior of the church at Hebron: see 'Abstract of Proceedings' appended to William Warburton, *A Sermon Preached before the Incorporated Society for the Propagation of the Gospel in Foreign Parts; at their Anniversary Meeting in the Parish Church of St. Mary-le-Bow, on Friday February 21, 1766* (1766), 23.

[81] For the Great Awakening in a broad context, see Thomas S. Kidd, *The Great Awakening: The Roots of Evangelical Christianity in Colonial America* (New Haven, 2007). For New England in particular, see Douglas L. Winiarski, 'Souls Filled with Ravishing Transport; Heavenly Visions and the Radical Awakening in New England', *William and Mary Quarterly*, 61 (2004), 3–41, and his '"A Journal of Five Days at York": The Great Awakening on the Northern New England Frontier', *Maine History*, 42 (2004), 47–85; Elizabeth C. Nordbeck, '"Almost Revived": The Great Revival in New Hampshire and Maine, 1727–1748', *Historical New Hampshire*, 35 (1980), 24–58. See also Clarence C. Goen, *Revivalism and Separatism in New England, 1740–1800* (New Haven, 1962).

[82] See Gilbert, *Religion and Industrial Society*. For a revised view see Jeremy Gregory, '"In the Church I will Live and Die": John Wesley, the Church of England and Methodism', in *Religion and Identity in Eighteenth-Century Britain*, ed. William Gibson and Robert Ingram (Ashgate, 2005), 147–78, and David R. Wilson, 'Church *and* Chapel: Parish Ministry and Methodism in Madeley, c. 1760–1785, with Special Reference to the Ministry of John Fletcher' (Ph.D. thesis, University of Manchester, 2010).

[83] Lambeth Palace Library, SPG Minutes IV, 1740–4, fo. 254, Caner to SPG, 10 Nov. 1743. An abstract of this was quoted in Philip Bearcroft, *A Sermon Preached before the Incorporated Society for the Propagation of the Gospel in Foreign Parts; at their Anniversary Meeting in the Parish Church of St. Mary-le-Bow, on Friday February 15, 1744* (1744), 43–4.

Whitefield fuelling it on his tour through New England in 1740),[84] and it was reported that Ebenezer Punderson, the itinerant SPG missionary in New England, had moaned that 'Enthusiasm had so unsettled many People from all sober and steady Principles, that great Prophaneness and Disregard for the instituted Means of Grace appear', and that 'though he had been constant in his Labours, and preached twice every Sunday, and once or more in every Week, the Success did not answer his Hopes'.[85] Nevertheless, compared with the endless splintering of Congregational congregations, and the divisions between Old Lights and New Lights – it has been calculated that over 170 new congregations emerged as a result of the Great Awakening[86] – the Church of England was a gainer rather than a loser from the revivalist fervour. From the 1740s, reaction to the Great Awakening was frequently cited as a reason for coming over to the Church, and a joint letter of the New England missionaries to the SPG declared that 'it is a Matter of great Comfort . . . to see in all Places the earnest Zeal of the People in pressing forward into the Church from the Confusions which Methodism has spread among them; in so much that they think nothing too much to do to qualify themselves for obtaining of Missionaries from the Society'.[87] In December 1744, Timothy Cutler reported that hardly a Sunday went by without some Congregationalists joining them in the Church service at Christ Church:

> multitudes being now inclined to examine, and look into both Sides of a Question which few comparatively could be persuaded to do heretofore, till the late Revival of Enthusiasm among them; and some Hundreds have thereupon been added to the Church, insomuch that in many Places, where Error, Confusion and every evil Work did abound, Grace through God's Mercy doth now much more abound.[88]

Cutler's understanding of the Great Awakening as a 'revival of Enthusiasm' – in typical Anglican fashion – portrayed the religious

---

[84] See *George Whitefield's Journals, 1737–1741*, ed. William Wale (Gainesville, 1969 reprint); Harry S. Stout, *The Divine Dramatist: George Whitefield and the Rise of Modern Evangelicalism* (Grand Rapids, 1991); Frank Lambert, *'Pedlar in Divinity'. George Whitefield and the Transatlantic Revivals, 1737–1770* (Princeton, 1994). See also Gerald J. Goodwin, 'The Anglican Reaction to the Great Awakening', *Historical Magazine of the Protestant Episcopal Church*, 35 (1966), 345–6.

[85] Quoted in the 'Abstract of Proceedings' appended to Bearcroft, *Sermon*, 44.

[86] Goen, *Revivalism and Separatism*, 157; John Butler, *Awash in a Sea of Faith: Christianizing the American People* (1990), 320.

[87] Quoted in the 'Abstract of Proceedings' appended to Samuel Lisle, *A Sermon Preached before the Incorporated Society for the Propagation of the Gospel in Foreign Parts; at their Anniversary Meeting in the Parish-Church of St. Mary-le-Bow, on Friday February 19, 1747* (1747/8), 54.

[88] Quoted in the 'Abstract of Proceedings' appended to Hutton, *Sermon*, 40. See also Douglas C. Stenerson, 'An Anglican Critique of the Early Phase of the Great Awakening in New England: A Letter by Timothy Cutler', *William and Mary Quarterly*, 30 (1973), 475–88. This is an edition of Cutler's letter of 28 May 1739 to Bishop Gibson's request for information about the recent outbreak of revivalism and contains his views on Jonathan Edwards' account of the religious revival in Northampton.

developments of the 1740s in New England as a recurrence of the religious enthusiasm that had caused such chaos in Old England in the 1640s and 1650s, and Anglicans in New England reminded their congregations of the political and social upheaval that had caused. Another clergymen noted:

> not only Teachers, but Taylors, Shoemakers, and other Mechanicks, and even Women, Boys and Girls, were become (as their term is) Exhorters. From all which, however, this Advantage hath by God's kind Providence arisen, that it hath remarkably engaged serious People's Attention to our Liturgy and the Doctrines of our Clergy, and this hath brought many considerable Families . . . to be added to the Church.[89]

Moreover, and perhaps with some irony, the Great Awakening allowed moderate Congregationalists ('Old Lights') to mirror this Anglican discourse by accusing their 'New Light' rivals of continuing the enthusiast tradition, while distancing themselves from it. Charles Chauncy, minister of the First Church of Boston and a leading New England Old Light spokesperson, preached and published a sermon in 1742, *Enthusiasm Described and Caution'd Against*, which reads remarkably like Anglican critiques of seventeenth-century Protestant nonconformists and eighteenth-century Methodists.[90] A recurring refrain during the 1740s was that moderate Congregationalists and other dissenting groups in New England were more charitable towards the Church because of the Great Awakening, and in 1751 Cutler claimed that the Church of England 'hath the second place in esteem with all the sects'.[91]

There were two main areas of Anglican growth in colonial New England, first the seaboard and coastal towns, such as Portsmouth,

---

[89] Quoted in Matthias Mawson, *A Sermon Preached before the Incorporated Society for the Propagation of the Gospel in Foreign Parts; at their Anniversary Meeting in the Parish-Church of St. Mary-le-Bow, on Friday, February 18, 1742–3* (1743), 41–2. On women in the revival, see Catherine Brekus, *Strangers and Pilgrims: Female Preaching in America* (Chapel Hill, 1998), Susan Juster, *Disorderly Women: Sexual Politics and Evangelicalism in Revolutionary New England* (Ithaca, 1996).

[90] Charles Chauncy, *Enthusiasm Described and Caution'd Against* (Boston, MA, 1742). Compare this with the tract attributed to Thomas Comber, prebendary of Durham cathedral, *Christianity no Enthusiasm, or, the Several Kinds of Inspirations and Revelations Pretended to by the Quakers Tried and Found Destructive to Holy Scripture and True Religion* (1678); George Hickes, *The Spirit of Enthusiasm Exorcised in a Sermon Preached before the University of Oxford, on Act Sunday, July 11 1680* (1680); and George Lavington, *The Enthusiasm of Methodists and Papists Compared, 3 Parts* (1749–51). Seventeenth-century English Presbyterians had also targeted those they considered enthusiastic sectaries: Thomas Edwards, *The First and Second Part of Gangraena, or, A catalogue and Discovery of Many of the Errours, Heresies, Blasphemies and Pernicious Practices of the Sectaries of this Time* (1646). On the durability of religious language castigating opponents, see Jeremy Gregory, 'Articulating Anglicanism: The Church of England and the Language of "The Other" during the Long Eighteenth Century', in *Religion, Language and Power*, ed. Nile Green and Mary Searle Chatterjee (2008), 143–66.

[91] Quoted in the 'Abstract of Proceedings' appended to Richard Osbaldeston, *A Sermon Preached before the Incorporated Society for the Propagation of the Gospel in Foreign Parts; at their Anniversary Meeting in the Parish Church of St. Mary-le-Bow, on Friday February 21, 1752* (1752), 37.

Newburyport, Boston, Falmouth, Bristol, Newport, Providence and New London. This included invitations to preach in such traditionally Puritan towns as Plymouth. In 1756 it was reported that Ebenezer Thompson had been

> invited by several of the good People of the Town Plymouth to come and officiate to them there, where the Liturgy of the Church of England (tho' that Town has been settled more than 120 Years) was never publickly used before, he went thither on the Feast of the Epiphany, and read Prayers and preached in the Court-house, the High Sheriff of the County and the Chief magistrates attending Divine Service, and about 300 persons more.[92]

That the Church of England liturgy was being used in such an iconic place in New England's religious heritage as Plymouth, and to such a large number of people, is indicative of the ways in which the old order was changing, and by 1758 there were three Anglican churches in Plymouth county (at Scituate, Marshfield and Bridgewater).[93]

But, second, by the 1760s the real headway was in new centres of population growth and what some saw as the industrialising hinterland, such as Lichfield county, Connecticut, with Anglican congregations emerging in Danbury, Sharon, Cornwell and Salisbury. These could rightly be claimed to be *pays de mission* (since there were no existing ministers of any denomination), and Anglican missionaries seem to have been adept in reaching out to new back-country settlements. Thomas Davies wrote from Lichfield county in 1762: 'People . . . seem to have lost their ancient bitter Temper, and think that Christianity is clearly taught in our Church, and are resolved to erect churches.'[94] He also noted:

> by advice of the Rev Mr Caner of Boston, a few families in Barrington, the westernmost settlement of that colony, sent their earnest desire that I would come and visit them. Accordingly in September last I went (it is sixty miles) and preached to a large concourse of people, and baptised some children and instructed them in the meaning, use and propriety of the Common Prayer Book. They informed me that many of them had long been dissatisfied with their dissenting instructors, being constantly taught rigid Calvinism, and that sin was of advantage and advanced happiness greatly in the world; that if the Church was introduced there they must pay tithes etc; that the Church was just like the papists; that the service book was taken from the mass-book etc.[95]

Davies put them right on these last points, and established an Anglican congregation.

---

[92] Quoted in the 'Abstract of Proceedings' appended to Frederick Cornwallis, *A Sermon Preached before the Incorporated Society for the Propagation of the Gospel in Foreign Parts; at their Anniversary Meeting in the Parish Church of St. Mary-le-Bow, on Friday February 20, 1756* (1756), 38.

[93] Quoted in the 'Abstract of Proceedings' appended to Johnson, *Sermon*, 38. On the iconic status of Plymouth, see John Seelye, *Memory's Nation: The Place of Plymouth Rock* (Chapel Hill, 1998).

[94] Quoted in the 'Abstract of Proceedings' appended to Egerton, *Sermon*, 53.

[95] Lambeth Palace Library, MS 1124/2, fo. 145, Davies to SPG, 28 Dec. 1762.

Although Anglicanism was intimately connected with New England's fashionable elite (and was satirised by Congregational clergy on these grounds),[96] it also made surprising successes with the lower levels of society and flourished in some of the remoter regions. John Wentworth, governor of New Hampshire, and himself an Anglican descendant of the Puritan William Wentworth, noted in 1750s that 'if the Church service was performed without Expense, or any zealous attempts to proselytise, the People would naturally flock to it'.[97] Anglicans in New England seem to have behaved not unlike Methodists in Old England, doing well in new areas of population growth such as Simsbury, where, by 1762, there were reported to be 2,000 people (many of whom had lately arrived from England to work in the copper mines).[98] Arthur Brown, the missionary in Portsmouth, reported success in the frontier settlements of New Hampshire.[99] The missionary at Hebron boasted in 1762 that he had ridden 2,000 miles that year (intimations of Wesley), at the request of various congregations, and had preached over 100 week-day lectures, on top of his usual Sunday services.[100] In reports such as these, SPG missionaries could be seen as itinerants. Itinerancy in both Old and New England was often viewed as a hall-mark of Evangelicalism, and moderate Congregationalists disapproved of the practice as much as did most Old England Anglicans.[101] But some SPG missionaries participated in this practice and competed for souls in an Evangelical way. Indeed at a certain level most SPG missionaries itinerated given that the area encompassed by their missions was frequently large and encompassed a number of settlements. From his Newport base, James Honeyman in the 1720s, 1730s and 1740s often visited Freetown, Tiverton and Little Compton, and at one point preached at the latter on week-days in a Congregationalist meeting house,[102] which is itself suggestive of a more accommodating relationship between Anglicanism and Congregationalism than Bridenbaugh's thesis implied. In similar vein, in 1763 Matthew Graves was asked to do duty in a Congregationalist

[96] See Noah Welles, *The Real Advantages which Ministers and People May Enjoy Especially in the Colonies, by Conforming to the Church of England; Faithfully Considered, and Impartially Represented, in a Letter to a Young Gentleman* (Boston, MA, 1762), which satirised the Church's links to politeness, moderation and financial gain (as well as to Popery).

[97] Quoted in Woolverton, *Colonial Anglicanism*, 88.

[98] Lambeth Palace Library, MS 1124/2, fo. 102, Davies to SPG, 3 July 1762.

[99] Lambeth Palace Library, MS 1124/1, fo. 152, Browne to SPG, 10 Sept. 1760.

[100] Lambeth Palace Library, MS 1124/2, fo. 134, Samuel Peters to SPG, 24 Dec. 1762. Joshua Bailey, the itinerant missionary on the eastern frontier of Massachusetts, rode between 600 and 700 miles in 1761: *ibid.*, fo. 169v, Bailey to SPG, 26 Mar. 1761.

[101] Timothy D. Hall, *Contested Boundaries: Itinerancy and the Reshaping of the Colonial Religious World* (Durham, NC, 1994).

[102] Berkeley, *Sermon*, 56.

meeting house because their minister was sick, and where he used the Anglican liturgy, with the consent of those present. He further reported that he had preached for several weeks in a private house belonging to a member of the Church who was ill: 'This Sunday Evening Exercise was attended with crowded audiences of various denominations.'[103] Likewise, in 1761 Ebeneezer Dibblee was asked by the dissenters at Greenwich, with the permission of the church people, to officiate to them.[104] Samuel Fayerweather, himself a former Congregationalist minister, and a Church of England conformist, reported that Congregationalists were now treating him pretty charitably, citing his practice of allowing total immersion at baptism as a reason for this.[105]

Reports from the 1760s noted that 'people of every Denomination, especially the young' were inclined to conform to the Church, indicative of the Church's ability to reach out to the rising generation,[106] suggesting that the long-term future for the Church in New England seemed favourable. Moreover, two high-profile Congregationalists conformed to the Church in the late 1760s, as if to demonstrate the ways in which the old order had indeed been refashioned. In 1767, Nathaniel Rogers, the descendant of the Puritan minister Nathaniel Rogers, who had emigrated to New England in the 1630s, and who was thus seen as coming from the purest Puritan stock, became a parishioner at the King's chapel.[107] Henry Caner, now rector there, characterised him as being from the first families in the country (by which he meant that Rogers was descended from the Puritan fathers), and noted that Rogers was believed to be related to John Rogers, the martyr in Queen Mary's time, as if to stress a common Protestant heritage for both Congregationalists and Episcopalians.[108] Caner further described Rogers as being 'warmly attached to the cause of liberty & particularly to that of the colonys, yet firm in his Duty & loyalty to the king & the British Government, and an enemy to the factious proceedings which have taken place, and are still too cherished'.[109] How far we are to infer from this that Rogers only conformed to the Church because he was dismayed by the tense political atmosphere of the late 1760s is unclear, but the statement does suggest

[103] Lambeth Palace Library, MS 1124/ 2, fos. 200–1, Graves to SPG, 20 July 1763.

[104] Quoted in 'Abstract of Proceedings' attached to John Hume, *A Sermon Preached before the Incorporated Society for the Propagation of the Gospel in Foreign Parts; at their Anniversary Meeting in the Parish Church of St. Mary-le-Bow, on Friday February 19, 1762* (1762), 44.

[105] Lambeth Palace Library, MS 1124/2, fo. 100, Fayerweather to SPG, 25 Dec. 1761.

[106] Lambeth Palace Library, MS 1124/2, fo. 89v, 'Petition from the Church of Warwick in the Colony of Rhode Island, 17 June 1762'.

[107] Cameron, *Letter-Book of the Rev. Henry Caner*, 239, Caner to Secker, 23 Oct. 1767.

[108] *Ibid.*

[109] *Ibid.*

the complex set of allegiances which people like Rogers were trying to hold together. In the spring of 1768 Mather Byles, a Congregational minister, the great-nephew of Cotton Mather, the great-grandson of Increase Mather, and the great-great-grandson of Richard Mather (who had fled England for Boston in 1635), and therefore a member of a family who arguably represented 'Puritan New England' more than any other, accepted the post of rector at Christ Church, Boston.[110] Byles maintained that he conformed on account of his reading (this was the most common reason given by former Congregational ministers who came over to the Church), and he told his former flock that he still believed the Congregational church to be a true church, and that he had only changed his views about the validity of Anglican ceremonies. 'There is not a sermon that I have preached in this place', he promised them, 'but what I shall in the Church of England'.[111] Again it is hard to know quite what to make of this statement, except to suggest that besides the large volume of Congregational and Episcopalian printed tracts and pamphlets which were directed at each other, there were other areas, such as the reformation of manners, on which clergy of all denominations could find common ground. It is also instructive to compare the reaction to Byles's conforming to the Church in 1768 with that experienced by Cutler, Brown and Johnson in 1722. The 'Yale apostasy' had provoked an enormous frisson in Congregational circles, whereas Byles's conforming nearly fifty years later, while provoking comment, did not create such as furore, even when the 'bishop controversy' had been at its most vehement, and when the political tensions in Boston were at a height. It is true that a number of satirical verses were written about Byles, largely accusing him of going over to the Church for financial reasons, and suggesting that he would end up in Rome, and on 25 April 1768, the *Boston Gazette* printed 'A Wonderful Dream',[112] where the spirit of Richard Mather prophesied bad things for his great-grandson and for any attempts to establish an

---

[110] On the Mathers see Robert Middlekauff, *The Mathers: Three Generations of Puritan Intellectuals, 1596–1728* (New York, 1971). For Byles's father, also called Mather Byles, see Arthur Wentworth Eaton, *The Famous Mather Byles: The Noted Boston Tory Preacher, Poet and Wit* (Boston, MA, 1914). For our Mather Byles, see Clifford K. Shipton, *Sibley's Harvard Graduates*, XIII, *1751–1755* (Massachusetts Historical Society, 1965), 6–26.

[111] MHS, MS N-1153: 'Life and Letters of Revd Mather Byles', 78.

[112] *Boston Gazette*, 25 Apr. 1768. For one colonial Anglican clergyman's positive response to Byles's conforming, see Samuel Peters, *Reasons Why Mr Byes Left New London, and Returned to the Bosom of the Church of England* (New London, 1768), but for an opposite view (highlighting the financial reasons for the move) see Benjamin Gales, *A Debate between the Rev Mr Byles, Late Pastor of the First Church in New-London, and the Brethren of that Church* (New London, 1768). It is worth noting that the bitter anti-British feeling of 1765–6 occasioned by the Stamp Act had abated somewhat between 1766 and 1770: Merrill Jensen, *The Founding of a Nation: A History of the American Revolution, 1763–1776* (New York, 1968), chs. 10–11.

episcopate in America, but it is significant that there was not even more vehement criticism.

If I am right to suggest that the Church was making some inroads into Puritan New England by the early 1760s, what went wrong? In large measure, as political, social, economic and cultural historians have emphasised, the broader context changed remarkably sometime in the mid-1760s (although there are large debates about the causes, nature and timing of those changes).[113] This is not the place to rehearse the debates about the impact of legislation from the Stamp Act onwards, and the economic and political and economic crises which followed; nevertheless it is clear that as anti-British government feeling grew, the Church of England clergy became victims of this, and the Church was viewed as an agent of an unpopular government.[114] But even in this changing context, the mid-1760s were not the mid-1770s. The missionary at Salem in 1764 felt that

> establishing missions in New England has contributed much to promote Peace and Harmony between Churchmen and Dissenters, and to wean the latter from their rigid notions and aversion to the Church . . . when they see our Service fairly set forth before their eyes, they are convinced that those things what they were informed concerning us are nothing. Ocular demonstration (and perhaps nothing else could) abates their prejudices and satisfies them that our Service is neither idolatorous nor superstitious.[115]

Moreover, overt and public displays of the Church's position did not seem to arouse much comment. A report to the SPG in 1766 noted that the Church of England Convention of New England clergy had met in Boston, with fourteen clergy attending. 'We made something of an appearance for this country, when we walked together in gowns and cassocks', the author recalled, 'but we have heard of no jealous or unfriendly remarks upon the occasion'.[116] In the abstracts of proceedings for that year, attached to the printed version of the annual sermons to the SPG, and containing reports from on the ground, some clergy were at pains to emphasise that they and their parishioners were on cordial

---

[113] For a useful overview, see John Shy, 'The American Colonies in War and Revolution, 1748–1783', in *The Oxford History of the British Empire*, II, ed. Marshall, 276–323, esp. 307–13. See Nathan O. Hatch, *The Sacred Cause of Liberty. Republican Thought and the Millennium in Revolutionary New England* (New Haven, 1977); Gordon S. Wood, *The Americanization of Benjamin Franklin* (New York, 2004); and T. H. Breen, 'Ideology and Nationalism on the Eve of the American Revolution: Revisions Once More in Need of Revising', *Journal of American History*, 84 (1997), 13–39.

[114] Bell, *War of Religion*, 160ff.

[115] William McGilchrist to SPG, 17 July 1764, in *Historical Collections relating to the American Colonial Church*, ed. Perry, III, 514–15.

[116] William McGilchrist to SPG, 27 June 1766, *ibid.*, 525.

terms with members of other denominations.[117] As late as 1773, reflecting on activities in 1772, it was noted at Simsbury, Cambridge, Scituate and Marshfield that 'there is more harmony than formerly' between members of the Church of England and 'the dissenters',[118] and in 1774, referring to 1773 at Norwich, the SPG missionary had 'the satisfaction to observe in the Dissenters a gradual increase of peaceableness and goodwill to the Church of England'.[119] There may, of course, be problems with this particular kind of evidence. Some clergy maintained that the secretary of the SPG who compiled the abstracts from information sent out to him from clergy working in America, misjudged or misunderstood what they had sent him (although in fact the originals of these letters in the SPG archives do say in these cases exactly what the digest claimed).[120] And J. C. D. Clark has warned us of the dangers of accepting these kind of statements at face value because they are hard to square with what would transpire over the next two or three years, and perhaps partly because they do not fit into his picture of denominational rivalry.[121] Nevertheless I would be wary of dismissing them altogether. If, as other kinds of research indicate, people took different paths to Revolution, then it may be that in some places the Church was simply not the issue as it was elsewhere.

But, it is certainly true that by the early 1770s, as in other areas of New England life, attitudes were hardening considerably. Henry Caner saw the Massachusetts Marriage Act of 1773 – which meant that ministers could be fined if they did not know the couple whom they were marrying – as an attack on the Church: 'it is utterly impossible', he claimed, 'for any clergyman to know all the seafaring and low people who ask them to marry them'.[122] Worse, in October 1774 he lamented that Samuel Peters, the SPG missionary at Hebron, had been 'driven by violence' from his parish by people who called themselves the 'Sons of liberty'.[123] The following month, Ezra Stiles noted that the Episcopalians in Cambridge

---

[117] Quoted in the 'Abstract of Proceedings' appended to John Ewer, *A Sermon Preached before the Incorporated Society for the Propagation of the Gospel in Foreign Parts; at their Anniversary Meeting in the Parish Church of St. Mary-le-Bow, on Friday February 20, 1767* (1767), 48ff.

[118] Quoted in the 'Abstract of Proceedings' appended to Jonathan Shipley, *A Sermon Preached before the Incorporated Society for the Propagation of the Gospel in Foreign Parts; at their Anniversary Meeting in the Parish Church of St. Mary-le-Bow, on Friday February 19, 1773* (1773), 22.

[119] Quoted in the 'Abstract of Proceedings' appended to Edmund Law, *A Sermon Preached before the Incorporated Society for the Propagation of the Gospel in Foreign Parts; at their Anniversary Meeting in the Parish Church of St. Mary-le-Bow, on Friday February 18, 1774* (1774), 27.

[120] I have checked the digests of the letters printed in the 'Abstracts of the Proceedings' added to the printed sermons preached to the SPG with the originals in Rhodes House Library, Oxford.

[121] Clark, *Language of Liberty*, 216–17.

[122] Cameron, *Letter-Book of the Rev. Henry Caner*, 250, Caner to Terrick, 29 Sept. 1773.

[123] *Ibid.*, Caner to Terrick, 258, 7 Oct. 1774. For Peters, see Sheldon S. Cohen, *Connecticut's Loyalist Gadfly: The Revered Samuel Andrew Peters* (Hartford, 1976).

had not observed Thanksgiving Day that year,[124] which was indicative of a cultural split, and a departure from the last eighty years where members of the Church of England in New England had observed the November Thanksgiving Day (itself suggestive of how something that had roots in a 'Puritan' context had in the recent past been able to transcend possible anti-Church of England connotations). Yet even at this juncture Stiles could observe that the Church of England congregation at Christ Church, Boston, who had been annoyed that their rector, Mather Byles, had not opened the church for a service on that day, were 'more for liberty' than any episcopal congregation north of Maryland.

During the next year, and those that followed, Church of England clergy were harried from their parishes, and church building were damaged, or used as store rooms, or even as Congregationalist meeting rooms. From then on, the reports back to England from Church of England clergy in New England were almost universally grim, and in 1777, after detailing the sufferings inflicted on clergy in New England and elsewhere during the previous year, the secretary of the SPG claimed that

> were every instance of this kind faithfully collected, it is probable that the sufferings of the American clergy might appear, in many respects, not inferior to those of the same order in the great rebellion of the last century; and such a work would be no bad supplement to Walker's *Sufferings of the Clergy*.[125]

Evidence such as this would fit well into the model of a Church which had been roundly rejected by Congregational New England. But as I have tried to demonstrate this should not be seen as the only possible way to understand the Church's place in New England, particularly from the 1730s. Indeed by the early 1760s, the Anglican Church was doing rather well in the colonial religious market place (benefiting perhaps from consumer choice, which, in a recent analysis of pre-Revolutionary America, Timothy Breen has argued was an overriding factor in American culture),[126] and, in its way, the Church of England was becoming embedded in New England life. As one of Mayhew's Anglican critics told him: 'Pray sir be calm, is this not our country, and the native country of most of us, as well as yours?'[127] If nothing else, the evidence I have produced might provide us with a richer context – a thicker description – with which to evaluate the significance of the 'bishop controversy', and relations between Congregationalists and Anglicans.

[124] *Literary Diary of Ezra Stiles*, ed. Dexter, II, 502, 20 Dec. 1774.

[125] Quoted in the 'Abstract of Proceedings' appended to William Markham, *A Sermon Preached before the Incorporated Society for the Propagation of the Gospel in Foreign Parts; at their Anniversary Meeting in the Parish Church of St. Mary-le-Bow, on Friday February 21, 1777* (1777), 58.

[126] Timothy Breen, *The Marketplace of Revolution: How Consumer Politics Shaped American Independence* (New York, 2004).

[127] Henry Caner, *A Candid Examination of Dr. Mayhew's Observations on the Charter and Conduct of the Society for the Propagation of the Gospel in Foreign Parts* (Boston, MA, 1763), 89.

Above all, it might make us wary of the temptations of teleology. Because of the events of the years after 1776, it has been easy for some historians to discern necessary links between anti-Britishness, anti-Anglicanism and anti-Episcopalianism.[128] But New England Anglicanism was not an oxymoron in Puritan New England, and both it (and bishops) found a small home in the United States after 1784.[129]

---

[128] Bridenbaugh, *Mitre and Sceptre*.
[129] Frederick V. Mills, *Bishops By Ballot. An Eighteenth-Century Ecclesiastical Revolution* (New York, 1978).

Transactions of the RHS 20 (2010), pp. 113–25 © Royal Historical Society 2010
doi:10.1017/S0080440110000071

THE INSTITUTIONALISATION OF ART IN EARLY VICTORIAN ENGLAND
The Colin Matthew Memorial Lecture

By Charles Saumarez Smith

READ 11 NOVEMBER 2009 AT GRESHAM COLLEGE

ABSTRACT. This article explores the political and intellectual circumstances which led to the efflorescence of cultural institutions between the foundation of the National Gallery in 1824 and the National Portrait Gallery in 1856: the transformation of institutions of public culture from haphazard and rather amateurish institutions to ones which were well organised, with a strong sense of social mission, and professionally managed. This transformation was in part owing to a group of exceptionally talented individuals, including Charles Eastlake, Henry Cole and George Scharf, accepting appointment in institutions to foster the public understanding of art. But it was not simply a matter of individual agency, but also of coordinated action by parliament, led by a group of MPs, including the Philosophical Radicals. It was much influenced by the example of Germany, filtered through extensive translation of German art historical writings and visits by writers and politicians to Berlin and Munich. It was also closely related to the philosophy of the utilitarians, who had a strong belief in the political and social benefits of the study of art. Only the Royal Academy refused the embrace of state control.

In writing about the early history of the National Gallery, which I was asked to do while I was its director, I became interested in the extraordinary rapidity with which it transformed itself from a fairly amateur operation, established apparently rather casually by Lord Liverpool's government in 1824 and occupying in its early days a private house in Pall Mall, looked after as its keeper by William Seguier, who was certainly knowledgeable about works of art, but as a professional adviser to connoisseurs and aristocratic collectors. At the beginning there was not a very clear mandate for its operation. There were no formal meetings of its Board of Trustees, who were in the early days merely a sub-set of the trustees of the British Museum. And yet the National Gallery transformed itself in the space of only about thirty years from being a rather casual, haphazard operation into being a much more disciplined, coherent, scholarly and professional organisation, occupying grand and stately premises on the north side of Trafalgar Square.

What, I asked myself, were the mechanisms and processes, the ideas behind its formation, which led to the institutionalisation of art in early Victorian England?

In my book, I adopted a purely narrative and descriptive approach.[1] I recorded the ways in which, in the late 1820s, the trustees of the National Gallery, when Robert Peel was appointed to their number, became somewhat more organised in their meetings, keeping minutes for the first time and recognising that the building which they originally occupied was wholly inadequate to the task of displaying works of art and that they must therefore commission a new one – larger and grander and more public in its orientation and with a proper order and sequence of public galleries. I described how, in the 1830s, parliament became interested in the issue of the education of public taste and the role that a National Gallery might play in improving the public's knowledge and awareness of the principles of fine art by the establishment of a parliamentary committee in 1835 to look at, and investigate, the processes of training in fine art for the improvement of British manufacture. I discussed how, in 1843, when the first keeper, William Seguier, died, the trustees appointed Charles Eastlake, a painter, who had spent the 1820s living in Rome and who came to the task of running the National Gallery with a much more scholarly and, indeed, more academic knowledge of the history and study of art than his predecessor.

In the 1840s, Eastlake got fed up with the amount of public criticism he faced for all his actions as keeper of the National Gallery, his acquisitions and his policies of conservation of the pictures, and it was only in 1855 when he returned as a fully fledged *director* of the National Gallery that he was able to establish its operation on properly professional lines with an orderly structure, a commitment to the scholarly study of the works of art which had been acquired, a procedure of cataloguing, a description of how the relationship between the director and the Board of Trustees was expected to operate and a budget which enabled Eastlake to go on buying trips in Italy every autumn, so that he was able to transform the National Gallery from an amateurish collection of Old Master paintings, which betrayed its origins in the Grand Tour taste of its Board of Trustees, into one of the greatest, small-scale collections in Europe of works of art which were properly illustrative of the history of western European

[1] Charles Saumarez Smith, *The National Gallery: A Short History* (2009). The lecture in the form that it was originally delivered (including reference to Colin Matthew) is available on the Gresham College website and an abbreviated version has been published as 'Civilising Servants', *Standpoint* (Jan./Feb. 2010), 19, 80–3. In writing about the National Gallery, I remain indebted to the work of Jonathan Conlin, including 'The Origins and History of the National Gallery, 1753–1860' (Ph.D. thesis, University of Cambridge, 2002) and his subsequent monograph, *The Nation's Mantelpiece: A History of the National Gallery* (2006).

painting, including those by the early Italian masters alongside some of the greatest works of the seicento.

This process of transformation of the National Gallery from a small-scale, amateurish and somewhat haphazard operation into a much more ruthlessly efficient system for the study and care of works of art all happened quite quickly. In the book I describe the process of formation of the National Gallery. But I do not record the fact that this was also the period when the National Portrait Gallery was founded, also by parliamentary action, and, in the case of the National Portrait Gallery, as a result of a very obvious process in the professionalisation of the writing of history, whereby Thomas Carlyle, in writing about the actions of the great men of the past, realised that study of them would be greatly enhanced by images of them, or, as he wrote – in words which are redolent of the great Victorian confidence in the power of images to illuminate the public understanding of history:

> Often I have found a Portrait superior in real instruction to half-a-dozen written 'Biographies', as Biographies are written; or rather, let me say, I have found that the Portrait was a small lighted *candle* by which the Biographies could for the first time be *read*, and some human interpretation be made of them.

These words, written by Thomas Carlyle in 1854 in a letter to David Laing, the great Scottish bookseller and honorary professor of antiquities to the Royal Scottish Academy, led in the space of two years to a series of debates in the House of Lords, led by Lord Stanhope, in which Stanhope quoted the words of Charles Eastlake how

> 'whenever I hear of portraits for sale of historical interest I cannot help wishing that a gallery could be formed exclusively for authentic likenesses of celebrated individuals, not necessarily with reference to the merit of the works of art. I believe that an extensive gallery of portraits with catalogues containing good and short biographical notices would be useful in many ways and especially as a not unimportant element of education.'

By December 1856, a National Portrait Gallery had been established with government funding, a well-qualified secretary and keeper, George Scharf, who was then occupied in organising the great Manchester exhibition of works of art and who had indeed been a candidate for the post of director of the National Gallery the previous year and who, like Eastlake, had many of the same attributes of careful and scrupulous scholarship, a meticulous concern for the documentation of works of art, and an interest in establishing the new institution on properly scholarly lines.[2]

The 1850s was, of course, also the decade of the Great Exhibition, the greatest display of artefacts from all over the world, organised in the space of eighteen months in a huge, glass, temporary palace in Hyde Park with

[2] For the foundation of the National Portrait Gallery, the most recent account is in David Cannadine, *National Portrait Gallery: A Brief History* (2007). There is also a description of its origins in Charles Saumarez Smith, *The National Portrait Gallery* (1997).

a huge, popular and public interest in seeing the wonders of the world, but also an extraordinary feat of management. The Great Exhibition led, the year afterwards, to the establishment of a Museum of Manufactures in Marlborough House and, in 1857, to its organisation on a much more permanent footing in South Kensington, once again with the security of parliamentary funding and an extremely able and powerfully engaged director, Henry Cole, who, like Charles Eastlake, had a finger in every pie of arts management during this period, beginning his professional career in the Public Record Office, working as an assistant to Rowland Hill in the introduction of the Penny Post, writing a popular guide to the National Gallery under the pseudonym Felix Summerly, editing *The Journal of Design and Manufactures* and, in 1849, involving himself in the *Select Committee Report on the Government Schools of Design*, before working as one of the commissioners under Prince Albert in the organisation of the Great Exhibition and taking up the post of general superintendent of the newly established Department of Practical Art under the Board of Trade in 1852.[3] The role of the Department was to administer the Schools of Design and to set up 'museums, by which all classes might be induced to investigate those common principles of taste which may be traced in the works of excellence of all ages'.

This is also the period of the establishment of the Royal Commission on the Promotion of the Fine Arts (normally known as the Fine Arts Commission), set up in October 1841 under the aegis of the young Prince Albert to supervise issues of public taste and the commissioning of didactic frescoes in the recently completed Palace of Westminster. As Peel described its mandate, it was 'to be composed of Members of each house of parliament selected without reference to party distinctions, whose attention has been directed to the Cultivation of the Fine Arts, and including two or three distinguished artists'. Who was appointed as its first secretary? None other than Charles Eastlake, recommended in the year before he was appointed keeper of the National Gallery by Sir Robert Peel?[4]

All of these facts are perfectly well known to historians of this period, as well as to art historians, and are closely related to the professionalisation

---

[3] Henry Cole's autobiography is entitled, very appropriately, *Fifty years of public work of Sir Henry Cole KCB, Accounted for in his Deeds, Speeches and Writings* (2 vols., 1884). There is a brief, but suggestive discussion of his significance in Michael Conforti, 'The Idealist Enterprise and the Applied Arts', in Malcolm Baker and Brenda Richardson, *A Grand Design: Art of the Victoria and Albert Museum* (1997), 28–33, and full biographies in Ann Cooper, 'For the Public Good: Henry Cole, his Circle and the Development of the South Kensington Estate' (Ph.D. thesis, Open University, 1992), and Elizabeth Bonython and Anthony Burton, *The Great Exhibitor: The Life and Work of Henry Cole* (2003).

[4] There is a good discussion of the views of the Fine Arts Commission in Emma Winter, 'German Fresco Painting and the New Houses of Parliament at Westminster, 1834–51', *Historical Journal*, 47 (2004), 291–329.

of the study of history in the same period.[5] They are important aspects of the culture of early Victorian England. But what I am not convinced has previously been satisfactorily analysed or explained, even in spite of a great deal of recent research by a group of younger cultural historians, including Jonathan Conlin, Emma Winter and Holger Hoock, is the extreme rapidity of this transformation, the exact process of the institutionalisation of art.[6]

Let me spell out the issue as clearly as I can. From a period in the 1820s when the management of culture consisted of not much more than the rather old-fashioned practices of the trustees and staff of the British Museum, who were in charge of an extremely miscellaneous and highly eclectic set of collections which mingled antiquities with works of natural history and which was only visitable by persons 'of decent appearance' on three days a week, suddenly, during the 1830s and 1840s, there was a much more energetic determination on the part of parliament, the crown and a small number of public officials, like Charles Eastlake and Henry Cole, to bring order and system and supervision to the realm of art. Instead of being a free market, subject to the vagaries of public taste and the whims of private patronage, with the only public institutions of fine art being organised as an act of free enterprise by groups of private individuals, as happened in the establishment of the British Institution in 1805, the world of fine art, its study and practice, suddenly came within the scope of parliament to organise, finance, supervise and control.[7] The acquisition and display of works of art became much more systematic.

---

[5] For writing about historians, see, for example, P. Levine, *The Amateur and the Professional: Antiquarians, Historians and Archaeologists in Victorian England, 1838–1886* (1986).

[6] The pioneer in writing about this topic was Janet Minihan (née Oppenheim), *The Nationalization of Culture: The Development of State Subsidies to the Arts in Great Britain* (1977), and there is a briefer, but also suggestive analysis, in Nicholas Pearson, *The State and the Visual Arts: A Discussion of State Intervention in the Visual Arts in Britain, 1760–1981* (Milton Keynes, 1982). However, they are both fairly broad-brush. For Janet Minihan's approach to the subject, see Peter Mandler, Alex Owen, Seth Koven and Susan Pedersen, 'Cultural Histories Old and New: Rereading the Work of Janet Oppenheim', *Victorian Studies*, 41 (Autumn 1977), 69–105. More recently, there has been much investigation of the period by a group of younger cultural historians, influenced by the writings of John Brewer and Peter Mandler. For broad overviews, see Peter Mandler, 'Art in a Cool Climate: The Cultural Policy of the British State in European Context, c. 1780 – c. 1850', in *Unity and Diversity in European Culture c. 1800*, ed. T. Blanning and H. Schulze (Oxford, 2006), 101–20, and Holger Hoock, 'Reforming Culture: National Art Institutions in the Age of Reform', in *Rethinking the Age of Reform: Britain 1780–1850*, ed. A. Burns and J. Innes (Cambridge, 2003), 254–70. In thinking about these issues, I am exceptionally grateful for informal advice at an early stage from Professor Peter Mandler and Emma Winter, both of whom guided my interpretation, and for comments on the final text from Professor Tim Barringer.

[7] For a description of the phase in which it was assumed that art institutions were more likely to be established by private than by public initiative, see Peter Funnell, 'William Hazlitt, Prince Hoare, and the Institutionalisation of the British Art World', in *Towards a Modern Art World*, ed. Brian Allen (London and New Haven, 1995), 145–56.

Works of art were studied, documented, classified and interpreted in a way that they had not been before. The teaching of art was subject to an iron discipline in a way that it had not been previously. Art was treated as a didactic instrument to teach the public about British history. Throughout the British Isles and not just in London, there was a belief that art could be managed in the same way as other areas of the public realm.

So, why did this happen? Why was it that in the space of only about thirty years attitudes towards the study and enjoyment of Old Master painting changed from being the private pleasure of a small number of connoisseurs and collectors to being a public duty enjoyed by large numbers of citizens – in the National Gallery in 1859 as many as a million a year, equivalent to ten a minute – in free public galleries? Why was it that, during the 1820s, the enjoyment and appreciation of Old Master paintings was concerned above all with an appreciation of their visual qualities, without particular regard for their date or attribution, whereas by the 1850s there was a much stricter regard for their documentation and history, so that works of art could be properly studied in terms of their historical development? Why was it that, during the same period, historians recognised that works of art could become useful documents of study, helping the task of interpretation? Why was it during this period that it was acknowledged that it would be beneficial to the public to be able to study objects of manufacture, as well as works of art, from other parts of the world in order to give them a better understanding of the mysteries of taste, so that they would be better able themselves to produce works of art to compete in a global marketplace? Why was it, in short, that the institutionalisation of art took place?

I am going to attempt an analysis of this phenomenon and to try to pick out and establish some of its most obvious characteristics in search of an explanation. First, it is impossible to ignore the role of a small group of highly energetic, well-trained individuals, who saw themselves as public servants in a way which did not exist in the previous generation. Charles Eastlake was trained in the Royal Academy Schools in the early part of the century, but he then lived in Rome during the 1820s, where he came into contact with German artists and German art historians.[8] He seems to have absorbed some of the intellectual and moral discipline of his German friends, including J. D. Passavant who wrote the first biography of Raphael and Gustav Waagen, the art historian who was appointed director of the Altes Museum in 1832, as well as the wide range of their intellectual and academic reference. As a result of living in Italy and

---

[8] For the life of Charles Eastlake, see David Robertson, *Sir Charles Eastlake and the Victorian art world* (Princeton, 1978), and Christopher Hodkinson, 'In the National Interest: Sir Charles Eastlake and the National Gallery's Collection of Italian Renaissance Paintings' (MA dissertation, Lancaster University, 2004).

travelling on the Continent, Eastlake approached works of art, not simply aesthetically, to be appreciated visually, but as having a history which was susceptible to intellectual study and analysis. In 1840, he published a translation of *Goethe's Theory of Colours*. In 1842, he published a translation of Franz Kugler's book on the Italian schools of painting. In 1847, he published his magisterial *Materials for a History of Oil Painting*, a book which is still in print for the information it supplies about the early history of the materials and techniques of painting, and the following year he published a compilation of articles under the title *Contributions to the Literature of the Fine Arts*. In other words, he was a scholar as well as a public official, highly industrious and productive in publishing work alongside his public duties, a model of the high-minded Victorian public servant.

Think now about the characteristics of Henry Cole. Educated at Christ's Hospital, he entered public service aged fifteen as an assistant to Francis Palgrave, the early student of public records and who was such a significant figure in the establishment of the Public Records Office. Cole seems to have inherited from Palgrave some of his powerful determination to reform public organisations, including, in Henry Cole's case, the postal service, the system of art school teaching, the Royal Society of Arts and the ways in which manufactures and public taste could be improved by their systematic display, first in Marlborough House and, from 1857 onwards, much more ambitiously in the South Kensington Museum. Both Palgrave and Cole, if faced by obstacles, were capable of being pretty bruising in the ways in which they treated colleagues: that was the way they got things done.[9]

George Scharf, who was the key figure in the foundation of the National Portrait Gallery, was perhaps a slightly less bullish public servant, but the range of his intellectual interests was still fairly formidable, travelling as the official artist on Charles Fellows's expeditions to study Lycian antiquities, compiling a catalogue of the pictures owned by the Society of Antiquaries, helping to organise the Greek, Roman and Pompeian courts when the Crystal Palace moved to Sydenham, and appointed as the secretary to the great Art Treasures Exhibition at Manchester in the same year that he took up the post of secretary to the trustees of the National Portrait Gallery when it was established in 1857 in a small, private house in Great George Street, close to the houses of parliament.

We have got used in recent years to the idea of the professional bureaucrat as a term of abuse, as if all bureaucrats are intellectually second rate, interested only in the perpetuation of systems of existing management and not in innovation. But these art bureaucrats of early Victorian England were something else: tirelessly hard-working, writing

---

[9] There is a good description of Cole's personality in H. T. Wood, *A History of the Royal Society of Arts* (1913), 359.

books in the morning, serving on committees in the afternoon, endlessly networking and socialising in the evening, with a dedicated sense of mission to create and reform institutions of art for the educational benefit of a broad public. And it is surely not accidental that their activities, their sense of moral purpose, coincided with the reform of the civil service itself, the sweeping away of systems of patronage through the Northcote-Trevelyan Report of 1854. The tidying of procedures, the organisation of systems of public management, the idea of public duty, were not confined to art history.

However, as a system of historical explanation, to say that a widespread historical phenomenon such as the institutionalisation of art was only the result of the agency of a small number of highly motivated individuals may well be viewed by historians as intellectually suspect. There were very obviously wider forces at play.

The first of the wider forces was the agency of parliament. It is impossible to ignore the fact that it was parliament which, following quite heated argument and debate, agreed to the foundation of the National Gallery. It was not just a small group of self-interested individuals who were themselves already deeply involved in the art world, like George Beaumont and Sir Thomas Lawrence, the then president of the Royal Academy, who led the move to found a National Gallery, but the prime minister Lord Liverpool himself, who wrote to the duchess of Devonshire in support and chose to have himself painted by Sir Thomas Lawrence with the original charter of foundation in his hand. The chancellor of the exchequer, Frederick Robinson, known as 'Prosperity' Robinson, was able not only to give grants for the foundation of the National Gallery, but also in nearly the same year towards the new building by Robert Smirke for the British Museum. And a young backbench MP like George Agar-Ellis, later Lord Dover, combined his service in parliament with trusteeships of both the British Museum and the National Gallery alongside the formation of a collection of British art and editing Horace Walpole's letters.

In the 1830s, in the period after the Great Reform Bill and as a direct consequence of it in bringing into parliament a new class of idealistic and reforming MPs, there was a tremendous amount of involvement of parliament in state policy towards the arts. Robert Peel took a close personal interest in the development of a new building for the National Gallery. There was detailed discussion of its design and cost in debates in the House of Commons. In July 1835, parliament established a select committee which was appointed 'to enquire into the best means of extending a knowledge of the Arts and Principles of Design among the people (especially the Manufacturing Population) of the Country; also to enquire into the Constitution of the Royal Academy, and the effects produced by it'. It asked for evidence to be heard from both Gustav Waagen, who spoke forcefully in favour of wider public access to the arts and to 'the employment of artists in public buildings', and from Leo von Klenze, the architect of the Glyptothek and the Alte Pinakothek in Munich.

Nor did this level of parliamentary interest in arts policy diminish in the 1840s. The requirements of decorating the newly built houses of parliament was what led to the establishment of the Royal Fine Arts Commission. Prince Albert brought a very Germanic view of the importance of the arts to his role as Prince Consort, collecting the works of Winterhalter and Landseer, and acting as chairman of the Royal Fine Arts Commission.[10] Gladstone, in his book on *The State in its Relations to the Church*, wrote how the state was able to offer 'to its individual members those humanizing influences which are derived from the contemplation of Beauty embodied in the works of the great masters of painting'.[11] There were further select committees to investigate the possible relocation of the National Gallery. Throughout these discussions and debates there was a keen awareness of the educational benefits of museums and galleries and the improving advantages of wider public access to great works of art, which seems to have crossed the political spectrum, such that in 1844 Joseph Hume, the radical parliamentarian, was able to boast of the fact that:

> The notion that the English people were only fit to be trusted in particular places – that museums were only intended for the visits of the rich, and that those collections so calculated to improve the mind, and promote science, should only be open to men of birth and fortune, had wholly gone by.

Although there is a presumption that parliament became much less interventionist during the 1850s, less troubled by the prospect of social subversion, there does not seem to have been much reduction in the cultural activities of the legislature in the establishment of institutions of art during the 1850s. In 1850, another select committee was established to decide the fate of the Vernon Collection. Lord John Russell as prime minister pledged public funds to relocate the Royal Academy into new premises apart from the National Gallery. In 1853, parliament established yet another select committee, this time, 'To inquire into the management of the National Gallery; also to consider what mode the collective monuments of antiquity and fine art possessed by the nation may be most securely preserved, judiciously augmented, and advantageously exhibited to the public.' The committee took evidence for four months before publishing its *Report* which consisted of over 1,000 pages of evidence. It was parliament, not the trustees, which was responsible for establishing

---

[10] The best discussion of Prince Albert's influence on the arts remains Winslow Ames, *Prince Albert and Victorian Taste* (1967).

[11] For Gladstone's views of art, see Jonathan Conlin, 'Gladstone and Christian Art, 1832–1854', *Historical Journal*, 46 (2003), 341–74.

the organisation and management of the National Gallery on a properly professional footing through the issue of a treasury minute in March 1855.

So, it was not just the officials who were industrious. They were under the close scrutiny of members of parliament who took a personal interest in all aspects of arts policy, including the conservation of paintings and – not always helpfully – the price of works of art and the arrangements for their acquisition. The institutionalisation of the arts was not a product of private initiative, but of the application of public policy to the improvement of the lives and welfare of the citizenry. Few areas of life were now immune from parliamentary action and members of parliament took a much broader view of their responsibilities.

It will be evident throughout this analysis that another motivator of change was competition with, and awareness of, what was happening in, Germany.[12] It was the Germans who taught the British the discipline of art history, including Karl Friedrich von Rumohr, whose *Italienische Forschungen* introduced the discipline of connoisseurship to the study of early Italian art, and Johann David Passavant, whose *A Tour of a German Artist in England*, published in 1836, revealed the wealth of works of art in private collections and whose 1839 monograph on Raphael was digested by Eastlake in the *Quarterly Review*. Both had known Eastlake in Rome, as had Gustav Waagen, who wrote his doctorate on Hubert and Jan van Eyck, addressed the 1835 select committee (in German) on the virtues of the Berlin museum system and published *Works of Art and Artists in England* in a translation by Eastlake in 1838. Waagen remained a close friend of Eastlake and his wife, visited England nearly every year during the 1850s, produced his more comprehensive four-volume *Treasure of Art in Great Britain* between 1854 and 1857, and was said to be Prince Albert's candidate to be director of the National Gallery.[13]

Nation states were in competition in their cultural policy as they had been on the battlefield. There was a cartoon published in the 1820s comparing the miserable accommodation of the National Gallery with the glories of the Louvre. There was a strong awareness amongst the intellectual leaders of the 1830s, particularly in the universities, where young men inspired by the writings of Coleridge, Kant and Schlegel would go to study in the university of Heidelberg, of what was being achieved in terms of the display of art in both Munich and Berlin. Schinkel's great

[12] The influence of German ideas on British culture is the subject of Emma Winter, 'The Transformation of Taste in Germany and England, 1797–1858' (Ph.D. dissertation, University of Cambridge, 2005).

[13] For the influence of German writing on art history, see Francis Haskell, *Discoveries in Art: Some Aspects of Taste, Fashion and Collecting in England and France* (1976); Michael Podro, *Critical Historians of Art* (1982); and, most recently, Christopher Hodkinson, 'A Question of Attribution: The Evolution of Connoisseurship during the Nineteenth Century' (Ph.D. dissertation, Lancaster University, 2009).

building for the Altes Museum on the banks of the Spree and Leo von Klenze's purpose-built Alte Pinakothek were the models for what could be achieved through a dynamic policy towards the display of art for public benefit. Younger members of parliament were aware of, and inspired by, the essentially German idea that cultural institutions could provide symbolic value to the effectiveness of the nation state.

My final determinant in what led to the institutionalisation of the arts is the culture of utilitarianism. It was the writings of Bentham and John Stuart Mill which led to the belief in the improving role of art for wider purposes of public education. It was parliamentarians like William Ewart, Benjamin Hawes and Joseph Hume, the so-called Philosophical Radicals, who led to the provision of public institutions of art, under the influence of utilitarian beliefs. They believed that art had a wide social, political and educational value, should be taken away from the clutches of the traditional connoisseurs and used, instead, as an instrument of social amelioration. It was they who suggested the establishment of the Select Committee on Arts and Manufactures in 1835, who introduced the bill which led to the establishment of the Fine Arts Commission and supported the Museums Act in 1845. Someone like Henry Cole definitely worked under the influence of the utilitarians and, indeed, met Jeremy Bentham just before his death in 1832, knew John Stuart Mill reasonably well (certainly well enough to borrow money from him) and was quite a close associate of Edwin Chadwick. It was this circle of utilitarians which helped to inspire Cole's belief in the need for a reform of English design. Indeed, in writing in support of his programme of teaching at South Kensington, Cole was to quote the words of John Stuart Mill, who he described as 'the first and most liberal of English writers on Political economy':

> It is only necessary to refer to his work, where he proves that education is one of those things which it is admissible in principle that a government should provide for the people, and that help in education is help towards doing without help, and is favourable to a spirit of independence.[14]

I have so far made very little reference to the Royal Academy of Arts, and of what happened to it during this period.

The reason is that the Royal Academy offers a very different model to the role of institutionalisation to that which I have described. The Royal Academy is an institution not of the early Victorian period, but classically of the reign of George III. Founded in 1768, it was the result not of parliamentary action, but of the community of artists going privately to the king and it was the king – without the intervention or involvement of parliament – who asked them to draw up a set of rules for their

---

[14] Henry Cole, *Introductory Addresses on the Science and Art Department* (1857), no. 1, 9.

operation and who agreed remarkably generously to pay off any debts
they incurred, which he did consistently in the Academy's early years.[15]
In the 1830s, parliament was extremely irritated by the independence of
the Royal Academy and it was attacked by writers like George Foggo and
the artist Benjamin Robert Haydon, who viewed it as an instrument of
private privilege, rather than of public benefit.[16] The Royal Academy was
wary of being incorporated into a new government building in Trafalgar
Square as part of the National Gallery and felt that it was being coopted
by the state. Parliament asked for information about the finances to be laid
before it and Sir Martin Archer Shee, the then president, simply refused.
He regarded the Royal Academy as a private institution, which should
not necessarily be subject to public regulation. When appearing before
the select committee, he was sceptical that the creation of better premises
for the National Gallery would necessarily produce an improvement in
the state of art and criticised the creation of the National Gallery on the
grounds that, as he described it

> the Royal Academy [is] a much more important institution to the nation than the
> National Gallery; I look upon it that a garden is of more consequence than a granary;
> and you may heap up a hortus-siccus of art without producing any of the salutary effects
> which never fail to result from the operations of such a school as the Royal Academy.

In other words, the Royal Academy stuck two fingers up at those who
believed in wider public access to the arts and felt that providing better
facilities for the study of art would not necessarily improve its practice;
and, indeed, there is a case to be made that the institutionalisation of art
did, indeed, greatly increase the public knowledge and interest in art, but
did not necessarily at the same time improve its creative practice.

A final reflection is that, as we approach the prospect of a likely change
of government and as the two parties face the problem of what they are
going to do about the arts in an environment of substantially reduced
availability of public funding, there may be benefits in looking back at the
issues and debates faced by government and the House of Commons in
the 1830s and 1840s.

We have had an administration over the last decade whose attitude
towards the arts has been essentially utilitarian, sometimes nearly
Benthamite in its belief that the essential value of the arts lies in its

---

[15] In *The King's Artists: The Royal Academy of Arts and the Politics of British Culture 1760–1840*
(Oxford, 2003) Holger Hoock provides a revisionist account of the Royal Academy as a
national cultural institution as if it were an arm of the Hanoverian state. It and his recent
monograph *Empires of the Imagination: Politics, War, and the Arts in the British World, 1750–1850*
(2010) argue against an idea that state-funded art institutions in Britain were a creation of
the post-Napoleonic era.

[16] There is a useful description of the views of the opponents of the Royal Academy in
Peter Funnell, 'The London Art World and its Institutions', in *London – World City 1800–1840*,
ed. Celina Fox (London and New Haven, 1992), 164–5.

purposes of social amelioration. But alongside those who espoused these utilitarian beliefs in the 1830s were others who had a stronger and more idealistic belief in the arts as a source of moral and intellectual and, indeed, in many cases, religious uplift – a way of improving society through its culture.

We have in many ways lost the language of how to describe these idealising purposes of art in public discourse. But parliamentarians in the 1830s did not feel so constrained. They perfectly understood that there were a set of ideas and beliefs which derived from the writings of Kant and Coleridge and which were capable of providing a source, as well as a language, of public belief. I conclude by suggesting that it may perhaps be helpful in considering the sometimes arid language of current aesthetic discourse to go back to those writers and thinkers for whom these issues were a subject of intense public debate and to think, once more, about the emblematic and moral value of arts institutions, instead of just their instrumental purpose.

Transactions of the RHS 20 (2010), pp. 127–39 © Royal Historical Society 2010
doi:10.1017/S0080440110000083

THE POOR INQUIRY AND IRISH SOCIETY – A CONSENSUS THEORY OF TRUTH

By Niall Ó Ciosáin

READ 26 JUNE 2009 AT THE QUEEN'S UNIVERSITY BELFAST

ABSTRACT. The most detailed contemporary ethnographic representation of early nineteenth-century Ireland can be found in the reports produced by the Poor Inquiry of 1833–6. Despite their richness, however, these reports remained marginal to contemporary policy discussions and public debate. This is normally, and correctly, attributed to the unpopularity and impracticability of the specific recommendations of the Inquiry. This paper argues that the marginalisation of the reports was also due to their discursive originality. It focuses on the voluminous oral evidence which was collected and published by the Inquiry. This evidence was taken in public from large groups representing all social classes, and much of it was printed verbatim. This method was unique among state reports of the nineteenth century in the United Kingdom, and unusual in social discourse more generally. It emerged from an equally unusual conception of truth as social consensus, a theory which the Inquiry adopted in order to overcome what it saw as the socially fragmented nature of representation in Ireland.

The Royal Commission on the Condition of the Poorer Classes in Ireland, which was active from 1833 to 1836, has a peculiar status within the history and the historiography of nineteenth-century Ireland. Usually known as the Poor Inquiry, it stands out as the most substantial and comprehensive examination undertaken of pre-Famine society. The investigation lasted almost three years, inquired into a huge range of issues and produced three reports and a vast amount of appendices, containing over five thousand pages altogether. This thoroughness and scale has made it uniquely valuable to historians. One could put together a substantial book of articles that are almost entirely based on some section of it, such as K. H. Connell's pioneering article on illegitimacy, Mary Cullen's study of the household budgets of labouring families and the geographical studies of diet by L. A. Clarkson and Margaret Crawford. Extracts from the Inquiry appear in five separate sections in the volumes of the *Field Day Anthology of Irish Writing* devoted to women's writing, on subjects such as begging and infanticide. For these topics, the Poor

Inquiry is not just the most detailed source, but sometimes the only one.[1]

This status in historiography is in marked contrast to the fate of the Inquiry within the debate on Irish society and poverty which took place in the 1830s and 1840s, and of which it should have formed a central part. In fact, despite its scale and detail, it was effectively ignored and marginalised. It is well known that the government paid little heed to its recommendations or to any part of its findings, but it also had little impact on the debate inside or outside parliament.[2] The Devon Commission, which investigated land tenure in Ireland only ten years afterwards, hardly refers to it, even though the Poor Inquiry had dealt with many of the same issues. In contrast, the Devon report makes a good deal of reference to a select committee of 1830 on the Irish poor, which was far more restricted in its scope than the Poor Inquiry. Even more revealing is the attitude of Thomas Bermingham, a land agent in east Co. Galway and a pamphleteer on Irish economic issues. Bermingham was an enthusiastic supporter of the Poor Inquiry. He gave evidence to several of its different investigations and wrote to newspapers in the west of Ireland exhorting people to cooperate fully with the Inquiry and to seize the opportunity to make their views known. Two years after the Inquiry had reported, however, Bermingham published a pamphlet on Irish poor relief which does not mention the Poor Inquiry at all. The debate on Irish poverty, in other words, continued as though the single largest contribution to that debate had never happened.[3]

Its impact on the contemporary ethnographic and economic literature was somewhat greater, but still relatively slight. Some commentators did praise the Inquiry for its realism. Gustave de Beaumont, who toured Ireland at the same time as the Poor Inquiry, thought that 'Les travaux immenses de cette commission lui ont paru mériter la plus grande confiance. Ils sont l'image la plus fidèle de l'Irlande. C'est encore voyager en Irlande que de les parcourir.' Similarly, a selection of extracts was published under the title *True Tales of the Irish Peasantry, as Related by Themselves*, by Christian Johnstone, editor of *Tait's Edinburgh Magazine*.

[1] K. H. Connell, *Irish Peasant Society: Four Historical Essays* (Oxford, 1968), ch. 2: 'Illegitimacy before the Famine'; Mary Cullen, 'Breadwinners and Providers: Women in the Household Economy of Labouring Families 1835–36', in *Women Surviving: Studies in Irish Women's History in the Nineteenth and Twentieth Centuries*, ed. Maria Luddy and Cliona Murphy (Dublin, 1989), 85–116; L. A. Clarkson and E. Margaret Crawford, 'Dietary Directions: A Topographical Survey of Irish Diet 1836', in *Economy and Society in Scotland and Ireland, 1500–1939*, ed. Rosalind Mitchison and Peter Roebuck (Edinburgh, 1988), 171–92; *Field Day Anthology of Irish Writing*, IV (Cork, 2002), 847, 903, V (Cork, 2002), 522–4, 611, 835.
[2] Peter Gray, *The Making of the Irish Poor Law 1815–43* (Manchester, 2009).
[3] *Connaught Journal*, 27 Mar. 1834; Thomas Bermingham, *Remarks on the Proposed Poor Law Bill for Ireland* (1838).

But the material was not used in the ethnographic literature on Ireland to anything like the extent that similar reports on industrial towns and cities in Britain and France were used by novelists such as Balzac, Hugo, Disraeli and Gaskell.[4]

I

If the Poor Inquiry is anomalous by virtue of the relative disproportion between its size and its impact, it is also anomalous as a text. Its genre is the parliamentary report, but it departs in many ways from the standard, almost universal, format of published parliamentary investigations in the nineteenth-century United Kingdom. In its printed form, the report of a royal commission or select committee was followed by the evidence collected during the investigation and on which the recommendations in the report were founded. The reports made continuous reference to this evidence in order to support and illustrate their analyses and recommendations.[5] On the first point, the Poor Inquiry complied with the formula of printed report and accompanying evidence. On the second point, though, it departed significantly from practice.

The overall recommendations of the Inquiry are contained in its third report, published in 1836. The first eight pages of that report contain an analysis of Irish poverty which is almost entirely deductive, based essentially on a comparison of the 1831 censuses for Britain and Ireland. It makes no reference to the mountain of evidence collected and printed by the Inquiry itself, and indeed could have been written without any investigation taking place at all. The various initiatives suggested by the commission are also discussed without reference to the evidence, with one odd exception. This is a section on emigration, which goes to the other extreme – its nine pages consist entirely of quotations from the evidence, with hardly any commentary. With the exception of this section, however, we can fairly say that the material collected by the Irish Poor Inquiry was marginalised even within that Inquiry itself. This becomes clearer if we compare the third report of the Inquiry with a pamphlet published in the same year by John Revans, *Evils of the State of Ireland*. Revans had been the secretary to the Inquiry but disagreed strongly with its conclusions and published his own views and recommendations. Revans's text is securely

---

[4] Gustave de Beaumont, *L'Irlande: sociale, politique et religieuse* (Paris, 1843, orig. 1839), 179. This passage does not appear in the English translation published in 1839, and consequently not in the 2006 reprinting of that translation by Tom Garvin and Andreas Hess; Christian Isobel Johnstone, *True Tales of the Irish Peasantry as Related by Themselves* (Edinburgh, 1836); Louis Chevalier, *Labouring Classes and Dangerous Classes in Paris during the First Half of the Nineteenth Century* (1973, orig. 1958), 41–53; Sheila M. Smith, 'Willenhall and Wodgate: Disraeli's Use of Blue Book Evidence', *Review of English Studies*, 13 (1962), 368–84; Patrick Bratlinger, *The Spirit of Reform. British Literature and Politics 1832–67* (1977).

[5] Oz Frankel, *States of Inquiry: Social Investigations and Print Culture in Nineteenth-Century Britain and the United States* (Baltimore, 2006).

founded in the evidence, and there are very few of its 150 pages which do not adduce some section of it. In purely stylistic terms, therefore, Revans's pamphlet could be described as the 'real' report of the Poor Inquiry, rather than the official reports themselves.[6]

Perhaps the most striking and unusual feature of the Poor Inquiry, however, and what makes it almost unique, is the nature of one major section of its evidence. It collected and published oral material, taken from conversations among representatives of all classes and occupations in particular parishes in Ireland, gathered together in large groups. The appendices to the Poor Inquiry, as printed, contain over 1,000 pages of such material, collected in one parish per barony in seventeen counties. It varies a good deal: in some parishes there is a short account of the evidence of two or three of the parish elite, while in others there is an an apparently verbatim transcription of a lengthy conversation featuring thirty or forty witnesses from all social classes, from landowners to beggars. This variation is partly geographic, with western counties tending to have more witnesses and longer conversations, but it is also due to differences among the different investigators themselves. Some of these clearly believed in gathering as many witnesses as possible and reporting their discussions with as little intervention as possible, so that the evidence often consists entirely of transcribed speech.

Looked at in this way, the report of the Poor Inquiry constitutes by far the largest oral archive documenting the words and beliefs of early nineteenth-century Irish people. It is not the only source of popular speech from that period. Early folklorists such as Thomas Crofton Croker were already active in the 1820s and 1830s. They tended, however, to collect longer narratives from recognised individual performers rather than record conversations, and, despite claims to 'reproduce the very words of the narrator', to present them in a stylised literary form.[7] Even within other parliamentary investigations, where one might not expect it, representations of popular speech were not entirely unknown. Some committees summoned witnesses who were well outside the usual elite. A select committee on a contested parliamentary election in Carrickfergus, Co. Antrim, in 1828, for example, briefly interviewed a fisherman, a sailor, a mason and others, some of whom could not write. Another type of parliamentary investigation which sometimes contained extensive non-elite oral narrative was that into crime. The English Constabulary Commission of 1839, for example, contains thirteen pages of confessions

---

[6] John Revans, *Evils of the State of Ireland, their Causes and Remedy: A Poor Law* (1837).

[7] Brian Earls, 'Supernatural Legends in Nineteenth-Century Irish Writing', *Béaloideas: The Journal of the Folklore of Ireland Society*, 60–1 (1992–3), 93–144.

from ordinary criminals, some obtained by the commissioners themselves and others by prison chaplains.[8]

These were different to the Poor Inquiry, however, in two respects. First, the Carrickfergus and constabulary witnesses were questioned individually, whereas the Poor Inquiry witnesses spoke in large groups. Secondly, the Carrickfergus witnesses were summoned to London, and found themselves well outside their familiar context, while the testimony of the criminals was given in prison, also an alien context one might say. The Poor Inquiry commissioners, in contrast, travelled to interview people in their own areas.

In the case of the constabulary report, moreover, including such accounts was less original than it might look, as the criminal confession, purportedly 'authentic' but often quite stylised, had been a staple of both popular and elite literature for centuries. It is also found in reports on prisons in other countries, such as that on the American penitential system by Tocqueville and Beaumont, also in the 1830s. These particular witnesses were therefore in a situation in which the divergences in power between the interviewers and the interviewed were stark, and where there were well-established norms of narrative of which the prisoners, the investigators and later the reading public would have been aware. In the Poor Inquiry, by contrast, there were nothing like the same constraints and expectations.[9]

A few examples can hardly begin to convey the extreme originality of the Poor Inquiry's oral evidence. There are lengthy personal accounts taken from beggars such as Mary Hanley and Catherine Flynn in Ballina, Co. Mayo. There are also disputes and arguments, sometimes between people of different classes, sometimes within the same class. An example of the former comes from the barony of Carbery, Co. Sligo. According to the rector of Drumcliff, Mr Yates,

> 'in the immediate neighbourhood of Sir R.G. Booth's residence there was as much employment given as anywhere, and yet threatening notices were of frequent occurrence there; and no later than this last spring a large stack of corn was burnt, and several ploughs maliciously broken.' Young Shaw [described as 'a small farmer'] replied, 'You forget, Mr. Yates, that the real reason of those outrages was that poor people were unhinged, and driven out of their land and dwellings at Ballygilligan; and that, besides, they are by no means constantly employed; they still consider themselves aggrieved.'

An example of a disagreement within the same class comes from Licarrow, Co. Roscommon. James Rattigan, a labourer and beggar, while describing his means of survival, said that he would rather be supported by others

---

[8] *First Report of the [Constabulary] Commissioners*, HC 1839 XIX; *Carrickfergus Forgeries Committee*, HC 1830–1 III.

[9] Michael Harris, 'Trials and Criminal Biographies: A Case Study in Distribution', in *Sale and Distribution of Books from 1700*, ed. Robin Myers and Michael Harris (Oxford, 1982), 1–36; *Tocqueville: œuvres complètes* Tome IV, Vol.I, ed. Michelle Perrot (Paris, 1984), 333.

than take roadbuilding work in the winter. A footnote tells us that 'Kenny, another witness [a labourer] who was present, when he heard this, was heard to remark with bitter scorn, "That is the worst word you ever spoke, unfortunate man!"' More dramatically still, in Kilkee, Co. Clare, Simon Curry, a nailer, claimed that some beggars hoarded money and became extortionate moneylenders. Then, 'whilst Curry was relating this story, a beggar woman, who was attentively watching the proceedings, suddenly pushed in her head, and cursed him violently for "telling tales, and not minding his own business"'.[10]

II

It was unusual, and not just in a state inquiry, to interview beggars about their lives or to record arguments among agricultural labourers. It was even more unusual to publish them with a minimum of intervention. The Poor Inquiry is distinguished therefore by both originality of research and originality of presentation. This originality is the consequence of two assumptions, both of which are laid out in the first report of the Inquiry.

The first assumption was that Irish society was fundamentally different to that of England. In particular, its social and occupational structure was different. 'In whole districts, scarcely one of that class of substantial capitalist farmers, so universal in England, can be found. The substantial tradesman is not to be met with at intervals of two or three miles as in England . . . and parochial authorities can scarcely be said to exist.' This meant that English social categories could not be used, because 'many of the ordinary distinctions of society are commonly merged in the same individual'. A related characteristic of Irish society which set it apart from English was the extent of poverty. In the words of the report, 'the poorer classes in Ireland may be considered as comprehending nearly the whole population'.[11]

The investigation was therefore conceived of as a type of anthropological fieldwork, and its aim was to represent one society to a reader from a completely different society. The strategy adopted is partly that which became known in later anthropological writing as 'the actor's model', the idea that a different worldview is best conveyed in the words of those who share that worldview. This was the second assumption of the Inquiry. In the words of the first report, 'none are so conversant with those matters which peculiarly or chiefly belong to any class, as the

[10] *Royal Commission on Condition of Poorer Classes in Ireland* (henceforth 'Poor Inquiry'), Appendix A, HC 1835 XXXII, 496 (Mayo), 516 (Roscommon), 626 (Clare) Appendix D, 1836 XXXI, 14 (Sligo).
[11] Poor Inquiry, 1st report, HC 1835 XXXII, vi–vii.

members of that class'.[12] The corrolary of this is that members of one class will not be perfectly conversant with the circumstances of other classes. Therefore an inquiry into a society will need to interview representatives of all classes.

However, these two working assumptions could have led to the Inquiry interviewing those socially representative types individually. Instead, it interviewed them collectively. To see why this happened, we need to examine the genesis of the Inquiry and of its working methods as well as the methodological principles outlined above.

The debate on poverty and the relief of poverty in Ireland was profoundly influenced by the contemporaneous debate on poor relief in Britain, and indeed is part of that debate. Irish immigrants were putting pressure on poor relief mechanisms in cities such as Liverpool, while English grain farmers objected to the competitive advantage given to their Irish counterparts by the fact that there was a poor law in England and not in Ireland.[13] Similarly, the Irish Poor Inquiry was directly influenced by the major inquiry into the poor law in England and Wales, which reported in 1834. Its overall procedures, in particular, were modelled on the English investigation, for which a novel approach had been devised. Instead of the standard method of interviewing expert witnesses in London, the commission adopted a double practice. Initially, questionnaires were circulated to each of the 15,000 parishes in England and Wales. Following this, twenty-six assistant commissioners were sent to various parts of the country. They were sent partly to encourage those parishes that had not replied to do so, but more importantly to verify the information and to evaluate the opinions contained in the questionnaires that had been returned. They were to submit the results of their investigations to the main commissioners in London every week.[14]

We can characterise the English investigation therefore as a form of verification by professional, centralised investigators of the information supplied by amateur local elites and poor law administrators, since the latter were too closely involved in the administration of the poor law to be reliable witnesses. This emphasis on personal verification was an important element in contemporary social investigation, particularly as concerned poverty. It is a powerful motif in one of the most influential discussions of poverty at the time, *The Visitor of the Poor*, by the Baron de Gérando, first published in French in 1820 and in English in 1832. One should never give to the poor without first examining their conditions for

---

[12] Ibid., x.

[13] Gray, *Making*, 37–47.

[14] Anthony Brundage, *The Making of the New Poor Law, 1832–39* (1978), ch. 2, 'The Royal Commission of Inquiry'.

yourself:

> It is in their dwelling-places that you must investigate which is the reality, and which is the phantom; and it is an investigation that requires attentive study. It is not enough that you are open-handed; you must open your eyes too. It is your own fault if you are deceived.[15]

In the English Inquiry, the words of the local elites are unreliable and they are verified through a physical examination by the visiting commissioner. In the Irish Inquiry, this approach is found in some parts of the evidence. It is very strong in the medical section of the report, which mainly deals with the dispensary system in rural areas. Here, the unreliable members of the elite are the dispensary doctors, many of whom were said to be neglecting the dispensaries in favour of more lucrative private practice. The medical assistant commissioners, who were eminent doctors, visited the dispensaries and examined the patients themselves. In Ardrahan and Gort, Co. Galway, they 'saw and examined the greater part of the patients', despite the fact that cholera was widespread in western areas at the time.[16]

In the more general parts of the Irish Inquiry, those dealing with the extent of poverty, its manifestations and its causes, the emphasis is totally different. Instead of conducting physical examinations of housing, diet or employment, the assistant commissioners collected enormous amounts of verbal testimony, which was then reproduced at great length in the report. The eye favoured by Gérando and the doctors was demoted and the ear put in its place; or, alternatively, the state was 'listening' instead of 'seeing'.[17] In many areas, the evidence consists only of speech, with no interpolation of description or interpretation whatever. This is true particularly of the parishes in counties Clare, Galway, Mayo, Roscommon and some of Cork.

III

This unusual mode of investigation and presentation was not explicit in the Poor Inquiry from the beginning, but seems to have evolved during the first six or nine months of its activities. Initially, it adopted the model of the English Poor Law Inquiry, circulating questionnaires to elites in every parish in Ireland and following these up by visits by the travelling assistant commissioners. Indeed, the published instructions to those assistant commissioners are very closely based on the instructions to the assistant commissioners in the English Inquiry.[18] Quite early in the Irish Inquiry,

---

[15] Joseph-Marie, Baron de Gérando, *The Visitor of the Poor* (Boston, MA, 1832), 15; Michelle Perrot, 'L'œil du baron ou le visiteur du pauvre', in Michelle Perrot, *Les ombres de l'histoire* (Paris, 2001), 101–8.

[16] Poor Inquiry, appendix B, 3.

[17] James C. Scott, *Seeing like a State: How Certain Schemes to Improve the Human Condition Have Failed* (1998).

[18] *Instructions to Assistant Commissioners*, HC 1834 XLIII.

however, this method ran into problems. Assistant commissioners were initially hired from England, some of them veterans of the English Inquiry. It soon became apparent to the Irish members of the main Poor Inquiry commission that these were insufficiently acquainted with Irish conditions to be accurate and competent observers, and they therefore began to hire assistant commissioners from Ireland. One of the first Irish assistants to be hired, however, caused the opposite problem. This was Mathew Flanagan, a Dublin Catholic priest, who accused the poorhouses that he was investigating of proselytism, and who resigned from the Inquiry when he was not permitted to ask questions about it.[19] In general, therefore, as far as the Poor Inquiry was concerned, observers of Irish conditions were either too far removed from them to understand them (the English), or else too closely involved in them to be impartial (the Irish). This was in contrast to England, where the objects of investigation were unreliable but the investigator was reliable; in Ireland, not only were the objects of investigation unreliable, but the investigators also.

The commission's answer to this problem appears initially straightforward and practical, and is generally treated as such by historians. It was to ensure that assistant commissioners would travel in pairs, one English and one Irish, and that their respective disadvantages would cancel each other out, or alternatively that their advantages would complement each other. The principle underlying this solution, however, is an unusual one in social investigation, and it structures the Inquiry as a whole. It is the assumption that a worldview is specific to a particular group, in this case a national group, and that the truth (or at least a more truthful view) is arrived at by creating a dialogue between different groups. As a result, it was a working rule of the Inquiry that the commissioners would accept evidence as valid only if it had been collected by both assistant commissioners, English and Irish, working together.

This principle was soon extended to the people being interviewed. All witnesses are unreliable because of their social position, but Irish ones particularly so, since Irish society was unusually divided, by wealth, by religion and by politics. As the first report put it,

> in an inquiry amongst a people the various classes of whom had long been at variance with each other, it became a matter of fearful moment to determine respecting whom the inquiry should be made, and from whom testimony could be received, which would not merely be impartial, but which would be admitted by all to be so.[20]

The Poor Inquiry dealt with this problem by taking evidence in the innovative way we have described. In some parishes, thirty or forty people gathered and held discussions on social and economic issues,

[19] Flanagan to Commissioners, 13 Jan. 1834, National Archives of Ireland, Chief Secretary's Office, Official Papers 1836/212.
[20] Poor Inquiry, 1st report, vii.

with apparently the minimum of intervention from the investigators. Descriptions of these sessions are unfortunately rare, but we can get a sense of them from a fairly hostile report in the Londonderry Sentinel:

> Instead of finding, as we expected, the various Clergymen of the City, or the members of the Mendicity Board called upon to give evidence, there sat the youthful Commissioners, surrounded by some 70 or 80 persons, nine-tenths of whom were themselves mendicants and the rest, with very few exceptions, unemployed tradesmen, who were glad to find refuge from the inclemency of the weather. But the mode of examination was the most novel part of the scene – instead of interrogating any person singly, all were at liberty to answer as they pleased, and certainly the motley group evinced as charitable feelings as any equal number of individuals in His Majesty's dominions, for they described the begging tribe as the most honest, virtuous and honorable body in the kingdom.[21]

Truth, in this method, emerges in a state of society. This is underlined in the first report by the way in which Irish society is described:

> In a community which had long been divided into politico-religious parties, each regarding the other with jealousy and animosity, it was extremely difficult to find persons who would be able, even if they were desirous, to divest themselves of every partial feeling, nurtured as they had been in an anti-social state.[22]

Anti-social, in this context, appears to mean segregated and mutually suspicious. What the investigation did, therefore, was to create temporarily an ideal state of society that would enable the inquiry to understand Irish society better.

Both unreliable informants and unreliable investigators have therefore had their prejudices overcome, or at least diminished, through finding themselves in company with those who differed from them. However, to be consistent, the principal commissioners would have to regard themselves as also being prejudiced in the interpretation of this evidence, due to their social and cultural position. It is true that the denominational and national composition of the commission was deliberately mixed, and it included both the Anglican and the Catholic archbishops of Dublin as well as the Presbyterian clergyman James Carlile, as well as a selection of both Irish and English members. All of the members, however, were well off and had little experience of the rural economy or indeed of being poor, so that, by their own judgement, they would not have fully understood the experience of poverty.

In the event, the commissioners were indeed consistent, and this is visible in the way they dealt with the evidence that was being sent to them. Their first reaction was not to draw any conclusions from it, or indeed to interpret it in any way. It was, instead, to publish it more or less in the form in which it had been sent to them. The first report was published in 1835, and it contained a methodological statement of

---

[21] Quoted in *Mayo Constitution* 3 Nov. 1834.
[22] Poor Inquiry, 1st report, ix.

14 pages followed by nearly 800 pages of mainly oral evidence taken in the manner outlined above, and also by 400 pages of the original questionnaires to which the oral hearings had been the follow-up. Before this, the commission had published a shorter collection of evidence in a form that was more directed at the general public, or at least at the more comfortable members of the public – an octavo instead of the folio of a parliamentary report, and apparently at a few shillings a copy, although it contained over 400 pages.[23]

The commission's intent in publishing the selection of evidence was to promote a public discussion of the issue. As the secretary of the commission, John Revans, wrote to the Irish chief secretary, Edward Littleton, in November 1834 when he was requesting permission to publish, the commission 'expect that the very general expression of public opinion, which will be induced upon the perusal of the proposed extracts, will greatly assist them in the formation of a correct judgement upon the important subjects entrusted to their consideration'.[24] By opening out the discussion on policy to a wider reading public in this way, the commission was putting into practice the same theory of truth that had guided the collection of evidence. Publication would create a community of interpretation whose greater size and variety would benefit the discussion. At all levels, therefore, the work of the commission was structured by a social consensus theory of truth. Such a theory was unusual in the 1830s, although hints of it can be found in some other aspects of contemporary state activity in Ireland. The Ordnance Survey, for example, initially adopted as far as possible the form of a placename on which local experts were most agreed, while the content of the textbooks produced by the Commissioners of Education (whose membership overlapped significantly with that of the Poor Inquiry Commission) was designed to meet the approval of all churches. Nowhere, however, does the principle of consensus determine both methods and presentation as completely as in the Poor Inquiry.[25] A full-scale consensus theory of truth is also unusual outside the context of the 1830s, but not unknown. The most influential modern proponent of a consensus theory of truth is Jürgen Habermas, and the Poor Inquiry's procedures correspond well to some of his categories. The public hearings could be viewed as an attempt to construct a type of 'ideal speech situation', the context in which Habermas suggests that truth will emerge, while the conception of the print sphere as a privileged arbiter of truth, implicit in the publication of the *Selections*,

---

[23] *Selections of Parochial Examinations relative to the Destitute Classes in Ireland* (1835).

[24] Revans to Littleton, 5 Nov. 1834, N.A.I. C.S.O. O.P. 1834/4681.

[25] J. H. Andrews, *A Paper Landscape: The Ordnance Survey in Nineteenth-Century Ireland* (Oxford, 1975), 119–21; D. H. Akenson, *The Irish Education Experiment* (1970), 235.

concurs with Habermas's emphasis on the importance of the circulation of print in the creation of a public sphere.[26]

Such wide consultation, while democratic, was not necessarily very practical. Littleton for one was not impressed and seems to suggest that the commission had abdicated its primary responsibility: 'The observation contained in it, that the expression of public opinion will greatly assist them in the formation of a correct judgement on the subject committed to their consideration, is a singular observation to come from a Commission.'[27]

IV

Littleton's view suggests some distance between the assumptions and procedures of the Poor Inquiry and those of normal parliamentary investigation, and may give some idea why the Inquiry was so rapidly marginalised. Of course, the political failure of the Poor Inquiry can be explained by the fact that its policy recommendations would not have satisfied opinion either inside or outside parliament. But the marginalisation is also epistemological, and the extreme originality of the procedures of the Inquiry meant that its representation of Ireland and of Irish poverty did not fit readily into the various contemporary discourses about society.

In the first place, it is hard to classify relative to one of the principal early nineteenth-century debates about social analysis, that is, whether such analysis should be empirical and inductive, deriving numerical regularities from the new array of statistics that were beginning to be collected at the time; or whether it should be primarily deductive in the style of Ricardo or the early Malthus, building an entire system on the basis of a few fundamental axioms about wages or population dynamics.[28] The evidence of the Poor Inquiry was certainly inductive, but it was unlike statistics in that what was being deliberately sought were opinions rather than measurable facts. Indeed, it is fair to say that the use of numbers in the *Third Report* is simplistic and even cavalier. In the second place, the Inquiry did not adopt the developmental approach characteristic of most contemporary discussions of society. Its reports contain little historical analysis, for example not discussing the idea, common in contemporary discussion, that Ireland in the 1820s and 1830s was at the same stage of

[26] Jürgen Habermas, *On the Pragmatics of Social Interaction* (Cambridge, 2001), 97–9; Jurgen Habermas, *The Structural Transformation of the Public Sphere* (Cambridge, 1989, orig. 1962).

[27] Littleton to Duncannon, 8 Nov. 1834, Stafford Record Office, Hatherton papers (National Library of Ireland MS microfilm 3027).

[28] Lawrence Goldman, 'The Origins of British "Social Science": Political Economy, Natural Science and Statistics, 1830–1835', *Historical Journal*, 26 (1983), 587–616; Theodore M. Porter, *The Rise of Statistical Thinking, 1820–1900* (Princeton, 1986), 31–9.

evolutionary development as England had been in the sixteenth century, before the introduction of the Elizabethan poor law.[29]

It might be suggested that the Inquiry is similar to early folklore collection, where the voice of lower-class narrators was also being discovered. Here also, however, there are substantial differences. Folklorists such as Crofton Croker, the Brothers Grimm and Elias Lonnrot collected lengthy narratives from individual narrators whereas the Poor Inquiry recorded conversations. Moreover, folklore developed as part of a romantic nationalism, which saw peasant narrators as carriers of a single national spirit, and as representative of that spirit. The Poor Inquiry, in direct contrast, was based precisely on the idea that no one section of society was representative, and that all classes had to contribute to the synthesis which would constitute truth.[30]

The closest thing to a contemporary counterpart of the Poor Inquiry was ethnographic fiction about Ireland, in particular the works of William Carleton such as *Traits and Stories of the Irish Peasantry*. Here we find many of the same characteristics as in the Poor Inquiry evidence: the representation of a whole society through its speech, since for Carleton the term 'peasantry' covered a wide social spectrum; the importance of such a representation for good governance; and a linked conception of an Irish narrator as essentially unreliable, typified in Maria Edgeworth's *Castle Rackrent*. A close relationship with an ethnographic literature is also suggested by the title of the extracts from the evidence published by Christian Johnstone, *True Tales of the Irish Peasantry*. I am unaware, however, of any substantial impact of the Poor Inquiry material on ethnographic fiction, for example, although a good deal of further investigation would be necessary in order to verify that claim.[31]

Taken all together, therefore, the discourse of the Poor Inquiry, or at least of its oral hearings, was quite removed from that of contemporary textual representations of Irish society, or indeed of society more generally. This may well be another reason why the Poor Inquiry was so marginalised. Its voluminous reports had little impact on the public debate about poverty or on state policy, little impact on Irish ethnography and little impact on the genre of the official or parliamentary inquiry. The unique methodology employed by the Inquiry, however, offers the historian an extraordinarily rich record of all levels of pre-Famine rural society, and one that has scarcely begun to be exploited.

---

[29] George Stocking, *Victorian Anthropology* (New York, 1987); Revans, *Evils*, 111; 'A Poor Law for Ireland', *Tait's Edinburgh Magazine*, 4 (1837), 190.

[30] Peter Burke, *Popular Culture in Early Modern Europe* (Aldershot, 1978), 21–2; William A. Wilson, *Folklore and Nationalism in Modern Finland* (Bloomington, 1976), 25–61.

[31] The Poor Inquiry is not mentioned in a recent survey of this literature, Helen O'Connell, *Ireland and the Fiction of Improvement* (Oxford, 2006).

Transactions of the RHS 20 (2010), pp. 141–56 © Royal Historical Society 2010
doi:10.1017/S0080440110000095

IRISH SOCIAL THOUGHT AND THE RELIEF
OF POVERTY, 1847–1880

By Peter Gray

READ 26 JUNE 2009 AT THE QUEEN'S UNIVERSITY BELFAST

ABSTRACT. This paper investigates the way in which the 'problem of poverty' in Ireland was encountered, constructed and debated by members of the Irish intellectual and political elite in the decades between the Great Famine and the outbreak of the land war in the late 1870s. This period witnessed acute social upheavals in Ireland, from the catastrophic nadir of the Famine, through the much-vaunted economic recovery of the 1850s–1860s, to the near-famine panic of the late 1870s (itself prefigured by a lesser agricultural crisis in 1859–63). The paper focuses on how a particular elite group – the 'Dublin School' of political economists and their circle, and most prominently William Neilson Hancock and John Kells Ingram – sought to define and investigate the changing 'problem', shape public attitudes towards the legitimacy of welfare interventions and lobby state officials in the making of poor law policy in this period. It suggests that the crisis of 1859–63 played a disproportionate role in the reevaluation of Irish poor relief and in promoting a campaign for an 'anglicisation' of poor law measures and practice in Ireland.

Irish social thought was diffused and largely unfocused before the mid-nineteenth century. Public argumentation about social issues was of course widespread; pamphlets and the burgeoning newspaper and periodical press brought these debates in print form to a growing reading public, while the occasional treatise, written for a more select audience, might aspire to more than a polemical or instrumental treatment of matters such as social welfare. Intellectual environments existed in places such as Trinity College Dublin and in 'improving' bodies such as the Royal Irish Academy, the Royal Dublin Society and the Belfast Literary Society, where such questions might be debated. However, the formation in 1847 of the Dublin Statistical Society marked a new departure in Irish intellectual life, as this was both the first public body dedicated to applying a 'social scientific' methodology to the social and economic problems of Ireland and to disseminating its views and deliberations through the country by means of serial publications and public lectures. It paralleled and emulated in Ireland the work in Great Britain of the British Association for the Advancement of Science's Statistical Section (1833) and later the Social Science Association (1857), albeit on a much smaller scale and in a radically different political environment. This paper concentrates on the responses of the members of the Dublin Society (after 1864 renamed the Social and Statistical Inquiry Society of Ireland), and particularly of two of its leading 'public intellectuals' of the period, to the questions of poor relief between 1847 and 1880.

Established under the influence of Archbishop Richard Whately of Dublin, principally as a mechanism for inculcating the putative 'science' of political economy in Ireland, the Society has been regarded, at least in its origins, as embodying a 'colonial' ideological agenda.[1] It is certainly true that, from its foundation, it was dominated by the then and previous holders of the Whately chair in political economy at Trinity College and their equivalents at the new Queen's Colleges, and that the dominant tone of its debates reflected the free-trade liberal, *laissez-faire*, preoccupations of this core of intellectuals drawn predominantly from the liberal-unionist professional middle classes. One leading dissentient from this economic and political orthodoxy, Isaac Butt (holder of the Whately chair 1836–41), was largely excluded from its deliberations, due to both his deviance on the core doctrine of free trade and his tory, and later home-rule, politics. Nevertheless, the 'Dublin School' of political economists associated with the Society, overwhelmingly Irish in nationality, came in time to diverge significantly from Whately's economic principles and develop a distinctly 'Irish' (albeit liberal-unionist) political economy by the 1860s. The purpose of this paper is to suggest that a distinct strand of 'social thought' on welfare policy also evolved within the society between the Famine and the land war, and was communicated more widely to the political community in Ireland through the society's publications and the press more generally. This strand was far from uniformly endorsed even within the Society and was not without its ambivalences and contradictions; nevertheless, it represented both a distinct contribution to the debate on the nature of Irish society and the responsibility for and regulation of social welfare within it.

While many members contributed to the Society's debates on social welfare, discussion was dominated both quantitatively and qualitatively by two Ulstermen, both founding members and officers of the Society, liberal-Protestant polymaths with a commitment to applying a positivist 'social science' to the perceived problems of Ireland. These were William Neilson Hancock and John Kells Ingram. Hancock was the more precocious and intellectually specialised of the two. Elected to the Whately chair of political economy in 1846 at the age of twenty-six,

---

[1] Thomas A. Boylan and Timothy P. Foley, *Political Economy and Colonial Ireland* (1992), 1–5.

he was prime mover in the founding of the Dublin Statistical Society the following year and its first joint secretary; on taking up the chair of jurisprudence and political economy at Queen's College Belfast in 1849 he promptly established the Belfast Social Inquiry Society in that town, which was later merged with the Dublin society following Hancock's return to the capital in 1853. For the remainder of his working life he combined an active career at the bar with a series of secretaryships and other official appointments on Irish government and legal commissions. Although ostensibly politically independent from government, Hancock was, after 1853, what has been termed an 'official intellectual'.[2] Always a committed liberal, he became a trusted policy adviser to Liberal administrations, mentoring Gladstone on Irish land reform in 1868–70, while remaining in office under Conservative administrations. Like most of his circle he combined 'patriotism' with hostility towards Irish nationalism, and was credited by Ingram with coining the self-descriptive label 'liberal unionist' to describe his political position in 1880.[3]

Despite the youthful indiscretion of his ballad 'The memory of the dead', published in the *Nation* newspaper in 1843 in commemoration of the 1798 rising, J. K. Ingram's mature political outlook was similar to his friend's. Successively professor of oratory and Greek, librarian and then senior fellow of Trinity College, Ingram's intellectual range was extensive, and included a commitment to applying Comteian positivism to social questions, increasingly subordinating political economy to sociology and abandoning deductive (a priori) for inductive (observational) and historicising methodology in the process. The Statistical Society (of which he was president in 1878–80) received his enthusiastic support both as a platform for discussion and (through its public journals) for public dissemination. Indeed it might be seen as the ideal venue for the combination of practical patriotism and optimistic rationalism that Ingram associated with Comteianism.[4]

Hancock's interest in the Irish poor law began early through direct experience. As a student in 1838–9, he had acted as secretary to his father, William John Hancock, while the latter was employed as an assistant poor law commissioner charged with forming the new Irish

---

[2] T. Boylan and T. Foley, 'From Hedge Schools to Hegemony: Intellectuals, Ideology and Ireland in the Nineteenth Century', in *On Intellectuals and Intellectual Life in Ireland*, ed. L. O'Dowd (Belfast, 1996), 98.

[3] J. K. Ingram, 'Memoir of the Late William Neilson Hancock', *Journal of the Social and Statistical Inquiry Society of Ireland (JSSISI)*, 9 (1889), 384–93.

[4] R. D. Collison Black, 'John Kells Ingram', *Oxford Dictionary of National Biography*,www.oxforddnb.com/view/article/34104?docPos=12; G. K. Peatling, *British Opinion and Irish Self-Government 1865–1925* (Dublin, 2001), 28–31.

unions in Connacht.[5] This family connection (his father died in 1848 of famine fever, contracted while on poor law business) gave him a particular insight into the operations of the Irish system, although, as we shall see, Hancock's policy prescriptions evolved significantly over time in response to changing circumstances. After taking up the Whately chair, it is clear from an early stage that he diverged from his eponymous patron in supporting both an Irish poor law in principle, and its extension through the enactment of the Poor Law Amendment Act of 1847.[6] The coverage of the poor law question in his first major foray into practical economic analysis, delivered as Trinity lectures in early 1847 and published later in the year, largely coincided with the principles lying behind the extension act. Less-eligibility was for Hancock at this time the 'fundamental principle' of the system, requiring an extension of permanent and temporary workhouse accommodation alongside some 'emergency' toleration of outdoor relief for the 'aged and infirm' and the retention of the workhouse test for the able-bodied. The Speenhamland system of wage subsidies from the poor rates, he warned, had emerged in the midst of a similar national crisis in England in 1795: the same mistake should not be made in Ireland, and radical attempts to turn the poor law into an engine for improving the poor through wasteland reclamation or productive labour should be dismissed.[7]

Hancock's public statements in the latter stages of the Famine did not deviate from the line he had adopted publicly in early 1847. Commissioned to undertake a government inquiry into the causes of distress in the Skibbereen district in 1847, he delivered his conclusions in a public lecture to the statistical section of the British Association in 1850. The 'real cause' of mass mortality in west Cork (as elsewhere in Ireland) had not been the potato failure, he believed, but the acute backwardness of the rural economy, which in turn was rooted in the 'feudal' condition of land law preventing the development of capitalised agriculture.[8] The solution to Ireland's crisis, as Hancock and his associates constantly repeated in these years, lay in facilitating full free trade in land and contractual tenancy relations. The poor law was necessary as a mechanism for dealing with the consequences of previous misgovernment and social mismanagement, but must retain the deterrent principles evident in the

5 *Tenth Report from the Select Committee on Poor Laws (Ireland)*, House of Commons (HC) 1849 (301), XV, Pt 1, 48–9.
6 For Whately's continuing hostility to the Irish poor law, see Peter Gray, *The Making of the Irish Poor Law, 1815–43* (Dublin, 2009), 254–5, 333.
7 W. Neilson Hancock, *Three Lectures on the Questions, Should the Principles of Political Economy Be Disregarded at the Present Crisis? And if Not, How Can They Be Applied towards the Discovery of Measures of Relief?* (Dublin, 1847), 41–6.
8 W. Neilson Hancock, *On the Causes of Distress at Skull and Skibbereen during the Famine in Ireland* (Dublin, 1850).

1847 act. It is thus not surprising that, when called to give evidence before the Select Committee on the Irish Poor Law in 1849, Hancock joined his Statistical Society colleagues Mountifort Longfield and James Lawson in concentrating principally on the remedialist agenda of recommending further 'defeudalising' land reforms to follow up the Encumbered Estates Act of that year.[9] His only really substantive statement on the poor law in this period, read to the British Association in 1851, was reactive. It offered a refutation of the proposals of George Poulett Scrope, W. P. Alison and others that able-bodied paupers be employed on reproductive work (principally on land improvement). A poor law was a moral responsibility of a civilised society, but must not be more than residualist; 'poor laws are necessary', he commented, 'as a measure of police, as part of the duty of Government to protect against fraud and violence'.[10] However, the causes of pauperism were external to and mostly irremediable by the poor law, and it was to these that the 'scientific' social thinker must devote his attention.

The 1850s were a decade of extraordinary optimism for the 'Dublin School' of social and economic thinkers associated with the Statistical Society. The benign providentialism and faith in free-trade liberalism they had espoused during the Famine appeared vindicated by the statistics of agricultural recovery and 'natural' population adjustment (through significant but falling emigration) in that decade. A virtuous equilibrium appeared to liberal observers to have been attained in the wake of the necessary if painful crisis of the Famine; the dangerous heterodoxies of protectionist, radical and nationalist economics had (it appeared) been seen off, and *laissez-faire* policy on land tenure had reached its apogee in the 1860 Cardwell-Deasy legislation (which Hancock, now an administrative insider, helped frame).[11]

In this changed climate, the Statistical Society accorded increasing attention to the 'moral' as opposed to the 'material' problems of Irish society. Hancock had briefly alluded to the moral responsibilities of the state towards pauper children in 1851, but when he returned to the subject of the poor law in 1855 it was treatment of the 'dependent' categories of the population that concerned him. This to some extent reflected the changed reality of poor law demography. In the later stages of the Famine, very large numbers of 'able-bodied' men and their families had received relief within the overcrowded workhouses or in the outdoor relief

[9] *Tenth Report on Poor Laws (Ireland)*, 48–75.

[10] W. Neilson Hancock, *Should Boards of Guardians Endeavour to Make Pauper Labour Self-Supporting, or Should they Investigate the Causes of Pauperism?* (Dublin, 1851), 4.

[11] Peter Gray, 'The Making of Mid-Victorian Ireland? Political Economy and the Memory of the Great Famine', in *Victoria's Ireland? Britishness and Irishness, 1837–1901*, ed. P. Gray (Dublin, 2004), 157–9.

workyards. By the mid-1850s outdoor relief had all but disappeared, and able-bodied men were a small minority of workhouse inmates. Given the toll of death, dislocation and family disintegration left by the catastrophe, it is hardly surprising that a high proportion of those remaining were those with little ability to gain from the opportunities of rising wages or emigrant remittances – children (many orphaned or abandoned), widows, the disabled and the elderly.

Hancock's treatment of the case of women and children in his 1855 essay was informed by high Victorian patriarchalism. It was, he asserted, 'plain, ... that the spontaneous and universal recognition of the principle that women ought naturally to be supported by men, implies a condemnation of the Poor Law doctrine of applying the workhouse test to women and children'. An ideal family model, in which fathers supported and controlled their dependants and mothers cherished their offspring, was juxtaposed to the rigid internal classification by sex and age in the workhouse and incarceration of the fatherless and husbandless within its walls. It followed that both orphans and widows with children would be better relieved out of doors, preferably in forms that promoted the reconstitution of family bonds. This suggested a significant softening of his own previous declarations on outdoor relief, not necessarily reflecting any shift in gender ideology, but rather a belief that the social context that had required the harsh deterrent principles of 1834 and 1838 had been transformed – at least so far as women and children were concerned.[12]

Hancock's concern for orphans in particular was developed in further papers to the Society, read in 1859 and 1862. His preoccupation with the model family led him to reject the alternatives of state or charitable orphanages or industrial schools in favour of extended 'boarding-out' or fostering of workhouse children.[13] Although the principle of boarding-out was partially accepted by the Irish authorities in the 1862 Poor Law Amendment Act (mainly, it appears, out of alarm at consistently high rates of infant mortality in many workhouses), Hancock rejected its limitation of boarding-out to eight years of age and was increasingly preoccupied with combating the preference for separate institutionalisation of orphans in district residential schools sought by many commentators in both England and Ireland. Archbishop Paul Cullen and the Catholic hierarchy placed a particularly high value on the latter, and a challenge to Hancock's position was voiced within the Society by the barrister (later judge)

---

[12] W. Neilson Hancock, 'The Workhouse as a Mode of Relief for Widows and Orphans', *Journal of the Dublin Statistical Society* (*JDSS*), 1 (1855), 84–91.

[13] W. Neilson Hancock, 'On the Importance of Substituting the Family System of Rearing Orphan Children for the System now Pursued in our Workhouses', *JDSS*, 1 (1859), 317–33; 'The Mortality of Children in Workhouses in Ireland', *ibid.*, 3 (1862), 193–8.

John O'Hagan, who concluded that 'so far as Catholic children are concerned an efficient substitute may often be found in religious institutions in which, together with a discipline and an education of the intellect, the personal kindness and attention of the members to the children may, perhaps, supply the place of family ties'.[14] The negative consequences of this strand in Catholic social thought have become evident in contemporary Ireland.

Hancock's prioritisation of the moral integrity of the (patriarchal) family over both institutionalisation and the principle of less-eligibility has been described by some observers as embodying a more general 'feminising' turn in Irish social thinking in the 1850s embracing both a new paternalistic emphasis on female and child vulnerability outside the traditional family structure, and the active inclusion of women within this discourse – reflected in the admission of women members to the Society from 1861.[15] That this may be an oversimplified argument is suggested by subsequent developments. I have argued elsewhere that the Irish agricultural crisis of 1860–4 – which amounted in some parts of the west to a 'near-famine' – had a more profound effect on Irish economic thought and debate than its rather limited demographic effects might suggest. The crisis had the effect of pulling the rug from under the complacent optimism of the 1850s, of stoking the raw memories of famine in Irish society and assisting the revival of the radical nationalist tradition.[16] Within the Statistical Society the crisis provoked intense debate, with the intensely pessimistic 'declinism' articulated by Denis Heron in 1862 and 1864 eliciting defensive but worried ripostes from Hancock and others associated with the optimistic liberal orthodoxy of the previous decade. Hancock privately assured the long-serving Irish under-secretary Thomas Larcom in 1863 that he was confident that Ireland would bounce back from the crisis, but that its ability to progress was dependent on an improved degree of class cooperation, which in turn required greater official encouragement.[17] The crisis offered at least the opportunity (and for many a stimulus) for sections of the 'Dublin School' to begin to distance themselves from *laissez-faire* classicism and move towards a more contingent historicist economics that took practical form in growing support for an interventionist land reform recognising

---

[14] John O'Hagan, 'Observations on Dr Hancock's Plan for Rearing Poor Orphans in Families, instead of Placing them in the Workhouses', *JDSS*, 2 (1859), 331–3. Hancock had been at pains to cite instances of Catholic employment of the 'family system' alongside his model of the Protestant Orphan Society.

[15] Boylan and Foley, 'From Hedge Schools to Hegemony', 98–9, 108–9.

[16] Gray, 'Making of Mid-Victorian Ireland?'.

[17] National Library of Ireland, Larcom Papers (hereafter Larcom Papers), Hancock to Larcom, 17 Aug. 1863, MS 7606/4.

Irish difference from British norms.[18] Hancock was evidently reluctant to abandon his previous public pronouncements, but he was quietly shifting his ground on social welfare as early as 1862.

Hancock had, before 1860, restricted his criticism of the poor law to its failure to recognise and accommodate the needs of vulnerable categories of inmates defined by gender and age. A June 1862 paper took the critique substantially further by, for the first time, adding 'unemployed workmen' to the groups deserving more favourable treatment.[19] The stimulus for this discussion lay in the highly contrasting response made by the English poor law authorities to those suffering from the Lancashire 'cotton famine' in 1861–2, and the rigid stance taken by the Irish poor law commission towards both urban and rural labourers improverished by the economic crisis. For the first time, Hancock abandoned the rationalist justification for a poor law in favour of a historicist one (stealing, in a sense, the clothes of critics such as Poulett Scrope, whom he had previously dismissed). Paradoxically, while the turn towards historicism in the field of land policy pointed increasingly towards the acknowledgement of Irish socio-economic difference, in that of poor relief – for both Hancock and Ingram – the lesson was assimilationist. The centuries in which Ireland had been denied the 'old' Elizabethan poor law had, Hancock now claimed, seen its society descend into disorder and malaise, while that of England had prospered and advanced. Despite the introduction of a workhouse system in 1838, Ireland still lagged far behind in the march of social progress – a fact brought painfully home by the contrasting social states of the countries in the early 1860s: a 'liberal and charitably administered poor law', he was now convinced, 'is the best safeguard against disturbance of social order by the poorer classes' – that is to say, by unemployed male labourers.

Hancock also took the opportunity of this essay to write sympathetically of the plight of the South Dublin Union girls victimised for rioting against the workhouse regime (and confirming the case he had made previously about the unsuitability of the workhouse for such cases); this controversial incident has been highlighted and analysed by Anna Clark.[20] Arguably, however, the most important element in his 1862 intervention was Hancock's case for a real 'right to relief' to be extended to able-bodied adult men and women in Ireland, and for the huge discrepancy in outdoor relief rates (86 per cent of all relieved in England in January 1861, in contrast to only 6 per cent in Ireland) to be redressed. These

[18] Gray, 'Making of mid-Victorian Ireland?'.

[19] W. Neilson Hancock, 'The Difference between the English and Irish Poor Law, as to the Treatment of Women and Unemployed Workmen', *JSSISI*, 3 (1862), 217–35.

[20] Anna Clark, 'Wild Workhouse Girls and the Liberal Imperial State in Mid-Nineteenth-Century Ireland', *Journal of Social History*, 39 (2005), 389–410.

figures indicated that George Nicholls's vision of a rigid workhouse test in England had evaporated, and that it was anomalous that it was still adhered to in Ireland.

This new-found enthusiasm for a 'generous' non-pauperising form of relief for the able-bodied was not shared by all members of the Statistical Society; Hancock's father in law, the moral reformer and temperance campaigner James Haughton, for one, rejected the concession of outdoor relief to any classes save orphan children and famine victims.[21] It also signalled a sharp break between Hancock and Larcom, who had combined the role of an Irish poor law commissioner with active membership of the Statistical Society. While prepared to see some extension of the Irish poor law – the 1862 act granted non-pauperising medical relief by opening the workhouse infirmaries to 'the poor' at large, and a limited form of boarding-out of young children – Larcom agreed wholeheartedly with the orthodox chief poor law commissioner, Alfred Power, that outdoor relief to adults should be avoided as far as possible. The official position within the Irish commission is succinctly expressed in a letter from Assistant Commissioner Edward Senior to the lord lieutenant in 1862 deprecating the campaign for outdoor relief in the west that had been provoked by the subsistence crisis:

> I have no doubt . . . that the old and young alike, of the vagrant classes, in the remote and neglected districts would prefer to live . . . crouching in ditches and existing on an insufficient dole of meal rather than sacrifice their habits and submit to the order, cleanliness, labour, education and restraints of a workhouse, the rules of which are however in all respects identical to those in England and Scotland.[22]

For Power and his colleagues, holding the line on the workhouse test for the 'able-bodied' poor was crucial.

Although a member since 1847, John Kells Ingram made no recorded contribution to the Statistical Society's proceedings until 1863. On becoming vice-president that year, however, he began a series of public interventions on a range of topics, probably encouraged by the incipient 'turn' in the intellectual environment from classicism towards the historicist modes of social thought he found more conducive. In a vice-presidential address in late 1863, Ingram acknowledged that the present agricultural crisis was the gravest since 1847. Reluctant to accept the argument of the 'declinists' that rising emigration was 'unnatural' and that no real progress had been attained since the Famine, he nevertheless urged state-led reforms to revive agricultural development in Ireland, and

---

[21] James Haughton, 'Observations on a Paper on Poor Relief, by Dr Dowling, of Tipperary', *JSSISI*, 3 (1862), 158–62. His position had not changed by 1864, 'Discussion', *JSSISI*, IV (1864), 60.

[22] Larcom Papers, Edward Senior to Carlisle, 1 July 1862, MS 7784/59.

identified the poor law as key to this. Ensuring social security was to him key to maintaining the stability required for progress – and the contrast between recent English and Irish experience was plain to see. 'Common sense', he observed:

> dictates that, if temporary relief is to be given, it should be given in such a way as to be effectual for its purpose, and to disturb as little as possible the domestic life of the labourer. And this is precisely what is effected by the outdoor relief, which protects the English working classes in seasons of distress, and tranquillises their minds at all times by the guarantees it affords them against the inevitable vicissitudes of their condition.[23]

Unspoken but implicit here was the rising threat of Fenianism. Ingram at this point appears still to have supported George Cornewall Lewis's agenda of treating the poor law as a mechanism for weaning the 'surplus' smallholding peasant off the land, but insisted that only a full right to relief (preferably outdoors) would realise that objective, while at the same time countenancing an alternative 'Continental' small-farm model of landholding should this fail (and by 1870 both Ingram and Hancock appear to have swung fully behind advocating the consolidation of such a 'peasant' model of landholding).[24]

Despite their increasing support for the idea that Irish difference in historical development should be recognised in land law, both Ingram and Hancock adopted an assimilationist rhetoric on the poor law, regularly repeating (to 1880 at least) their mantra that Irish law and practice must be made identical with the English, and that any grounds for difference had long disappeared. Ingram's model for Ireland was the 'elastic' Out-relief Regulation Order of 1852, which applied to most of the northern and industrial areas of England (although he noted that even the more restrictive 1844 Prohibitory Order applied elsewhere gave much more discretion to boards of guardians than was permitted in Ireland).[25] All recent poor law legislation appeared to have seen Ireland 'outstripped in the race of improvement', leading to both unnecessary inhumanity in the treatment of its poor and 'a waste of social power' arising from the irrational welfare distinctions maintained between parts of the United Kingdom.

Ingram's addresses were widely discussed. In the Society itself his call for a resolution of the poor law question was strongly endorsed by the Quaker Jonathan Pim, who had been heavily involved in charitable initiatives during the 1860s subsistence crisis and had urged the government

[23] John Kells Ingram, 'Considerations on the State of Ireland, an Address Delivered at the Opening of the Seventeenth Session', *JSSISI*, 4 (1864), 22.
[24] For Lewis, see *Remarks on the Third Report of the Irish Poor Inquiry Commissioners ... by George Cornewall Lewis*, HC 1837 [90], LI, 241.
[25] J. K. Ingram, 'A Comparison between the English and Irish Poor Laws with Respect to the Conditions of Relief', *JSSISI*, 4 (1864), 43–61.

also to be more generous.[26] However, other members wrote to the papers to distance themselves from his 'dangerous' doctrines on outdoor relief.[27] Once out of the rarified air of the Statistical Society and in the wider public domain, Ingram's opinions inevitably became politicised. The Conservative *Daily Express* explicitly contrasted his 'scientific' understanding of emigration with what it dismissed as the conspiracy theories peddled by the Catholic Archbishop John MacHale of Tuam.[28] In contrast, the high-Tory *Dublin Evening Mail* mocked Ingram as a professor of *belles lettres* and erstwhile Young Irelander, whose visionary scheme would 'impoverish the industrious by a grinding poor-rate, to support the sluggard, and arrest the emigration of those who are willing to seek a field for work elsewhere'. What he urged amounted to social revolution – potentially even 'communism' – dressed up in maudlin sentiment and academic abstraction.[29] From the other end of the political spectrum, the *Nation* criticised Ingram's failure to admit that the causes of emigration were principally coercive, and that his assimilationist case for the poor law fitted neither current English sentiment nor Irish specificities; to the openly pro-Fenian *Irishman* the professor was simply a west British 'quack'.[30] Despite some (not uncritical) support from the liberal *Dublin Evening Post* and (a probably counterproductive) eulogy in the London *Times*, Ingram's hope that the 'social scientific' discourse of the Society might transcend political polarities and class interest was clearly misplaced.[31]

Ingram's 1863–4 intervention made little immediate impact on official policy. It was publicly endorsed by Denis Phelan, the experienced former assistant commissioner who had done much to promote non-pauperising medical relief since the late 1830s and who had sought to reopen the 'outdoor relief' debate in 1859, but Phelan now held little political influence.[32] Thomas Henry Burke, private secretary in the Irish chief secretary's office, urged Larcom to read the Society's papers, but this appears to have made little difference when countered by the rigid orthodoxy of Chief Poor Law Commissioner Power, who feared the Catholic clergy might take up outdoor relief as a crusade.[33] In 1865 Power concluded:

[26] *Express*, 19 Nov. 1863; Larcom Papers, Pim to Larcom, 19 June 1863, MS 7785/21.

[27] Letter, *Dublin Evening Mail*, 23 Nov. 1863.

[28] *Express*, 19 Nov. 1863. The *Irish Times* (19 Nov. 1863) took a more hostile line towards Ingram.

[29] *Dublin Evening Mail*, 19, 21, 23 Nov. 1863.

[30] *Nation*, 21 Nov. 1863; *Irishman*, 28 Nov. 1863.

[31] *Dublin Evening Post*, 24 Nov. 1863, 11 Feb. 1864; *Times*, 4 Dec. 1863.

[32] Phelan letter in *Freeman's Journal*, 4 Mar. 1864. For his 1859 initiative, see Virginia Crossman's article in this volume.

[33] Larcom Papers, T. H. Burke to Larcom, 7 Mar. 1864, MS 7607/1; University College London Archives, Chadwick Papers, Power to Chadwick, 3 Oct. 1863, 1605/40.

if outdoor relief should at any time hereafter be as liberally administered in Ireland as it is now in England, it may be expected that the same amount of demoralisation, to say the least, should result from it . . . as in England. The injury to property would be much greater, for there is a class of Unions in Ireland which with their present proportion of rental to population could not support even a very restricted system of out-door relief . . . A system of out-door relief which is economical is one especially dangerous to the poor themselves.

In fact, he asserted, allowing greater outdoor relief would amount to cruelty given the miserly amounts currently allowed by some boards of guardians. The poor were better off, for the most part, he concluded, within the protective and improving confines of the workhouse.[34]

Despite this reverse, both Hancock and Ingram regularly returned to these arguments over the following decades, mutually reinforcing each other's contributions. In 1871 Hancock excoriated the laws facilitating the removal of Irish paupers from Great Britain, again drawing attention to the inequity of treatment (a topic which regularly incensed Irish observers). It reflects the peculiarities of his own intellectual journey by this stage that he cited both Adam Smith and the ancient Irish Brehon Laws (which he was then joint-editing for publication) in support of his case for creating an 'inter-kingdom machinery for adjusting inter-kingdom claims of chargeability'. An ideal 'British' poor law should take the best aspects from each national legislation (the absence of powers of compulsory removal was, he thought, one of the few instances of Irish 'best-practice'); both the Anglo-Scottish and Anglo-Irish unions could not be deemed complete until this uniform social welfare system was adopted.[35] Nine years later he addressed the Trades Union Congress, then meeting in Dublin, to a similar end, reinforcing the message that the working classes throughout the United Kingdom had a shared interest in a uniform and generous poor law.[36] Legal discrepancies relating to electoral division rating, he asserted (at a time when the land war was commencing), offered a 'temptation and motive to clearances' in rural areas, while the improvements in metropolitan administration in London far outran those in Dublin. William Alison, Hancock's bugbear of 1852, was now praised as a great Scotch philanthropist and reformer, especially for his highlighting the suffering of the Irish poor in urban Scotland. The failure to protect the right of the Irish migrant labourer to equitable poor

[34] Larcom Papers, Power to Larcom, 7 Jan. 1865, MS 7781/6.

[35] W. Neilson Hancock, *The Law of Poor Removals and Chargeability in England, Scotland and Ireland; with Suggestions for Assimilation and Amendment* (Dublin, 1871). A similar argument, focusing on the consequences of the harsh removal clauses in Scotland for the health of Irish migrants there, is made in W. Neilson Hancock, 'Some Statistics and Researches on the Poor Removal Question, with Special Reference to the Removal of Persons of Irish Birth from Scotland', *JSSISI*, 6 (1878), 356–61.

[36] W. Neilson Hancock, *On the Anomalous Differences in the Poor Laws of Ireland and England* (Dublin, 1880).

relief in the English and Scottish communities that his work had enriched, Hancock concluded, was as important as the land question in propelling the crisis of 1880, and required equally radical means of redress.[37]

While their stance on outdoor relief to the able-bodied had shifted considerably, both Ingram and Hancock also continued to press for special treatment for the 'vulnerable' categories of pauper they had previously identified, especially female children, and to pursue full implementation of the boarding-out system (or the nearest equivalent) to the exclusion of further institutionalisation.[38] Both social commentators were aware of the neo-moralising turn in English social discourse in the 1870s, which led in that country towards a reemphasis on the workhouse test for the able-bodied. This was exemplified by the English liberal public intellectual Henry Fawcett's 1870 lectures on pauperism, in which he identified a moral crisis arising from the 'leniency and want of firmness' of English outdoor relief.[39] While this new mood ran counter to the agenda of the Dublin commentators (indeed it threatened to undercut their case for greater liberality in Ireland), they were happy to borrow elements from the drive for voluntary moral supervision associated with it. Ingram pressed for a 'Voluntary Supervising Committee of Ladies', independent of the board of guardians, to oversee boarding-out, and this was strongly endorsed by Isabella Tod in a paper she read to the British Association in 1878.[40] Also at Ingram's instigation, the Statistical Society established in 1876 a Dublin branch of the Charity Organisation Society in emulation of similar developments in London, in New York State and at Elberfeld in Germany.[41] Yet whereas this developed elsewhere as an 'inquiring body' of voluntary philanthropists established to advise guardians on the moral status of applicants for relief and to offer some non-pauperising assistance to the 'deserving' poor, in Ireland the opportunity to 'check abuses' was limited, and the branch appears principally to have been concerned with monitoring international developments, and recommending extensions rather than contractions of the Irish poor law system. An exception, however, was the case of vagrants – a category of 'undeserving poor' that the committee

[37] W. Neilson Hancock, 'On the Equal Importance of Education, Poor Law, Cheap Law for Small Holders, and Land Questions, at the Present Crisis', *JSSISI*, 7 (1880), 52–61.

[38] J. K. Ingram, 'Additional Facts and Arguments on the Boarding-Out of Pauper Children', *JSSISI*, 6 (1876), 503–23. An 1869 bill had extended the maximum age of boarding-out to ten (Ingram pressed for sixteen), but a large number of unions were still failing to board-out even the younger children as permitted under the 1862 act, *Freeman's Journal*, 11 Jan. 1876.

[39] Alan Kidd, *State, Society and the Poor in Nineteenth-Century England* (1999), 45–6.

[40] Isabella Tod, 'Boarding out of Pauper Children', *JSSISI*, 6 (1878), 293–9.

[41] J. K. Ingram, 'Address at the Opening of the Twenty-Ninth Session: The Organisation of Charity, and the Education of the Children of the State', *JSSISI*, 6 (1875), 449–73.

thought should be treated more rigorously than at present.[42] Similarly, those who became destitute due to 'drunkenness, immorality, or loss of character' required reformation in the workhouse, but this would only be feasible if the 'respectable' were relieved elsewhere.[43]

Despite serving as 'the most important forum in Ireland in the nineteenth century for the discussion of social and economic questions', the Statistical Society and its leading lights ultimately made remarkably little impact on the making of social welfare policy during the period under review. This might suggest the impotence of a middle-class talking shop, but this would be belied by the success of the Society and its dominant personalities in shaping legislation on law reform, civil registration and above all land reform during the period. Hancock, in particular, had a hand in drafting all three of the principal land acts between 1860 and 1881.[44]

What then might explain the failure of 'social science' discourse to make much legislative impact on Ireland in the 1850s–1870s? Most obviously, resistance from the landed interest (or large sections of it) was an obstacle to the liberalisation of the law, as can be witnessed in the bulk of the Conservative press's hostile reaction to Ingram's 1863–4 interventions. At a time when landed proprietors still dominated most boards of guardians as *ex officio* members, this was a serious obstacle, and explains Hancock's preference for granting the Irish poor law commission, rather than the boards, discretionary powers over poor relief. The liberalisers might have sought support from the powerful and assertive Catholic clerical lobby, but were hesitant to do so. Many Catholic clergymen, perhaps most vocally Fr James Maher, had been strong advocates of outdoor relief as a 'right' of the respectable poor and actively campaigned for this in the wake of the 1860–4 crisis. However, the overtly Catholicising moralistic agenda for poor law reform pursued by Paul Cullen (discussed by Virginia Crossman in this volume) was antipathetic to the Statistical Society's 'rationalist', and in practice predominantly Protestant, position, and collaboration was therefore impractical.[45]

Both institutional and ideological factors help explain Ingram and Hancock's failure on the poor law. Crucially important was the sustained refusal of the Irish poor law commission (later the local government board) to engage in more than the most limited of changes to law or practice.

---

[42] 'Reports of Charity Organisation Committee of the Statistical and Social Inquiry Society of Ireland', *JSSISI*, 6 (1876), 538–40; 'Reports of Charity Organisation Committee', *ibid.*, 7 (1876), 29–38; Jonathan Pim, 'Report on Houseless Poor, Other than Destitute Wayfarers and Wanderers', *ibid.*, 39–41; W. Neilson Hancock, 'Notes as to Proceedings of the State Charities' Aid Association of New York', *ibid.*, 51–4.

[43] Hancock, 'Some Statistics and Researches on the Poor Removal Question', 360.

[44] Boylan and Foley, 'From Hedge School to Hegemony', 105, 110–11.

[45] Gray, *The Making of the Irish Poor Law*, 336–8.

Alfred Power, chief commissioner from 1849 to 1872 and vice-president of the local government board from 1872 to 1879, was an orthodox Benthamite, personally close to Edwin Chadwick, and a stalwart upholder of George Nicholls's less-eligibility principle throughout his long career. Power also appears to have believed genuinely in the morally reformative power of the workhouse regime, and if anything sought the restoration of this principle in England also.[46] Yet, as Virginia Crossman has suggested, many boards of guardians were equally reluctant to abandon workhouse relief for outdoor-relief alternatives, even in the case of children – most of whom were still relieved 'indoors' in 1900.[47]

Independently of the conservatism of the Irish poor law authorities, the years 1868–70, a key reformist 'moment' in the governance of Ireland, may have been the principal period of both opportunity and failure for Hancock and Ingram. In 1867 Hancock had urged the Conservative Chief Secretary Lord Naas to consider the political dangers arising from too rigid an administration of relief in years of distress.[48] While this appears to have had little impact, he probably anticipated a more receptive audience from an incoming ministry committed to 'pacifying Ireland' through responsive reforms. Hancock evidently had Gladstone's ear from 1868, writing numerous memos to shape the prime minister's thought and speeches on the church and land reform measures.[49] Hancock also worked closely with Gladstone's other key adviser at this time, John Lambert – an English liberal Catholic with extensive experience of English poor law administration. Lambert prepared a plan for the extension of the scope of the Irish poor law's operations in 1869, principally through the creation of new specialised institutions for medical relief, care and training of the disabled, support for reformatory schools, the funding of an 'outdoor' midwifery service and the transfer of insane paupers to greatly expanded asylums.[50] The greater emphasis on indoor and institutional expansion was not quite what Hancock had argued for, but he was prepared to support what was intended to be a major expansion in the funding of social welfare.[51] Unfortunately for its advocates, the initiative was predicated on the appropriation of the surplus of the Church

---

[46] Alfred Power, *A Paper on Out-Door Relief in Ireland: Prepared at Earl Spencer's Request* (1875).

[47] Virginia Crossman, 'Cribbed, Contained and Confined? The Care of Children under the Irish Poor Law, 1850–1920', *Éire-Ireland*, 44 (2009), 37–61.

[48] National Library of Ireland, Mayo Papers, W. Neilson Hancock, Reports on the leading indications of the state of Ireland in August 1867, 4 Oct. 1867, MS 11,221.

[49] See numerous memos by Hancock in British Library, London, Gladstone Papers, Add. Mss 44,610 and 44,613.

[50] Gladstone Papers, Lambert to Gladstone, 5 Jan. 1869, Add. MS 44,235, fo. 33; Lambert memo, 8 Feb. 1869, *ibid.*, Add. MS 44,609, fos 27–40, Lambert memo, 6 May 1869, *ibid.*, Add. MS 44,610, fos 38–44.

[51] Hancock memo, 16 July 1869, *ibid.*, fos 190–5.

of Ireland under the disestablishment bill, and when this was curbed by parliamentary amendments to the bill, the welfare dimensions were lost.

Nearly simultaneously with the failed appropriation initiative, G. J. Goschen's 'Minute' on English poor law practice began the determined process of ratcheting back on outdoor relief and poor law expenditure that characterised the following decade. Thus, paradoxically, Hancock's and Ingram's assimilationist case for Anglicising the poor law administration of Ireland was pursued at a time when English administrators were intent on Hibernicising the English law, seeking to revive the 'pure' form previously maintained in Ireland. Elizabeth Hurren identifies the Liberal viceroy Lord Spencer and Alfred Power as key figures in promoting this idealised image of the Irish system in England in the 1870s.[52] While historicising rationales for Irish legislation could exert leverage over British governments in this era, assimilationism was (at least so far as the poor law was concerned) a non-starter.

By 1880 profound changes in the Irish poor law were already underway, driven not by 'social science' inquiry or by government innovation, but by takeover of boards of guardians by mobilised tenant-ratepayer electorates. The mechanisms and consequences of this have been reviewed by William Feingold and Virginia Crossman.[53] The debates of the Statistical Society became wholly irrelevant in this hostile environment, but they remain important to historians as a source of commentary on poor law policy, mapping changing attitudes towards society and the economy among liberal intellectual elite of Ireland in a period of intense political polarisation and social change.

[52] Elizabeth T. Hurren, *Protesting about Pauperism: Poverty, Politics and Poor Relief in Late-Victorian England, 1870–1900* (Woodbridge, 2007), 28–30.

[53] William L. Feingold, *Revolt of the Tenantry: The Transformation of Local Government in Ireland, 1872–86* (Boston, MA, 1984); Virginia Crossman, *Power, Pauperism and Power in Late Nineteenth-Century Ireland* (Manchester, 2006).

Transactions of the RHS 20 (2010), pp. 157–69 © Royal Historical Society 2010
doi:10.1017/S0080440110000101

'FACTS NOTORIOUS TO THE WHOLE COUNTRY': THE POLITICAL BATTLE OVER IRISH POOR LAW REFORM IN THE 1860s*

By Virginia Crossman

READ 26 JUNE 2009 AT THE QUEEN'S UNIVERSITY BELFAST

ABSTRACT. This paper focuses on the campaign to reform the Irish poor law in the 1860s. Debate on poor law reform highlighted fundamental divisions over the principles underlying the New Poor Law as well as widespread dissatisfaction with the poor law system in Ireland particularly within the Catholic community. Led by the leading Catholic cleric, Archbishop Paul Cullen, critics of the Irish poor law sought to lessen reliance on the institution of the workhouse and to expand outdoor relief thus bringing the system closer to its English model. The poor law authorities supported by the Irish landed elite fought successfully to maintain the limited and restrictive nature of the system fearful of the consequences of extending local discretion. The paper reveals the contested nature of poor relief both in principle and in practice, and the centrality of social issues to Irish political debate in decades after the Great Famine.

In contrast to the history of the New English Poor Law which was, until recently, largely understood as a story of progressive improvement,[1] Irish poor law history has generally been seen as regressive, with the manifest failure of the system during the years of the Great Famine (1845–50) representing its lowest point. This perception has its roots in the belief that, as an importation from England, the new system was fundamentally unsuited to Ireland. Irish popular culture, it was claimed in 1892, was antipathetic to institutional relief and favoured almsgiving.[2] More recently, Gerard O'Brien has speculated that cultural acceptance of begging encouraged the poor to regard themselves as entitled to outdoor

---

* This article draws on research generated by the ESRC project, 'Welfare regimes under the Irish poor law 1850–1921'.
    [1] This is best exemplified in S. Webb and B. Webb, *English Poor Law History* (1927–9). For a more recent example, see Lynn Hollen Lees, *The Solidarities of Strangers: The English Poor Laws and the People, 1700–1948* (Cambridge, 1998).
    [2] *The Irish Peasant: A Sociological Study by a Guardian of the Poor* (1892), 69.

relief and thus to reject the workhouse.[3] The extent to which Irish people rejected the workhouse has, however, been called into question. In his study of the parish in England and Wales, Keith Snell argues that it would have been impossible for the other parts of the United Kingdom to move to an indoor system of poor relief such as that which existed in Ireland because public opinion would have revolted.[4] But whilst it is true that the Irish poor law system was more limited than its English equivalent, a fact indicative both of the way Ireland was governed and of what Irish society was prepared to tolerate, it would be wrong to assume that the system operated unchallenged. The 1860s saw a prolonged and vigorous public debate in Ireland over the nature and purpose of the poor law. Critics of the system made a concerted attempt to introduce reforms that would have fundamentally changed the character of the Irish poor law, making it more like the English system. Whilst these attempts failed, the conduct and content of the debate reveals both deep divisions over the principles of poor relief and widespread dissatisfaction with the poor law system particularly within the Catholic community.

The 1860s remain a neglected period in Irish history. Writing in 1965, E. R. Norman noted that this was generally seen as 'an uneventful decade', disturbed only by the Fenian uprising of 1867 and 'characterized by the weariness of Irishmen and their despair of securing any worthwhile concessions from the Government by legal means'. This, he argued convincingly, was a false impression that ignored other expressions of political activity, most importantly 'the agitation of the Catholic hierarchy and priesthood' led by Archbishop (later Cardinal) Paul Cullen.[5] Appointed archbishop of Armagh in 1849 and subsequently of Dublin in 1852, Cullen was determined to reform and discipline the Catholic Church in Ireland whilst also promoting a role for the Catholic middle class in the government and administration of the country. A meritocrat and moderniser, he sought to wean the Catholic lower classes away from Fenianism by demonstrating the ability of constitutional nationalism to achieve practical reforms. To this end he was prepared to engage with government, seeking to influence legislation and to get Catholics appointed to official positions. Fearful of the spread of radical political ideas throughout Europe, Cullen was convinced that a healthy (and devout) body politic offered the best defence against revolution. In Ireland, he saw the social fabric being destroyed by poverty and

---

[3] Gerard O'Brien, 'Workhouse Management in Pre-Famine Ireland', *Proceedings of the Royal Irish Academy*, 100, 86 (1986), 132–4. See also Helen Burke, *The People and the Poor Law in Nineteenth Century Ireland* (Littlehampton, 1987), p. 284.

[4] K. D. M. Snell, *Parish and Belonging: Community, Identity and Welfare in England and Wales 1700–1950* (Cambridge, 2006), 334–5.

[5] E. R. Norman, *The Catholic Church and Irish Politics in the Eighteen Sixties* (Dundalk, 1965), 3.

disease. By failing to make adequate provision for the poor, successive governments had demonstrated a lack of humanity and statesmanship: 'The government that leaves the poor here without protection', he was to predict in 1864, 'will some day or other suffer for its neglect.'[6] Cullen regarded poor law reform as the most pressing political issue of the day. As he explained to a colleague in 1861, 'I think it is of the utmost importance that we should make an effort to get the present [poor law] system corrected. Perhaps no more important question was mooted for the last thirty years.'[7]

Introduced in 1838 and modelled on the New English Poor Law, the Irish poor law constituted the primary source of poor relief for almost a century.[8] In the early years of the system, relief was only available within the workhouse. Under the threat of mass starvation the system was extended in 1847 to allow poor law boards to grant outdoor relief to the sick and disabled, and to widows with two or more legitimate children.[9] Outdoor relief could only be granted to the able-bodied if the workhouse was full or a site of infection. As Ireland began to recover from the Famine, and numbers receiving poor relief fell back to pre-Famine levels, public attention began to focus on the management, effectiveness and cost of the poor law system. Critics highlighted both the appalling conditions in many workhouses and the relatively low levels of relief provided. In an influential pamphlet published in 1859, Denis Phelan, a former assistant poor law commissioner and one of the few Catholics to have been appointed to the poor law commission, demonstrated that the level of provision in Ireland was far lower than that in England and Wales or Scotland, concluding that relief as then administered in Ireland was insufficient. Phelan called for fundamental reform and the introduction of 'a mixed system of workhouse and outdoor relief similar to that practiced in England', where outdoor relief was 'the general rule, indoor the exception', arguing that this system was generally approved of as being 'humane, politic and economical'. Making the poor law more humane, he argued, would reduce political discontent by persuading working people that that they lived in a country where 'in age, infirmity, and disease, they are assisted'.[10] Sending a copy of the pamphlet to the

---

[6] Cullen to McCloskey, 2 Jan. 1864, Archives of the Archdiocese of New York, McCloskey Papers, A22. (I am immensely grateful to Colin Barr for providing me with a copy of this and other letters from Cullen's correspondence.)
[7] Cullen to Keane, 1 Mar. 1861, Cloyne Diocesan Archives (hereafter CDA), Keane Papers, 1796.04/21/1861.
[8] For an overview of the history of the Irish poor law, see Virginia Crossman, *The Poor Law in Ireland 1838–1948* (Dundalk, 2006).
[9] 10 Vict. c. 31.
[10] Denis Phelan, *Reform of the Poor Law System in Ireland; or Facts and Observations on the Inadequacy of the Existing System of Poor Relief* (Dublin, 1859), 35–6.

under secretary at Dublin Castle, Thomas Larcom, Phelan informed him that it was written 'under a strong conviction that poor relief is defective in this country and that the subject requires to be reconsidered'.[11]

Phelan's pamphlet received a generally favourable and universally respectful reception in the Irish and British press. Given his extensive practical experience, commentators argued, Phelan's views had to be taken seriously.[12] In an effort to neutralise the impact of the pamphlet, Phelan's former employers, the poor law commissioners, sent an annotated version containing a point-by-point refutation of his arguments to every poor law union in the country. Whilst acknowledging Phelan's expertise, Benjamin Banks, chief clerk to the commission, rejected his conclusions, noting that he did not appear 'to have derived from his poor law experience, however extensive, any notion of the nature or value of New Poor Law principles'. Banks maintained that contrary to Phelan's assertion, poor relief was sufficient, and was applied 'directly and exclusively to its object'. Since indoor relief could be granted in almost all cases of application without danger to property or encouragement to indolence or vice, such relief was rarely refused. The availability of indoor relief gave people who would otherwise waste time and energy importuning guardians for outdoor allowances the 'courage to struggle successfully against adversity'. Who should get relief, Banks suggested, was a question best left to the applicants themselves rather than placed at the discretion of administrators. The problem with any extended system of outdoor relief was that 'a great part of it goes to those who do not most need it; by force either of impunity, imposture or interest'.[13]

By the summer of 1860, pressure for reform of the poor law was mounting. Scandals concerning conditions in the Cork and Dublin workhouses had focused public attention on the workhouse system and generated public concern,[14] and there was growing dissatisfaction with what was seen as the unrepresentative nature of the Irish poor law commission, whose upper ranks were dominated by Protestant Englishmen.[15] Furthermore, with the poor law commission's five-year

[11] Phelan to Larcom, n.d. (1859), annotated copy of Phelan, *Reform of the Poor Law System in Ireland*, National Library of Ireland (hereafter NLI), Pamphlets, P475.

[12] *Dublin Evening Post*, 13 Aug. 1859, 16 Aug. 1859, 20 Aug. 1859; *Packet*, 16 Aug. 1859; *Daily Express*, 26 Aug. 1859, 10 Sept. 1859; *Freeman's Journal*, 22 Nov. 1859, 21 Dec. 1859.

[13] Annotated copy of Phelan, *Reform of the Poor Law System in Ireland*.

[14] For Cork, see John Arnott, *The Investigation into the Condition of the Children in the Cork Workhouse with an Analysis of the Evidence* (Cork, 1859); Colman O Mahony, *Cork's Poor Law Palace: Workhouse Life 1838–90* (Cork, 2005), 184–90. For Dublin, see Anna Clark, 'Wild Workhouse Girls and the Liberal Imperial State in Mid-Nineteenth Century Ireland', *Journal of Social History*, 39 (2005), 389–410.

[15] Memorandum on articles in the Dublin Evening Post relative to the Poor Law Commission (1857–8), NLI, Mayo Papers, MS 11,030. See also *Freeman's Journal*, 16 Mar. 1861; *Dublin Evening Post*, 27 June 1861.

term up for renewal, some measure of legislation was essential. Ministers were open to the idea of incorporating additional provisions into the renewal act, encouraged by the poor law commissioners who were anxious to see certain changes introduced. The latter had been arguing for some years that treatment in workhouse hospitals should be extended beyond the destitute, and that provision should be made for the boarding out of infants.[16] They were, however, determined to resist more radical reforms.

Reporting on the prospects for reform in June 1860, Cullen's representative in London, Canon John P. Farrell, was optimistic.[17] However, when Farrell attended a meeting between a number of Irish MPs, the Irish chief secretary, Edward Cardwell, and the chief poor law commissioner, Alfred Power, to discuss the framing of a poor law bill, he discovered that the manifest failings of the poor law system were far from manifest to the poor law commissioners. Having outlined what he believed to be 'the two great evils of the Dublin Workhouses, the mortality amongst the young and the immorality amongst the females', Farrell had explained that the Catholic clergy believed the remedy to lie in 'outdoor support for the young of both sexes and for the females at least up to sixteen years'. Power's response was uncompromising, and to Farrell deeply shocking. For 'barefaced mendacity', Farrell reported, Power's reply 'exceeded anything we ever heard of – he said the plan proposed would not do, could not work and he denied its necessity', insisting that workhouse children were as healthy and moral as any other children. It was impossible, Farrell complained later, 'to deal with a man who will deny, obstinately deny, facts that are notorious to the whole country'.[18]

Forced to abandon the poor law bill in the face of procedural objections, Cardwell sought to appease the reform lobby by agreeing to the appointment of a select committee to investigate the administration of the poor law.[19] Having been infuriated by Power's refusal to accept there was anything amiss with the existing system, reformers were determined to expose its failings and thus to prove him wrong. To this end they set about collecting evidence and preparing witnesses. Cullen circulated a questionnaire on poor law administration to workhouse chaplains in his diocese and wrote to a number of his fellow bishops requesting that they

[16] 2nd Annual Report of the Commissioners of the Irish Poor Law on the Medical Charities Act (Dublin, 1854), 242; Banks to Larcom, 12 May 1857: National Archives of Ireland, Chief Secretary's Office Registered Papers (hereafter NAI, CSORP), 1860/11908; Banks to Larcom, 23 Jan. 1860: NAI, CSORP, 1860/11907.
[17] Farrell to Cullen, 20 June 1860, Dublin Diocesan Archive (hereafter DDA), Cullen Papers, 333/4/1.
[18] Farrell to Cullen, 22 June 1860, 11 July 1860, ibid., 333/4/2, 333/4/10.
[19] A number of MPs objected to the principle of introducing substantive new clauses in a continuance bill: Hansard 3, CLX, 149–50 (24 July 1860), CLX, 1031–3 (10 Aug. 1860), CLXI, 861 (22 Feb. 1861).

do the same. As he explained to William Keane, bishop of Cloyne, the questionnaire 'would serve to point out some of the matters that ought to be examined. If your Lordship would think it worth your while to get the questions answered by the chaplains, some useful information might be gleaned'.[20] Cullen was anxious to make a strong showing before the committee. It was important, he argued, 'to get some person of weight to state our grievances. If the system be not now corrected, it will destroy the poor.'[21] He offered himself as a witness and urged his colleagues to give evidence. 'If the bishops go over', he observed to Keane, 'it will show that we are in earnest.'[22]

In the event, Cullen was the only member of the Catholic hierarchy to appear before the select committee. Drawing on the information he had gathered, Cullen presented a powerful call for a more humane and compassionate approach to poor relief. Poverty, he observed, was not a crime yet convicts received a better diet in a common prison than workhouse inmates received. When reminded of the principle of less eligibility, he observed that the poor were 'creatures of God' and as such should be treated, 'as we would wish ourselves to be treated; and I would treat them in that way, let it cost what it might to the rate-payers'. He rejected the suggestion that an outdoor relief system would be liable to abuse, commenting that he thought there was 'no great inclination to take relief'. Indeed he thought, if anything, people were 'rather too proud in that respect'. The respectable poor, Cullen maintained deserved to be treated with humanity, and in ways that would preserve their self-respect. But he had little sympathy for the undeserving poor. Poverty in itself, he told the committee, 'is most honourable ... but when poverty is brought on by profligate courses, that is another case'.[23]

Cullen argued for a more discretionary system of poor relief, combining specialist institutional care organised on a denominational basis and outdoor relief. The classes he envisaged being supported outside the workhouse but within institutions included the deaf, dumb and blind, and lunatics, as well as prostitutes who were to be sent to reformatories. The respectable, deserving poor could be given outdoor relief, but anyone who had led 'a reckless profligate life' should be excluded, as should anyone who was able but unwilling to work, such as 'vagrants and sturdy

---

[20] Cullen to Keane, 20 Mar. 1861, CDA, Keane Papers, 1796.04/22/1861. For the replies, see Secular clergy, 1861, DDA, Cullen Papers, 340/1/1; Workhouses: Reforms, Elphin Diocesan Archives (hereafter EDA), Bishops, Section III C.

[21] Cullen to Keane, 1 Mar. 1861, *ibid.*, 1796.04/21/1861.

[22] Cullen to Monsell, n.d., NLI, Monsell Papers, MS 8317(3); Cullen to Gillooly, 19? Mar. 1861, EDA, Gillooly Papers, NLI Microfilm, P.7622; Cullen to Keane, 20 March 1861, CDA, Keane Papers, 1796.04/22/1861.

[23] *Report from the Select Committee Appointed to Inquire into the Administration of the Relief of the Poor in Ireland*, Parliamentary Papers, 1861 (408), X, Q3997, Q4098.

beggars'. Outdoor relief should only be given in cases where 'giving it would bring about the re-establishment of the person in his situation in life in a short time again, or where a person had led such a life that he was not deserving to be thrust into a workhouse'.[24] It was important, Cullen argued, to keep the undeserving or dissolute poor apart from respectable, decent people. For if the respectable poor were innately moral and thus could be trusted not to abuse the system the non-respectable represented not merely a bad example but a direct threat to society. Unlike the poor law commissioners who presented workhouses as places where people could be trained in good habits and thus restored to society as useful and productive citizens, Cullen held out little hope of redemption. The language Cullen used in referring to the immoral suggests that for him they had forfeited any real claim to humanity. In response to a suggestion that there were opportunities of reformation within the workhouse, he commented that 'contagion of example' prevented people from being reformed, adding that the 'more you increase a mass of filthiness, the more it ferments; it is the same with vice and evils when accumulated together'. Furthermore, he found it difficult to conceive of some people ever fulfilling a useful function either within the workhouse or outside: 'Take a beggar man out of the streets, and put him to nurse a sick man, how', he wondered, 'would he go through his duties?'[25]

Led by Cullen, the reform lobby made an effective case before the committee. They were, however, followed by a succession of witnesses who argued equally forcefully for maintaining the system essentially as it was. These witnesses included poor law guardians, elected and *ex officio*, and poor law officials, both Catholic and Protestant, including the Catholic master of the North Dublin Union whom Cullen himself had praised as doing an excellent job. Moreover, the chair of the North Dublin Board of Guardians, Henry MacFarlane, repeatedly cited the Catholic workhouse chaplain as endorsing the North Dublin Board's refusal to grant outdoor relief, undermining reformers' efforts to present the Catholic community as united in their support for an extension of outdoor relief. Farrell admitted that MacFarlane's evidence had been 'most damaging to us – he was at variance with your Grace on every point. His tone and manner were most plausible and apparently free from prejudice.'[26]

Cullen and his supporters were seeking a comprehensive reform of the poor law system. Changes sought ranged from the extension of outdoor relief and the introduction of boarding out for children up to the age of fifteen, to an improved dietary regime and the provision of separate accommodation in the workhouse for elderly couples. District schools

[24] *Ibid.*, Q4093.
[25] Ibid., Q4047, Q4039.
[26] Farrell to Cullen, 11 June 1861, DDA, Cullen Papers, 340/1/1/80.

were proposed for the education of 'the more permanently destitute of the juvenile classes', together with specialist institutions for the physically and mentally disabled and refuges for prostitutes and unmarried mothers. To counter alleged Protestant bias in the administration of the poor law, reformers demanded greater representation of Catholics on poor law boards and on the poor law commission, as well as increased provision for denominational education and specially designated spaces for Catholic worship.[27] In its final report, the select committee rejected calls for radical change concluding that Irish poor law guardians had sufficient powers of affording relief and that no alteration of the poor laws 'in that respect is necessary or desirable'.[28] The committee's recommendations formed the basis of the Poor Law Amendment Act of 1862 which introduced significant albeit limited amendments.[29] These included provision for the boarding out of orphan and deserted children up to age of eight years and the opening of workhouse hospitals to those who were poor but not destitute, thus establishing the basis of a comprehensive, free medical service under the poor law both inside and outside the workhouse.[30] Poor law critics were disappointed at the limited nature of the reforms introduced, but not surprised. Noting 'the latest victory of foreign legislation above our wants and necessities – above our poverty and suffering', the *Nation* concluded that the only hope was 'national independence'. The Conservative *Dublin Evening Mail* on the other hand welcomed the frustration of Catholic hopes, dismissing the leaders of the reform lobby as 'these philanthropic clamourers for greater personal power and political influence'.[31]

The select committee hearings presented two opposing views of poor relief and social welfare. The first, propounded by the poor law commissioners and supported by the majority of Irish landowners, was based on New Poor Law principles and stressed the need for minimal relief in order to provide an incentive for thrift and industry. The second, propounded by the Catholic hierarchy and supported by Irish nationalists and liberal unionists, rejected the New Poor Law model as inappropriate for Ireland, and called instead for a more humane but also more discretionary system of relief. Significantly, the proponents of both points of view were convinced not only that their analysis was correct and that what they advocated was in the best interests of Ireland, but also that they enjoyed the support of educated public opinion. Poor law commissioner Edward Senior caused outrage in the Catholic press when

[27] 'Select Committee of the House of Commons upon the Irish Poor Law', n.d. (1861), DDA, Cullen papers, Poor Law, 43/8.

[28] *Report [on] the Administration of the Relief of the Poor in Ireland*, 3.

[29] 25 & 26 Vict. c. 83, s. 9.

[30] Burke, *The People and the Poor Law*, 252–6; Laurence M. Geary, *Medicine and Charity in Ireland 1718–1851* (Dublin, 2004), 206–16.

[31] *Nation*, 2 Aug. 1862; *Dublin Evening Mail*, 19 Mar. 1862.

he airily dismissed criticism of the commission as 'vulgar clamour'.[32] As the *Freeman's Journal* commented in 1862, if poor law administration was 'so "satisfactory" why the constant demands of the Irish people for its revision on a sounder and less exclusive basis?'[33]

But as well as underlining and reinforcing the deep divisions between the pro- and anti-reform lobbies, the select committee also revealed a striking degree of unanimity about some aspects of poor relief. All the witnesses declared themselves strongly opposed to indiscriminate outdoor relief. Indeed, it became apparent that the prejudice against outdoor assistance was so strong that many guardians were unclear what their powers in this respect actually were. Nicholas Mahony, an elected guardian from Cork, was surprised to be told that boards of guardians already had the power to grant outdoor relief to the family of a sick man, stating that he had been unaware of this.[34] Critics maintained that outdoor relief was officially discouraged. Cullen claimed that the poor law commissioners had, 'in every instance ... thrown difficulties in the way of giving out-door relief, so that the guardians, in many places, think they cannot give that relief'.[35] The commissioners denied this, but their regular pronouncements on its dangers certainly encouraged many guardians to believe that outdoor relief was not only unwise but illegal.

There was similar unanimity on the desirability of encouraging industry and self-reliance amongst the Irish people. Supporters of the existing poor law argued that it had had a very positive effect in promoting self-reliance, something that, according to John Vandeleur Stewart, chair of the Letterkenny Board of Guardians, 'was always wanting in the Celtic character. The poor law throws upon everybody a moral responsibility, which tends to cultivate it.'[36] Even those advocating reform used the language of self-help. It was the workhouse that was demoralising Irish society, they asserted, and outdoor relief that would encourage people to struggle to remain independent. A judicious system of outdoor relief, one Drogheda poor law guardian asserted in 1861, benefited everyone, relieving the ratepayer and helping the poor. Give people a small weekly allowance and they would make an effort to bring themselves through, 'but lock the poor man up in a poor house and he becomes useless to all society, and, losing caste, he becomes broken-hearted, and dies in a short-time'.[37]

Much of the anxiety provoked by the idea of indiscriminate outdoor relief focused on the possibility of abuse and reflected a deep-seated suspicion of the Catholic peasantry and the Catholic clergy. Writing in the *Dublin University Magazine*, J. A. Scott warned that any system based

[32] *Nation*, 6 July 1861.
[33] *Freeman's Journal*, 26 Mar. 1862.
[34] *Report [on] the Administration of the Relief of the Poor in Ireland*, Q2007–9.
[35] *Ibid.*, Q3993.
[36] *Ibid.*, Q6172.
[37] *Daily Express*, 14 June 1861.

on outdoor relief would require discretion to be left with local guardians. From this 'necessarily extensive latitude', he argued,

> enormous abuses cannot but spring . . . Idle and vicious persons would find no difficulty in making good market of their self-inflicted misery. Pious and feeling clergymen, a class proverbially easy to be imposed upon, would use their influence on behalf of questionable claimants, and the rates would be burdened with the support, and, still more seriously, with the parental responsibilities, of worthless individuals.[38]

That a discretionary system would put more power into local hands and thus potentially into the hands of the Catholic middle class was a significant factor motivating both those agitating for change and those seeking to prevent it. Many Protestants feared that the Catholic Church was using the issue, as it used welfare more widely, to boost its own influence and authority among the people.

Protestant criticism of Cullen's reform campaign reveals a deep suspicion of Catholic involvement in politics. The careful and organised efforts of the reform lobby to collect evidence and find witnesses did not go unnoticed in the Protestant press. Thus the *Packet* reported in 1861 that the ultramontane party led by Cullen was 'proving adept at politics'. Cullen, it claimed, wished to upset the poor law system in order to accomplish the endowment of Popery by quasi-philanthropic schemes. To this end, he 'organizes his forces, gets up his case, procures a parliamentary committee, sends over his witnesses, and then, to make the organisation complete, convenes his representatives in order that he may browbeat them into compliance with his purposes'. Cullen's ultimate aim, the *Packet* believed, was to take control of the poor law system. Reporting on a meeting at Cullen's residence to discuss poor law reform in January 1862, the *Packet* speculated on the outcome of a successful campaign:

> Dr Cullen and his clergy, after obtaining the power in the management of the workhouses which is here sought, after making themselves the administrators of a vast and demoralising system of outdoor relief, and after substituting their nominees as poor law guardians for the holders of property and large occupiers, would in point of fact be the poor law system themselves.[39]

Ministers and their officials were equally suspicious of Catholic intentions, arguing both publicly and privately that Catholic critics of the poor law should direct their energies to persuading the people to accept indoor relief. Thus Larcom claimed in 1862 that the real difficulty in relieving distress in the west lay not with levying rates or providing provisions, but in

> inducing the people to enter the workhouse, which certain influential leaders prevent by every means – their object apparently being not the benefit of the suffering poor but the

---

[38] J. A. Scott, 'The Irish Poor Law Inquiry', *Dublin University Magazine*, 58 (1861), 60–1.
[39] *Packet*, 24 Jan. 1862.

increase of their own power and influence which they suppose would be diminished by the people resorting to legal charity as a lawful right instead of depending upon them for alms.[40]

It would be wrong, however, to present the issue of poor law reform in narrowly sectarian terms. A desire to counter both the influence of the Catholic Church and Catholic disaffection prompted some Protestants to argue for a more extensive and generous system of poor relief. Only if Britain could be seen to be responsive to the interests and needs of the Irish people would its administration of the country be either secure or justifiable. The apparent inadequacy of the poor law in the face of recurring distress in the far west in the late 1850s and 1860s was seen by some observers as revealing a fundamental flaw in the system. In a pamphlet published in 1862, William Ansell Day criticised the Belmullet Board of Guardians for refusing to grant outdoor relief to assist people suffering from temporary distress. The guardians' desire to keep poor rates down was inducing 'a line of action to the pauper, which, to say the least, is harsh and repulsive, and we ask ourselves, whether a system so administered, can adequately meet the requirements of a pauperised community'. Poor law boards, Day argued, should be obliged by law to grant outdoor relief where they could do so legally. Forcing people to rely on charity was putting power into hands of Irish priests. This was a dangerous course since the peasant then compared 'the zeal of his priest with the indifference of everyone else', and, 'not unnaturally, clothes that church exclusively with the attributes of charity, love and truth'.[41]

The following year in a vice-presidential address to the Social and Statistical Inquiry Society, John K. Ingram argued for the assimilation of the Irish poor-relief system with that in England and Wales. This would benefit Irish agriculture by promoting the consolidation of agricultural holdings. For consolidation to take place, Irish labourers had to be secured against bad seasons as the English labourer was. The labourer needed to be confident that,

> if he should be overtaken by calamity, he will be liberally assisted until the crisis has passed away; that his home will not be broken up, and his aged parents, his wife and his children forced to enter the workhouse, but that he and those who depend on him will be relieved at his own dwelling.

If this was not done, Ingram predicted, 'it will produce general popular discontent and social disorganisation'. Poor law reform could do more to change attitudes to government, Ingram suggested, than 'what are properly called political reforms', since social conditions affected the lower

---

[40] Larcom to Sir Robert Peel, 15 July 1862: NLI, Larcom Papers, MS 7785. See also Lord Naas to the Roman Catholic clergy of the Deanery of Westport, 11 July 1867, NLI, Mayo Papers, MS 11,218 (17).

[41] William Ansell Day, *The Famine in the West* (Dublin, 1862), p. 40.

classes 'far more nearly, and come more home to their business and their bosoms'.[42] The return of distress in 1867 prompted the political economist and founding member of the Statistical Society, W. Neilson Hancock, to reflect once again on the comparatively low level of relief given in Ireland. In an echo of Phelan's arguments, Hancock maintained that distress was not being adequately met by the poor law machinery and that the poor law was incapable of meeting 'any sudden emergency of temporary character'. There were, Hancock warned, political consequences to this since 'every recurrence of local distress or unfavourable season is seized on by disenchanted parties to show that Irish interests generally are in a state of decay'.[43] In identifying poor law reform as an essential component of social and economic development in Ireland as well as a crucial safeguard against political disaffection, 'social science' discourse on poverty and welfare as developed by Ingram and Hancock had much in common with Catholic social thought as espoused by Cullen. Despite this common ground, however, active cooperation to achieve reform was never a real possibility. As Peter Gray has noted, Cullen's 'overtly politicising agenda' made collaboration between Catholic activists and liberal unionists impractical.[44]

Government officials remained unmoved by critiques of the poor law, insisting that adequate relief could be provided if boards of guardians acted promptly and appropriately. Recalling the distress caused by crop failures in 1861–2, Larcom noted with satisfaction that the government's determination to rely on the powers and resources of the poor law had been justified by events: 'The operation of the poor law was seriously obstructed by the efforts to prevent the people availing themselves of the legal charity it afforded. But perseverance succeeded – not one death from destitution was proved to have taken place'.[45] Power remained equally confident that the system was essentially sound, and continued to resist any revision to the provisions regulating outdoor relief. Consulted in 1865 about a proposal to extend outdoor relief to some of the groups eligible to receive it in England, such as widows with one legitimate child or the wives of men serving in the armed forces, he acknowledged that outdoor relief was 'at all times more readily accepted by the lower classes' who were 'disposed to regard relief in the workhouse as degrading'. This view, he noted, was continually being 'urged on them by authorities who they look up to as not liable to error'. But so long as local rates were charged

[42] John K. Ingram, *Considerations on the State of Ireland* (Dublin, 1864), 14–15.

[43] W. Neilson Hancock, Reports on the leading indications of the state of Ireland in August 1867, 4 Oct. 1867, NLI, Mayo Papers, MS 11,221.

[44] See above, pp. 141–56.

[45] Note by Larcom, n.d., Poor Relief: Relief of Distress 1861–2, NLI, Larcom Papers, MS 7784.

with the expenditure, Power felt confident that guardians were unlikely to demoralise the poor or oppress the ratepayers by excessive expenditure:

> Perhaps the only real danger to be apprehended exists of the possibility of past experience being in time forgotten and that the arguments of those who contend that outdoor relief is not only the most acceptable form of relief to the poor but the most economical also to the ratepayers may some time or other prevail.[46]

If the poor law commissioners appeared to have won the battle over outdoor relief, however, their victory was more apparent than real. Throughout the 1860s the level of outdoor relief provided in Ireland climbed slowly but steadily upwards, although the proportion of the total number relieved in this way remained considerably lower than in England. Attitudes were changing, as Power realised that they might. Fading memories of the Famine had a part to play in this, but perhaps more significant was the publicity generated by the select committee. The growing willingness of boards of guardians to utilise the full range of their powers with regard to outdoor relief was most evident in the more prosperous unions in the south-east of the country. These were also the unions in which Catholic guardians were beginning to make their presence felt.[47]

The struggle over poor law reform in this period taught critics of the system a useful lesson. Attempting to alter the law was a mammoth task; altering local practices was far easier to achieve, since the decision-making power lay in the hands of local guardians. As Farrell had observed to Cullen in 1860, changing the law would not necessarily change the way relief was administered. Until Catholics had greater influence within poor law administration, 'no effective good can be achieved'.[48] It was not until the 1880s, however, that Protestant fears of a take-over of the poor law system were to be realised. And in the event, the campaign was to be spearheaded not by the Catholic Church, but by the nationalist movement under the leadership of Charles Stewart Parnell.[49] Nevertheless, without the public discussion and associated developments that took place in the 1860s, the transformation in both poor law administration and relief practices that took place in the 1880s could not have occurred.

[46] Power to Larcom, 7 Jan. 1865, *ibid.*, MS 7781.

[47] A good example is Enniscorthy Union. See Virginia Crossman, 'The poor law in Enniscorthy in the post-Famine period', in *History of Enniscorthy*, ed. Colm Toibin (forthcoming 2010).

[48] Farrell to Cullen, 11 Aug. 1860, DDA, Cullen Papers, 333/4/18.

[49] For an account of this transformation and its impact on poor law administration, see William F. Feingold, *The Revolt of the Tenantry: The Transformation of Local Government in Ireland 1872–1886* (Boston, MA, 1984); Virginia Crossman, *Politics, Pauperism and Power in Late Nineteenth-Century Ireland* (Manchester, 2006).

Transactions of the RHS 20 (2010), pp. 171–93 © Royal Historical Society 2010
doi:10.1017/S0080440110000113

THE AGE OF PROTHERO: BRITISH HISTORIOGRAPHY IN THE LONG *FIN DE SIÈCLE*, 1870–1920

The Prothero Lecture

By Michael Bentley

READ 1 JULY 2009

ABSTRACT. This paper revisits two generations of highly talented and significant historians who flourished in Britain between *c.* 1870 and 1920. George Prothero stood high among them and he, with his brother Roland, receives a good deal of attention at the centre of the argument here. But others stood still higher: Tout, Firth, Poole, Acton, the incomparable Maitland; and the purpose of the piece is to present a portrait of the British historical profession as a whole during a crucial period of its formation by using the Protheros' experience as a platform from which to depart. The journey inevitably begins with that Prothero experience seen as a microcosm of greater tendencies; but it soon winds away toward Germany and Scotland and France; we pause to admire fresh perspectives yielded in what had become an age of edition and what would become an age of economic and social history. Of course the track leads also to Sarajevo and the implications of European war for a fledgling profession. All this itinerary lends an opportunity, therefore, to think through some of the themes and characteristics which made this period of development distinctive; but it also warns and guards against reducing these years to a time of 'transition', remarkable only for what would follow it. The personalities and achievements discussed here deserve better of us and recommend that we devote more energy to considering the features of the age of Prothero, for their own sake and in their own terms.

I

Forty years ago, almost to the day and presumably near this spot, Charles Crawley of Trinity Hall, Cambridge, rose to deliver the first Prothero Lecture.[1] That ruby wedding between the Royal Historical Society and the Prothero family weighed with me in wondering whether his subject, George Prothero and his circle, might not be revisited. Revisited, but not repeated. Crawley had concentrated on what might be gleaned in

---

[1] Charles Crawley, 'George Prothero and his Circle', *Transactions of the Royal Historical Society*, fifth series, 20 (1970), 101–27. C. W. Crawley (1889–1992) had been vice-master of Trinity Hall, whose history he wrote, between 1950 and 1966. He married Augusta, daughter of Samuel Butcher, bishop of Meath. See G. W. Prothero, *Samuel Henry Butcher* (Tralee, 1911).

particular from Prothero's private diaries which had been in his hands since 1934 and which gave him special insight into his uncle by marriage; and it followed that his account has a strongly biographical and familial flavour.[2] My ambition is a different one. While in no sense seeking to transcend Crawley's helpful essay, I want to widen the lens and think more laterally and more generally about British historiography during Prothero's mature years. Rather than ask you to consider simply the time-line of the Protheros – for there are two of them – I intend to move your thinking sideways and to try to form an image of what was interesting and distinctive about the two generations of British historians who flourished in the fifty years after 1870, beginning always with events and contexts in the lives of the Protheros but then envisaging those environments as a place on which to build a structure that includes the two brothers but does not end with them. This means that, like all historians afflicted by periodisation and seeking escape, I shall speak of the long *fin de siècle*. The result will have neither the systematic virtues of a survey nor the immediacy of a single story but it may gain in atmosphere and flavour. Purists will say that an 'age' has no identity beyond that imposed in retrospect but I hope to propose that the age of Prothero yields significant characteristics that earlier and later periods sometimes reflect yet never fully share.

But first, the Protheros themselves. There were four brothers of whom two attract our attention: George, the eldest, born in the year of Revolution, 1848, and who died just after the First World War in 1922; and Rowland, the third son, born three years after George and who survived him by fifteen years. Why do they matter? G. W. Prothero became an influential historian of his generation; he played a major role in the Royal Historical Society (RHS) and was its president between 1901 and 1905. He spent the major part of his professional life as editor of the *Quarterly Review* in which post he succeeded his brother Rowland in 1899 and assumed the role of what nowadays we might call a public intellectual in the years before and during the First World War. R. E. Prothero was a professional author who did not hold a university post but wrote on a wide range of subjects from religion and poetry to the history of the countryside. After leaving the *Quarterly* he became a land-agent, later entered parliament as a Conservative and served as Lloyd George's minister of agriculture after

[2] The diaries have now been separated from the main collection of Prothero MSS held by the Royal Historical Society and have been deposited in the Archive Centre of King's College, Cambridge. A further *Nachlass* relating to Prothero's Edinburgh experiences is deposited in the Special Collections Department of the University Library in Edinburgh. 'Prothero MSS' will here denote the RHS material; 'Prothero collection' will relate to the Edinburgh deposit; 'Prothero diary' to the King's College manuscript diaries. In all quotations I have expanded the shorthand prose normally used by Prothero when writing for himself.

1916 when he was responsible for a programme to overcome the German blockade and feed the nation.[3] I have to say that it was the 'wrong' Prothero, Rowland, whom I came across first as a sixth-form schoolboy in the mid-1960s. Our A-Level bibliographies stood as monuments to the dead and out-of-print and I lacked the curiosity to notice that our text for rural economic history, Lord Ernle's *English Farming Past and Present* was in its sixth edition of 1961 which camouflaged an original date of publication in 1912. Nor did I have the remotest clue who Lord Ernle was. Only some years later, working on the politics of the First World War and beyond, did R. E. Prothero come into focus as the same man. His elder brother, 'our' Prothero, also remained no more than a name to me until I wrote about nineteenth-century historiography and realised that he had made sharp comments on the writing of history and participated in the nearest England ever got to a *Methodenstreit* concerning the right way to study it.

The brothers seem never to have been close. George cleaved to others in the family and Rowland as a younger child was left mostly to his own devices, a fate cruelly worsened when an ocular disease eventually led, with periods of remission, to total blindness.[4] Educational trajectories further separated George and Rowland for the former went off first to Eton and then King's College, Cambridge, to read classics since the Historical Tripos was not then available;[5] and Rowland to Marlborough, where he was unhappy, and Balliol College, Oxford, to read the new Modern History syllabus there and take a distinguished First Class followed by a Fellowship of All Souls. For all Rowland's achievements one senses a slight *de haut en bas* from George as the acknowledged family scholar and historian,[6] and an impression, compounded by Rowland's self-effacement, that the younger Prothero could claim competence as an author but little else. Yet they sprang into their careers from the same loving, clerical family, displaced from Wiltshire and Worcestershire where George and Rowland had been born, to Whippingham on the Isle of Wight where they spent their childhood. George, senior, their father, became a chaplain-in-ordinary to the queen and the family's

---

[3] His central achievement concerned the Corn Production Act of 1917 which encouraged the expansion of land under corn to meet wartime demand for food.

[4] Lord Ernle, *From Whippingham to Wetminister* (1938), 12–13, for childhood distancing. It is remarkable that Ernle's autobiography contains only two fleeting references to his brother.

[5] Between 1860 and 1869 Modern History figured only as a subject within the Cambridge Moral Sciences Tripos. After four years in the Law Tripos (1870–4), History became its own Tripos in 1875 but did not assume its modern shape for another ten years. See G. W. Prothero, *The Historical Tripos* (Cambridge, 1892).

[6] Witness his deprecation of Rowland's Life of Stanley: 'too long, some repetitions . . . somehow there is a lack of distinction about the book'. Prothero diary, 28 Mar. 1894, GWP/1/5.

proximity to Osborne meant that they saw much of her and the itinerant court. What the boys appropriated from Whippingham was, inadvertently, connection in its eighteenth-century form with a 'x' and, more consciously, churchmanship. That in itself became a further source of division because George took his Anglican stance around middle-stump and turned into a robust anti-ritualist when ritualism was the Church of England's obsession in the 1890s, while Rowland's position was, if not ritualist, then most certainly high and dry.[7] But the vicarage, home until their father died in 1894, united what religion sundered and formed both men, a fate frequently replicated in their generation.

Possibly this generation within the age of Prothero would prove the last to demonstrate so compellingly its origins in rectory, vicarage and manse and to issue in historians who, ecclesiastical or not in their focus, bore through their lives that indelible imprint. George's friend John Robert Seeley, from the generation before his own, still carried the virus of rationalist evangelicalism instilled at home and had produced not only an heretical life of Christ in *Ecce Homo* (1865) – 'vomited from the jaws of hell' as the dependable Lord Shaftesbury was heard to exclaim – and who went on to develop the idea of a National Church that had more to do with Stein's ambitions for the post-Napoleonic German lands than a realistic reading of British prospects.[8] Or bring to mind Samuel Rawson Gardiner, his eccentric childhood in the Catholic Apostolic Church and his later marriage to its founder's daughter. In the Prothero generation itself one thinks of the Plummers, Alfred and Charles, descended from the vicar of Heworth, once part of the parish of Jarrow with its echoes of Bede. Charles would hold the chaplaincy of Corpus Christi College, Oxford, from 1875 to his death in 1927 – fifty-two years! – whilst distinguishing himself in Anglo-Saxon history with his other hand.[9] Or perhaps of James Headlam-Morley, son of another vicar and brother of Arthur Headlam who became bishop of Gloucester. There are those historians of the Church itself: James Pounder Whitney, son of the perpetual curate of

[7] There is a hint that George, senior, had been underwhelmed by the Oxford Movement: see his commemoration address on the death of A. P. Stanley: 'A Sermon Preached at Whippingham on July 24th, 1881', published in London as *Arthur Penrhyn Stanley: A Sermon* (1881) 7, 11–13. But George, junior, conceded, for example, that Liddon had been 'a grt man' if not so 'grt' as Newman. Prothero diary, 10 Sept. 1890, GWP/1/5.

[8] Shaftesbury, quoted in Deborah Wormell, *Sir John Seeley and the Uses of History* (Cambridge, 1980), 23. Cf. R. T. Shannon, 'John Robert Seeley and the Idea of a National Church', in *Ideas and Institutions of Victorian Britain: Essays in Honour of George Kitson Clark*, ed. Robert Robson (1967), 236–67. George Prothero saw through the press Seeley's posthumous *The Growth of British Policy: An Historical Essay* (2 vols., Cambridge, 1895).

[9] Charles Plummer (1851–1927), *The Life and Times of Alfred the Great* (Oxford, 1902), and editions of Bede, the Anglo Saxon Chronicle and Sir John Fortescue. Alfred Plummer (1841–1926) wrote on early modern ecclesiastical history and was a distinguished commentator on the Gospels.

Marsden, ordained priest in 1885, and who after the First World War fused the Dixie Chair in Cambridge with the rectory of Wicken Bonhunt in Essex.[10] There was the terrifying H. M. Gwatkin, Whitney's predecessor and Mandell Creighton's successor in the Dixie Chair, who, following his four first degrees – how satisfying that he was placed in the First Class only in three of them – went on to compound a clerical childhood by taking Orders himself.[11] Then there were the churchmen who were also front-rank historians: Dean Stanley, son of a future bishop of Norwich, who wrote Dr Arnold's life; Dean Church, who made up for a secular father who had traded in Portuguese wines by writing the history of the Oxford Movement; Mandell Creighton who was bishop of London; William Cunningham, the economic historian, who became archdeacon of Ely; and of course, too early to count but too seminal to exclude, William Stubbs who moved from the Regius Chair in Oxford to its bishopric.[12] They join up with the Protheros, all these luminaries – not least through Rowland who wrote the life of Dean Stanley and a widely selling book on the Psalms.[13]

But they join together, too, through the mood of febrile concern over the future of English Protestantism and its relation to the state that so characterises the two decades either side of 1900. Those elements of the controversy that separated George and Rowland Prothero found their reflection in the wider historical community as the plain, unproblematic Protestantism of a James Anthony Froude or Edward Augustus Freeman encountered a more rampant version whose roots might equally lead down into evangelicalism or a newly aggressive Anglo-Catholicism that looked back on the Tractarians as a precious heritage. The sometimes farcical trial of the ritualist bishop of Lincoln, Edward King, in the late 1880s merely decorated some deeper attitudes that reached the thought and work of historians quite as much as others in the intellectual community; and those thoughts turned on possible doom for a church divided. George Prothero thought it likely, in the privacy of his diary, that schism must come out of the antics of ritualists and that disestablishment would follow.[14] Rowland, who had taken Holy Orders himself as the King

[10] J. P. Whitney (1857–1939), *The History of the Reformation* (1940), and works on Hildebrand.
[11] H. M. Gwatkin (1844–1916), *Selections from Early Writers Illustrative of Church History to the Time of Constantine* (1893).
[12] A. P. Stanley (1815–81), *The Life and Correspondence of Thomas Arnold* (1844); R. W. Church (1815–90), *The Oxford Movement: Twelve Years 1833–1845* (1891); Mandell Creighton (1843–1901), *A History of the Papacy during the Period of the Reformation* (5 vols., 1882–94); William Cunningham (1849–1919), *An Essay on Western Civilization in its Economic Aspects* (2 vols., Cambridge, 1898–1900).
[13] R. E. Prothero, *The Life and Correspondence of Arthur Penrhyn Stanley* (2 vols., 1893); R. E. Prothero, *The Psalms in Human Life* (1904).
[14] Quoted in Crawley, 'George Prothero and his Circle', 16.

trial proceeded, took the other side ten years later in telling the medievalist John Horace Round that 'the "cant" of the Evangelical makes me creep all over'.[15] For Montagu Burrows, a colleague of Rowland's at All Souls and holder of the Chichele Chair at Oxford, the Church of England was not the enemy; instead he focused on the Roman Catholics. Gathering that a proposal was imminent to make Lord Acton an honorary Fellow of his College in 1890, Burrows began his protest, as all bigots do, by proclaiming that he was not a bigot, and then quickly got into his stride:

> If he comes much to College we shall be liable to have his Romanist friends more with us than we may wish and ... they are 'all tarred with same brush'.... [A]nd if we elect Roman Catholics others will follow. The history of Oxford has surely not been written in vain.[16]

One begins to see why the young Lewis Namier's later rejection by the same College had a certain inevitablity about it since Jews were presumably more 'other' even than Catholics.[17]

Back at Whippingham in the 1860s the two Protheros knew nothing of these troubled waters gathering for the future and they made their way into their universities expecting to develop professional careers. George intended to become an academic historian and duly became one for a time. Rowland had ambitions in the Law but his eyesight deserted him and made it impossible. Both their wanderings throw light on some key tendencies. As a Fellow of King's College, Cambridge, George Prothero completed his first book, a biography of Simon de Montfort, in 1877. It is hard to know which predicament gave him the most difficulty: that Stubbs had not completed the second volume of his *Constitutional History* or that Reinhold Pauli had published his own life of de Montfort as Prothero wrote.[18] For whatever reason, Prothero's book was not very good, which is presumably why Cambridge University Press turned it down; it is remembered for youthful excess ('the pent up spirit of feudalism burst forth') and its echoing of Stubbs, who read the proofs, in identifying the parliament of 1295 as the embryo of all that followed.[19] But we have a better reason for remembering it. Prothero had wanted to teach for King's but the requirement was for medieval teaching: he wrote the book in order to teach its contents to undergraduates. Here is a rich and distinctive theme in the *fin-de-siècle* university. The development of professionalised

[15] R. E. Prothero to Round, 26 June 1898, Round MSS, University of London Library, IHR 924, 666.

[16] Burrows to Anson, 23 May 1890, Anson MSS, 79–80, All Souls College, Oxford. The Fellows elected Acton *pace* Burrows.

[17] Julia Namier describes the incident (with telling documentation from Pollard) in *Lewis Namier: A Biography* (1971), 99–101.

[18] Georg Reinhold Pauli, *Simon de Montfort: The Creator of the House of Commons* (Eng. trans. 1876).

[19] G. W. Prothero, *The Life of Simon de Montfort, Earl of Leicester* (1877), 1, 363.

dissemination in historical work produced the inverse of what we today regard as *de rigueur*. For in the age of Prothero it proved less important to supply research-led teaching than it did teaching-led research. So many streams fed into that development, the widest, perhaps, in a changing clientele. Memorising the text book would still do in many departments of history; but in the better schools and colleges a demand now existed for, at the very least, textbooks written by experts. Publishers drove that vehicle and expanded its range through their increasing contact with professional historians. And one did not write for Macmillans or Murrays or Longmans, or Duckworths: one wrote for Alexander Macmillan or John Murray or Charles Longman, or Gerald Duckworth; one knew those men personally; one dined with them at one's club. They knew what would sell and in an explosion of secondary and tertiary provision in education from the late 1880s a new market arose from the school and university syllabus. It was the beginning of a process that has come to dominate academic outputs in the twentieth century: the complex negotiation that makes academics write the things that they never wanted to write in the first place and which gives their books an intellectual patina that their publishers would gladly do without but on which academic historians insist for their own self-respect.[20]

A related and powerful feature of this environment arises in Prothero's third book, perhaps his best known. *Select Statutes and Other Documents Illustrative of the Reigns of Elizabeth and James I* appeared in 1894 but its inception dated from 1885 when regulations governing the recently introduced Historical Tripos in Cambridge allowed for the provision of a special subject; and the point of Prothero's collection of documents lay in presenting students with an array of constitutional documents for the purpose of mounting precisely that form of tuition. These years mark the apex of constitutional history, through which Prothero and colleagues in other universities could direct their advanced teaching. But this book also suggested something deeper. Prothero's collection stood among his contributions to editing texts and documents. Between them, he and Rowland played a lifelong tennis-match in edition: George edited Thierry's letters; but Rowland edited Gibbon's. George translated and edited some Ranke; but Rowland edited Byron in six volumes. George edited Voltaire on the age of Louis XIV; but then Rowland edited the Hispanist, Richard Ford. George and Rowland both edited the *Quarterly Review*. Deuce. But George edited the *Cambridge Modern History* and then, a crushing ace, the twenty-five volumes produced by the historical section of the Foreign Office after the First World War. Game, set and match. Whilst

[20] I am indebted here to my former research student, Paul Churchill, and his doctoral dissertation on 'The Production of History: Historians, Publishers and the Transfer of Knowledge in Britain, 1895–1960 (St. Andrews, 2007).

ever Rowland's eyes held out, not a year passed when the Protheros did not have in hand the work of editing and annotating and, though they may have been extreme in their devotion to that art, they reflected a generational imperative, for the age of Prothero was an age of edition.

It was a new *kind* of edition. Certainly the enthusiasm of an amateur devoting labour and love in order to interest others in a chosen subject still abounded: Joseph Gillow editing his English Catholics in five volumes; George Hill editing Boswell in six; Helen Foxcroft editing Halifax and Gilbert Burnet; Herbert Maxwell editing Creevey: it is not difficult to extend such a list.[21] Yet from that day in 1884 when Frederic William Maitland walked into the Public Record Office and emerged with his edition of *Pleas for the Crown in the County of Gloucester*, presaging the three volumes presenting and annotating Bracton's Note Book in 1887, history had changed for good.[22] This was not amateur enthusiasm; it was professional specialism and its rigours formed the contours of British historiography in this generation. Of course medievalists had Stubbs's *Select Charters* at their back[23] and knew the value of precise scholarship. The clinical eye of this generation, however, could encourage the congenital editor: a Plummer with his Bede, a Round with his Pipe Rolls, above all the phenomenon of W. H. Stevenson who between 1882 and 1916 staggered under the weight of paper he edited from the records of the boroughs of Nottingham and Gloucester and the eleven volumes of the *Calendars of Close Rolls* through his edition of Asser on Alfred to the index of place-names, his sole relaxation.[24] The early modernists were not far behind with Charles Harding Firth's editions of Lucy Hutchinson, Edmund Ludlow and the Clarke Papers, or J. R. Tanner's edition of Samuel Pepys's correspondence. The modernists, not an available mental category in this period, of necessity courted reticence because the material for editing was still sensitive, as those hoping to edit the queen soon discovered, and because documentary history stopped in 1815 where politics and journalism began. *Their* efforts swung away from texts and towards editing and contributing to the vast collective enterprises that

[21] *A Literary and Biographical History or Dictionary of the English Catholics from 1534*, ed. Joseph Gillow (5 vols., 1885–1902); *Boswell's Life of Johnson*, ed. George Birkbeck Hill (6 vols., Oxford, 1887); *The Life and Letters of Sir George Savile, First Marquis of Halifax*, ed. Helen Foxcroft (2 vols., 1898); *Supplement to the History of my Own Time*, ed. Gilbert Burnet (Oxford, 1902); *The Creevey Papers*, ed. Herbert Maxwell (2 vols., 1904).

[22] *Pleas for the Crown in the County of Gloucester before the Abbot of Reading and his Fellow Justices Itinerant* (1884); *Bracton's Note Book: A Collection of Cases Decided in the King's Courts during the Reign of Henry the Third* (1887).

[23] William Stubbs, *Select Charters and Other Illustrations of English Constitutional History from the Earliest Times to the Reign of Edward I* (Oxford, 1870).

[24] W. H. Stevenson (1858–1924) [ed.], *Calendars of Close Rolls* (11 vols., 1892–1908); *Asser's Life of King Alfred* (1904); etc.

dominated their day either side of the century's turn: the *Dictionary of National Biography* and the *Cambridge Modern History*.

Almost twenty years had gone into the original *DNB* when it was completed in June 1900 though the *Supplements* were still to come.[25] It had begun with an editor, George Smith, and had been carried forward, famously, by Sir Leslie Stephen who lived to see the end; but for the age of Prothero the significant forces would prove to be two assistants who shouldered the main burden in the later years: Solomon Lee, better known to an anti-Semitic society as Sidney Lee, and Albert Pollard who would go on to make the Tudor period his own. Lee contributed 820 articles to the *Dictionary*, frightening enough as a statistic but awesome when one of his articles, required by Queen Victoria's death in January 1901, ran to 94,000 tentative and wavering words. Pollard ran him close with 500 articles over his name. But the commitments ran far beyond the project's editorial team. Firth, for example, wrote over 200 articles for the venture, Tout some 240. The historical community as a whole became sucked into a remarkable success in editorial publishing. The *Cambridge Modern History* began also with an editorial vision, not from a publisher but from the teeming brain of Lord Acton who designed the shape of the project, commissioned many of its authors and wrote the celebrated letter of guidance to contributors, one of the most-quoted texts in modern historiography. He then died without writing a word of the venture he had brought into being.[26] The team left behind to prosecute the project through the eleven volumes that occupied the next ten years faced a back-breaking task of calling in chapters and making them ready for the press. Two of them did the the bulk of the work: Adolphus Ward who had just accepted the Mastership of Peterhouse, Cambridge, and who now had to manage both responsibilities; and the gay *bon-viveur* of Trinity College, Stanley Leathes. Between them these two scholars made regular contributions to the volumes as well as editing the whole. A third editor was today's hero, George Prothero, who had originally been asked to edit the whole thing by himself.[27] But he was in his third year of editing and writing for the *Quarterly*, as well as presiding over the RHS, and could find precious little time to write chapters for the *Modern History*. In fact he

---

[25] The original *DNB*, modelled on the *Biographie universelle* (40 vols., Paris, 1843–63), appeared in sixty-three volumes. A three-volume *Supplement* appeared in 1901 followed by ten chronological supplements from 1912. The project was taken over by Oxford University Press in 1917.

[26] For all the slightness of his contribution, George Prothero was the first of Acton's commissions, made before the venture had even been approved by the Syndics of Cambridge University Press. Acton to Prothero, from Tegernsee, 14 Aug. 1896, Prothero MSS, bundle 1/13.

[27] Prothero diary, 12 Oct. 1901, GWP/1/7.

wrote only for volume IV on the Thirty Years War.[28] Going beyond the editorial team into the contents pages of each volume is a journey into the heartland of English historical writing – some contributors writing several chapters, often far outside their specialisms – and increasingly, as the volumes proceeded, into many centres of European intellectual life for reasons to which we should return.

These interventions had cosmic size and significance but what did all this editorial effort *mean*? Description is easy, after all; explanation comes harder. Why now? Why a generational commitment to the editing, the annotating, the grounding of text? Simple availability has something to say about it. The opening of the Public Record Office in 1857, the work of the Rolls Series and many provincial societies dedicated to publishing local sources, the RHS in which Prothero took so great an interest, the British Academy's foundation in 1902, the Historical Association in 1906: all these developments accelerated the possibility of, as much as the need for, editions of historical material that would be reliable and form the platform for future study. Relatedly, their generation saw itself as working at the *beginning* of something important in historical work. They had read their Macaulay and Stubbs, their Freeeman and their Froude but they raised their eyes and their game: they wanted a more scientific understanding of the past which would place historians on the same level and in the same mental universe as those experimenters and inventors, mathematicians and philosophers who were changing the face of human knowledge in late Victorian Britain.[29] We have to ask our own questions, however, about the character of that knowledge. What the historians wanted, above all, was *facts*, the *motif* of these years. If they revered narrative any longer it was the grinding factuality of Samuel Rawson Gardiner's eighteen volumes that earned their admiration, constructed as they were within the walls of the archive and avoiding what he austerely called 'knowledge which has long been common property'.[30] Editions grounded that knowledge. Besides, narrative was transitory while editions seemed permanent. In a world convinced that all history began with its sources and their 'authorities' (what a significant word), texts formed the building blocks on which everything else must one day rest, part of a building-site where one could

---

[28] 'The Constitutional Struggle in England (1625–40)', IV, 265–85; and 'The First Two Years of the Long Parliament (1640–2)', *ibid.*, 286–301. His reading in history had also declined sharply as his own record of reading suggests in his diary for October 1902 to September 1905: GWP/1/8.

[29] For a survey, see *The Organization of Knowledge in Victorian Britain*, ed. Martin Daunton (Oxford, 2005).

[30] S. R. Gardiner (1829–1902). Vast narrative of English politics and religion between 1603 and 1656 rendered in a series of sub-periods and continued by C. H. Firth. For his austerity about knowledge, see Gardiner to Seeley, 4 Mar. 1887, with a disparagement of 'elegant writing' among the young. Seeley MSS, MS 903/1B/8, University of London Library.

make a difference to the solidity of what was coming to be thought of as a discipline. The Protheros played their small part in the process of change within that discipline and their early careers point to three of its locations, each significant in itself and all interesting for none of them having been English.

II

In 1873 George Prothero, now a Fellow of King's, set off for Bonn in the new German Reich with the intention of studying with Heinrich von Sybel. At this stage of his career Sybel, founder of the *Historische Zeitschrift*, soon to become director of the Prussian state archives, had not yet become part of the infamous trio: Sybel, Treitschke, Meinecke. Prothero's year there seems to have been less than happy and he came away with a critical view of German *Quellenkritik* in which, he thought, procedure did duty for creativity. The Germans were far too ready, he later complained to Oscar Browning, 'to stop at a collection of facts, to let the facts speak for themselves ... One wants a people with more imagination, with less caution, perhaps, to extract the essence from the material they collect, & that is what we ought to do in England.'[31] But the greatest German historian, Leopold von Ranke, had been extracting essence, the true referent for *eigentlich*,[32] for fifty years and was still going strong. It was his work, and not the inflamed writing of Sybel and his colleagues, whose translation into English had been organised by Stubbs: indeed George Prothero would himself translate part of the vast and unfinished *Universal History*.[33] The point is that Germany had established its reputation as the premier historical culture in Europe, soon to be challenged by the claims of Paris; and young scholars from England who felt serious about their work received encouragement to go there to learn the language and assimilate German method. Rowland Prothero followed his brother there a few years later, this time to Darmstadt, to improve his German. So did Headlam-Morley who worked under Treitschke and Delbrück in Berlin. Charles Harding Firth went, too, with portentous consequences a quarter of a century later when, as the new Regius Professor of Modern History at Oxford, he tried to impose on recalcitrant colleagues the advantages of German *Hilfswissenschaften* as ancillary tools for the historical research

---

[31] G. W. Prothero to Oscar Browning, 25 Mar. n.y., Browning MSS, i/Prothero, King's College, Cambridge.

[32] Ranke's ambition to represent the past *wie es eigentlich gewesen* has been consistently mistranslated 'as it actually was', though in 1825 the word 'eigentlich' meant something closer to 'essentially'. See G. G. Iggers's seminal article 'The Image of Ranke in American and German Historical Thought', *History and Theory*, 2 (1962), 17–40.

[33] Leopold von Ranke, *The Oldest Historical Group of Nations and the Greeks*, trans. G. W. Prothero (1884).

that he believed Oxford students should carry out.[34] An unimpressed Charles Oman soon put a stop to that if only through his knack of pronouncing *Hilfswissenschaften* to make them sound like a German sewage system.[35]

Yet in a sense Firth's battle was won though he died believing himself defeated. Curriculum reform had made some difference in the adoption of the special subject even if Belgium's other famous historian, Paul Fredericq, had found fault with English provision in his probing inspection in the early 1880s.[36] The English professoriate could not approach the German in number and quality, perhaps; but the size and range of the history schools in Oxford, Cambridge and Tout's Manchester broadcast a developing confidence by turn of century.[37] The real indicator of German success might be found in two particular events all the same: the founding of the *English Historical Review (EHR)* in 1886 on lines plainly reflecting the German model; and the appointment to Cambridge's Regius Chair of Modern History in 1895 of the man whose impenetrable article on 'German Schools of History' had launched the first number of the *EHR*[38] and who could claim to be Britain's most cosmopolitan, as well as most knowledgeable, student of history. *EHR*'s origins are too well known to rehearse here, though we might reasonably resist the idea that the founders were moved by 'exclusiveness': they merely held a view of factuality that outlawed imprecision, a trait shared by George Prothero, as we shall see in a moment.[39] Well established by 1900, the journal had become driven, through the later years of Mandell Creighton's editorship, by one of the most attractive and impressive men of his generation,

[34] C. H. Firth, *The Historical Teaching of History* (Oxford, 1904). This was the famous inaugural lecture for whose assertions and tone he was later made to apologise.

[35] When training young men in 'general knowledge of history', Oman alleged, 'the so-called "study of methods of investigation", and all the *Hilfswissenschaften* will be of comparatively little use'. Charles Oman, *Inaugural Lecture on the Study of History: Delivered on Wednesday, February 7, 1906* (Oxford, 1906), 20.

[36] Paul Fredericq, *L'enseignement supérieure de l'histoire: notes et impressions de voyage* (Ghent and Paris, 1899). For a recent study of him, see Jo Tollebeek, *Fredericq & Zonen: een antropologie van de moderne geschiedwetenschap* (Amsterdam, 2008).

[37] See Peter Slee, *Learning and a Liberal Education: The Study of Modern History in the Universities of Oxford, Cambridge and Manchester 1800–1914* (Manchester, 1986); Reba Soffer, *Discipline and Power: The University, History and the Making of an English Elite 1870–1930* (Stanford, 1994), and *History, Historians, and Conservatism in Britain and America: The Great War to Thatcher and Reagan* (Oxford, 2009); Michael Bentley, 'The Evolution and Dissemination of Historical Knowledge', in *The Organization of Knowledge*, ed. Daunton, 173–98.

[38] Lord Acton, 'German Schools of History', *English Historical Review*, 1 (1886), 7–42.

[39] Alan Kadish, 'Scholarly Exclusiveness and the Foundation of the "English Historical Review"', *Historical Research*, 61 (1988), 183–98. Cf. R. L. Poole, 'The Beginnings of the "English Historical Review"', *English Historical Review*, 36 (1921), 1–4; and Doris Goldstein, 'The Origins and Early Years of the "English Historical Review"', *English Historical Review*, 101 (1986), 6–19.

Reginald Lane Poole, who alone edited seventy-nine issues of *EHR* when teaching fifteen hours of tutorials and delivering six lectures every week in term and reading history in his five European languages or turning for relaxation to his studies in Latin, Greek, Hebrew and Arabic.[40]

George Prothero, meanwhile, had reason to resent Lord Acton's intrusion: he had nursed some hopes, in the reticence of his diary, that he himself might be appointed to the Regius Chair, if only as a Stop-Oscar-Browning candidate.[41] Acton's appointment brought none the less a sense that historical *thought* had arrived at the pinnacle of the profession. Acton's greatest critic and greatest supporter, Herbert Butterfield, reflected in 1954 that Acton's presence marked a turning tide and his premature death an ebbing one. '[H]e stands in 1900', Butterfield said in his Wiles Lectures, 'on the crest of what might be called a great wave of historical thinking; and perhaps it is not going too far to say that the wave has been receding ever since'.[42] Acton's illness and death brought a lesser man into the chair in J. B. Bury with his over-egged inaugural lecture hailing historical science 'no less and no more'.[43] Yet, again, Bury's cause needed no manifesto by 1902: it had become implicit in the way a younger generation thought about history and how to prosecute it.

Had Prothero's dream of the Regius Chair come to fruition he would have had to return to England from our second distant location. For in 1894 the University of Edinburgh had announced a new chair in history and Prothero decided to put forward his name. Why he wanted it remains unclear. Perhaps he felt that his Cambridge career had lost impetus; he had certainly associated himself with Seeley's reforms and turned into a young Turk. He may have felt that a fresh start would reinvigorate him pedagogically – he confessed to growing 'rather tired of going over the same subject so often'[44] – or at least enliven his *curriculum vitae*. There was an inside candidate in Peter Hume Brown, biographer of George Buchanan, author of a textbook on early modern Scotland

[40] R. L. Poole (1857–1939), *Chronicles and Annals* (Oxford, 1926), *Studies in Chronology and History* (Oxford, 1934), etc. Cf. G. N. Clark's introduction to Poole, 'The Origins of the "English Historical Review"', *English Historical Review*, 36 (1921), 1–4 at 1, and Poole to Round, 11 Apr. 1894, Round MSS, IHR 924 Round, 664.

[41] Prothero diary, 19 Apr. 1895. Acton and Bryce had learned from Creighton that Lord Rosebery had no intention of moving Prothero from Edinburgh so soon after his appointment.

[42] Herbert Butterfield, *Man on his Past* (1955), 97.

[43] J. B. Bury, *An Inaugural Lecture Delivered in the Divinity School, Cambridge, on January 26, 1903* (Cambridge, 1903). Prothero could not suppress his disappointment at being overlooked and felt 'rather bad about it all week', following the announcement: Prothero diary, 7 Dec. 1902, GWP/1/8.

[44] Prothero diary, 14 Oct. 1890, GWP/1/5.

and about to complete a life of John Knox.[45] Maybe these interests
suggested a temperament better fitted to Edinburgh's cultural climate.
But if Prothero, once appointed, had hoped for a better life, then those
hopes soon darkened in that first, dark winter. He tried to stay cheerful.
'Eight lectures a week', he told Seeley in December, 'give me plenty
of employment when added to the monthly exam[inatio]ns which the
classes have to go through.'[46] Optimism waned when he came to see
himself as nothing more than a machine for 'grinding out lectures'
and having no time to read or think,[47] which is doubtless why, when
his brother relinquished the editorship of the *Quarterly Review* in 1899,
Prothero responded positively to the chance of succeeding him.[48] His
own unhappiness in Edinburgh, fuelled by the greater sadness of his
wife, should not blind us, all the same, to the burgeoning significance
of Scottish historical culture[49] and its professionalisation within British
historiography as a whole. Just as Prothero moved to the Edinburgh
Chair, another Englishman, Richard Lodge, took the Chair of Modern
History, likewise newly created, at Glasgow; he then succeeded Prothero at
Edinburgh where he remained happily for a quarter of a century. Chairs
specialising in Scottish history then came into being in both Glasgow
and Edinburgh within a few years.[50] Or consider the less metropolitan
perspective offered by the Carlyles – Robert and Alexander – sons of the
manse from Brechin who witnessed to that fusion of experience between
Scotland and the Empire, about which John MacKenzie has reminded
us, before their great work on medieval political thought appeared in
the second half of their lives.[51] The Bryces, too, had highland roots and

[45] Peter Hume-Brown (1849–1918). He succeeded in his professorial ambitions in 1901
when appointed to the Sir William Fraser Chair at Edinburgh. 'A pleasant little man', said
Prothero in his patronising way, '& seems to bear me no grudge.' Prothero diary, 16 Jan.
1895, GWP/1/6.
[46] G. W. Prothero to Seeley, Seeley MS 903/1B/12, University of London Library.
[47] Prothero's diary, quoted in Crawley, 'George Prothero and his Circle', 109. It cannot
have enhanced *joie de vivre* that he also recorded '[i]ndigestion, cold, slight tendency to
giddiness sometimes, & a fit of rheumatism'. Prothero diary, 12 Oct. 1894, GWP/1/6. Writing his inaugural lecture – 'frightfully commonplace stuff . . . and not convincing either' –
perhaps deepened the gloom: *ibid.*, 9 Oct. For the published version, see *Why Should We
Learn History? An Inaugural Lecture Delivered at Edinburgh, 16th October 1894* (Edinburgh, 1894).
[48] He was not the first choice, even of own brother. Prothero diary, 5 Nov. 1898, GWP/1/7.
[49] Edinburgh was significantly the first institution – 'très florisante' – to be visited by Paul
Fredericq on his British tour: *L'enseignement supérieure de l'histoire*, 5.
[50] Edinburgh (1901), Glasgow (1913). Hume Brown's appointment to the former led only,
however, to 'the persistence of an older constitutional idiom'. See Colin Kidd, '*The Strange
Death of Scottish History* Revisited: Constructions of the Past in Scotland, c.1790–1914', *Scottish
Historical Review*, 76 (1997), 86–102 at 102.
[51] A. J. and R. W. Carlyle, *A History of Mediaeval Political Theory in the West* (6 vols., 1903–36).
See John M. MacKenzie, *Empires of Nature and the Nature of Empires: Imperialism, Scotland and the
Environment* (East Linton, 1997).

James might have been a happier man if they had remained attached there; but the family uprooted to Northern Ireland and the historian of American democracy discovered himself to be that formidable thing, an Ulster Presbyterian.[52] Ireland and Wales meanwhile deserve more than a footnote to the same story. When Bury arrived in Cambridge he did so from Trinity College, Dublin, and it was at the Queen's University, Belfast, that Maurice Powicke occupied his first chair before coming to Tout's Manchester. And would Tout's Manchester have become what it was without the crucial three years that Tout had spent at St David's College, Lampeter, where he learned how to teach? The impact of Bangor on H. W. C. Davis admittedly turned out harder to document. 'I know that ninety per cent of my pupils are fools', he wailed to the Warden of All Souls, 'but I always have the hope that with patience I may discover a genius among the other ten'.[53] He ran out of patience within the year and returned to Oxford.

But let us follow Prothero to Edinburgh and see what he was doing there as a microcosm of his age. We can do that because he left a detailed *Nachlass* of his lectures and reading from which a fascinating image focuses of how history was taught to undergraduates in the late 1890s. Prothero lectured on everything from the Greeks to the nineteenth century, with British coverage one year and European the next. He took close notes from what he still called 'authorities', many of which were general texts – Macaulay, J. R. Green, Freeman and so on – but also German texts: Below, Maurer, Eichhorn, Gfroerer.[54] He then made a time-line of parallel events across territory or category. The lectures themselves were written in almost unintelligible abbreviation but seem to have been mostly read out from his pencilled text. What they contained was information arranged in chronological order, not out of convenience but on principle. He told his audience this at the beginning of some lectures on Russian history in remarks that would have struck him as obvious:

> History is a study or science of the sequence of events. Thus *chronological order* is essential to history & the purpose of history is to relate and explain that chronological order, to say what the events were, and why this event followed and did not precede that, and why it was this event and not some other.[55]

One would have to go a long way to find a better adumbration of *l'histoire événementielle* as a positively charged doctrine, from a reader, incidentally,

[52] James Bryce (1838–1922), *The Holy Roman Empire* (Oxford, 1964 and many editions); *The American Commonwealth* (1888), etc.

[53] Davis to Anson, 1 Apr. 1897, Anson MSS 101.

[54] His Edinburgh material contains, for example, a catalogue from Oscar Schack of Leipzig in 1893 with substantial marginalia from Prothero's pen. Dk.5.59

[55] 'Lectures on the History of the Tsars', Prothero collection, Dk.5.44, University of Edinburgh Special Collections.

of Seignobos;[56] it speaks volumes for the epistemology, as well as the pedagogy, of Prothero's generation. The dependence on chronological knowledge also strikes up from his examination papers which we also have and which we should all assuredly fail, through ignorance in my case, through a failure to acquire speed-writing in yours. General British History, 19 March 1895. Two Hours. Answer not more than seven questions. Question 4: Write a short life of Clive or Wolfe. Question 7: Compare the positions of Walpole, Lord North and William Pitt as Prime Ministers. One begins to see where Sellar and Yeatman found their material.[57] February 1896: What do you know of the Statute of Gloucester, the Statute of Praemunire, Sir John Falstaff, the Treaty of Pecquigni, the Star Chamber? Behind the humour of our world lies distance from his and behind the distance a parallel universe of assumption about the nature of our subject.

In our own current context of the Anglo-American Conference of Historians it is a pleasure as much as a requirement to place beside the German and the Scottish a third historical culture of escalating importance as the nineteenth century became the twentieth. George Prothero again leads us there for in 1910 he went to deliver a course of twenty-eight lectures at Harvard on 'The Making of the British Empire', anticipating the visits of Harold Temperley in 1913 and Albert Pollard in the following year. The visit mattered to Prothero in opening lines of contact with senior figures in the American historical establishment, as we shall see in thinking about the impact of the war in 1914. But it also symbolised an emerging congruence. The new graduate schools at Johns Hopkins and Columbia had now produced a generation of home-trained scholars, some of whom directed their attention at British history. An older one had brought its expertise to bear on traditional British concerns: the empire and sea-power with Alfred Thayer Mahon. But, in the generations of Charles Gross, James Baldwin and C. H. McIlwain, we see a turn to British constitutional history that would make a fundamental contribution to its direction as a reverse side of what Peter Novick called American Anglo-Saxonism[58] and deserves a lecture to itself. One important export we might note from the British side was the Scot, Morse Stephens, a future president of the American Historical Association who emigrated

---

[56] For his lectures on modern European history, Prothero lists among his authorities Charles Seignobos, *Histoire politique de l'Europe contemporaine* (Paris, 1897). Edinburgh collection, Dk.5.45. Prothero met the author after the war.

[57] *1066 and All That* (1930).

[58] See Michael Bentley, *Modernizing England's Past: English Historiography in the Age of Modernism 1870–1970* (Cambridge, 2005), 34–6, and Peter Novick, *That Noble Dream: The 'Objectivity Question' and the American Historical Profession* (Cambridge, 1988).

to the US in 1894 and assumed an active historical career, first at Cornell and then for many years at Berkeley.

III

Where, then, in this widening gyre of historical sites and concerns do we find an impact in the nature of the writing itself? One might expect a new thrust towards the history of Germany and France, for example, but the expectation seems only patchily satisfied, as Professor Robert Evans reminded us in his recent Creighton Lecture.[59] Outside Adolphus Ward for whom Germany was home, that country's history, so far as British historians were concerned, remained in the hands of military men such as G. B. Malleson or those with German experience as in a James Headlam-Morley.[60] France hardly fared better. The ecclesiastical historian W. H. Jervis (*né* Pearson) contributed a general history; Louise Creighton, wife of Mandell, included a volume on France among her historical primers for the young.[61] Acton's lectures on the French Revolution came out posthumously in 1910. Yet the anniversaries of Oliver Cromwell and King Alfred came closer to home in the *fin de siècle* than had the centenary of the Revolution in 1889.[62] If anything the balance of power between Britain and the Continent swung the other way, as in the American case, with Frenchmen such as Charles Petit-Dutaillis, Charles Bémont and the young Elie Halévy taking an interest in British history and Germans making an impact on, say, eighteenth- century studies of British politics in the manner of Wolfgang Michael and Albert von Ruville.[63] An interesting project consists in counting how many essays on European or extra-European subjects for the *Cambridge Modern History* were written by British authors: frequent enough in the early volumes but scarcer by volume

---

[59] R. J. W. Evans, 'The Creighton Century: British Historians and Europe, 1907–2007', *Historical Research*, 82 (2009), 320–39 esp. 323–4, 326–7. For a more optimistic reading of a later period, see Richard J. Evans, *Cosmopolitan Islanders: British Historians and the European Continent* (Cambridge, 2009).

[60] G. B. Malleson, *The Refounding of the German Empire, 1848–71* (1893); James Headlam-Morley, *Bismarck and the Foundation of the German Empire* (1899).

[61] W. H. Jervis, *A History of France from the Earliest Times to the Fall of the Second Empire in 1870* (1902); Louise Creighton, *A First History of France* (1893).

[62] On these tendencies see Michael Bentley, 'Shape and Pattern in British Historiography, 1815–1914', in volume IV of *The Oxford History of Historical Writing*, ed. Daniel Woolf (5 vols., forthcoming, 2010–). The Cromwell and Alfred centenaries are considered respectively in Blair Worden, *Roundhead Reputations: The English Civil War and the Passions of Posterity* (2001); and Paul Readman, 'The Place of the Past in English Culture', *Past and Present*, 186 (2005), 147–99.

[63] Charles Petit-Dutaillis, *Studies and Notes Supplementary to Stubbs's Constitutional History* (Manchester 1908); *Chartes des libertés anglaises 1100–1305*, ed. Charles Bémont (Paris, 1892); Wolfgang Michael, *Englische Geschichte im achtzehnten Jahrhundert* (5 vols., Hamburg, 1896–1955); Albert von Ruville, *William Pitt, Graf von Chatham* (Stuttgart, 1905).

VI.[64] George Prothero had already borne witness to the problem in his final presidential address to the RHS in 1904. 'We in England', he said, 'are badly off for foreign histories in general – where are we to look for an adequate history of France or Germany or Italy or Spain or Russia, written in England for English readers and embodying the results of recent research?'[65]

Within English constitutional culture, meanwhile, it is important to locate absence as much as presence and in the age of Prothero one can hear four separate forms of silence. England possessed neither a Lamprecht nor yet a body professionally aspirant *Jungrankianer* to fret about one; so the bitterness of argument over method that disfigured German universities made virtually no impact in Britain outside the new field of economics, apart from raised eyebrows at the inaugural lectures of Bury and Firth.[66] England possessed, second, no Berr or Bloch or Febvre; and the proto-*annalistes* made no appearance across the Channel. England *did* have, for a time, Charles Beard;[67] but the forces that would take American academia in the direction of Paris after 1903 failed, thirdly, to generate in England. And finally where is the voice of women in this masculine and imperial age? John Richard Green's protégée, Kate Norgate (1853–1935), had won a reputation as a defender of Freeman against his detractors but strongest among female whispers at turn of century was that of Mary Bateson (1865–1906) of Newnham College, Cambridge, who achieved professional success through qualities of intellect but also through being a Bateson, daughter of the Master of St John's College and related through her elder sister to the Heitlands. Hers was a minority voice in this period, for all her distinction, and a brain haemorrhage swept even that away when she died at the age of forty-one

[64] The trend towards European authorship is especially marked in vol. VI on *The Eighteenth Century*, vol. IX on *Napoleon* and vol. X on *The Restoration*.

[65] G. W. Prothero, 'Presidential Address', *Transactions of the Royal Historical Society*, new series, 18 (1904), 12. Of course Bernard Pares would make his own impact on the Russian case within a few years.

[66] I have developed this comparative perspective in an essay, 'Historians Delivering Untheorized Truth: The Turn to Science', in *The Sage Handbook of Historical Theory*, ed. Sarah Foot and Nancy Partner (forthcoming, *c.* 2011). For the European perspective see Georg Iggers, 'The "Methodenstreit" in International Perspective. The Reorientation of Historical Studies at the Turn from the Nineteenth to the Twentieth Century', *Storia della storiografia*, 6 (1984), 21–32; and Lutz Raphael, 'Historikerkontroversen im Spannungsfeld zwischen Berufshabitus, Fächerkonkurenz und sozialen Deutungsmustern: Lamprechtstreit und französicher Methodenstreit der Jahrhundertwende in vergleichender Perspektive', *Historische Zeitschrift*, 251 (1990), 325–63.

[67] Charles Austin Beard (1874–1948). He spent two years based in Oxford, after graduation from DePauw University, and helped to found Ruskin Hall, forerunner of Ruskin College.

in the same year as Maitland.[68] It would be the next generation in which the voice of women gathered strength.[69]

It is all too easy, on the other hand, to amplify silences by starting in the wrong place, because in at least one respect Britain had, as we have seen, been feeling the weight of German historical culture for some years, not only in its constitutionalism but also in a new economic history that found a considerable audience in the country whose Industrial Revolution came first. The tradition says that the school of National Economy in Germany – principally List, Roscher, Schmoller, Knies and Hildebrand – became a model for economic historians in Britain.[70] Looking back on these currents of thought thirty years later, R. H. Tawney still thought them fundamental.[71] Whatever the inspiration, from the time of Arnold Toynbee's lectures on the Industrial Revolution published in 1884,[72] the concerns of economic history moved away from the wings of the national stage. They gained currency through the work of William Cunningham at Cambridge, William Ashley, in Toronto after 1888 but an habitué of Oxford and Göttingen, and a young Fellow of King's College, Cambridge, called John Clapham who fought a bitter war with colleagues to insist on the teaching of economic history within the Cambridge syllabus and who first professed it in 1928.[73]

This mode of working had its hard and technical side: some found it rebarbative. But there existed too a long tradition of humanist scholarship in economic thought, one running from Cobbett through Ruskin and Hobson and into a generation that voiced anxieties about modern capitalism and its effects on ordinary people unprotected by birth or private means. Here a junction existed between economic critique and a liberal, or at least social-democratic politics. It had an imperial wing, unsurprisingly in these years of the Boer War, Joseph Chamberlain's campaign for imperial preference in commercial policy and the benefactions of Rhodes and Beit establishing imperial history

---

[68] Mary Bateson (1865–1906). Prolific editor of medieval texts. Between 1890 and her death, according to her entry in the *Oxford Dictionary f National Biography*, she contibuted an article to *EHR* virtually every year.

[69] For an account of female emergence in the university system, see Bonnie G. Smith, *The Gender of History: Men, Women and Historical Practice* (Cambridge, MA, 2000); and for a suggestive study of a British example, Maxine Berg, *A Woman in History: Eileen Power 1889–1940* (Cambridge, 1996). A talented further exemplar, Caroline Skeel (1872–1951), lacks a biography.

[70] For an overview see Alun Kadish, *Historians, Economists and Economic History* (1989).

[71] R. H. Tawney, 'The Study of Economic History', *Economica*, 13 (1933), 1–21 at 5.

[72] Arnold Toynbee, *Lectures on the Industrial Revolution in England: Popular Addresses, Notes and Other Fragments* (1884).

[73] Sir William Ashley (1860–1927), *Introduction to Economic History and Theory* (1888); Sir John Clapham (1873–1946), *An Economic History of Modern Britain* (3 vols., 1926–38). For Cunningham, see n. 12.

securely if on a fairly narrow base. It also had a rural wing occupied by those who believed that urbanisation and enclosure of open fields had destroyed much quality of life for the rural poor in the early years of the nineteenth century. As the Great Depression, mythical or not, became a firm impression in the 1890s, the idea of an historical countryside worth reviving for a modern readership held an obvious attraction to authors and one of them was Rowland Prothero.

We left him trying to cope with incipient blindness in the early 1880s. He did so in a remarkable way. Gathering old clothes and boots and a little money, he set off to walk the length and breadth of France, living cheaply and resting his eyes on the French landscape, its farms and fields. When he returned with vision partially restored he decided to try his hand at writing for a living and contributed, among many other pieces, some articles to the *Manchester Guardian* on the rural depression. He had always taken an interest in farming since Whippingham days – the rectory had a bit of land attached to it – but on the cusp of the new century his life changed forever when the duke of Bedford invited him to become his land agent at a salary five times that paid by the *Quarterly* with a pension of a thousand a year and the run of and free accommodation in five country houses. The post gave him unparalleled access to farming practice and blended with a culture of rural commentary from Frederic Seebohm's influential meditation on *The Village Community* to an expanding documentary literature;[74] and as interest slid towards expertise he expanded an earlier manuscript into the book with which I began, *English Farming Past and Present* (1912). By that time he had competition, not least from a young female voice. In 1895, whilst Prothero was deep in writing and editing, a female examination candidate of Lady Margaret Hall in Oxford topped the Greats' class list in her year and met along the way Lawrence Hammond. The marriage of Barbara Bradby and Hammond produced one of those Edwardian powerhouses of writing alongside the Webbs and the Chesterbelloc. Their first major work, *The Village Labourer* (1911), a scream against the evils of enclosure, may stand with Prothero's blander survey of rural life. In its own way, and against the current of a far more powerful political, constitutional and legal historiography, the age of Prothero had begun a peculiarly English form of social history.

Rowland's excitements meant that when George Prothero accepted the presidency of the RHS in 1901, succeeding Adolphus Ward, he was already editing the *Quarterly* and hoping to ride both horses. His direction at the RHS was more eirenic than revolutionary but he did move forward

---

[74] Frederic Seebohm, *The English Village Community Examined in its Relations to the Manorial and Tribal Systems and to the Common or Open-Field System of Husbandry: An Essay in Economic History* (1884). For documentary literature see Richard Jefferies, *Hodge and his Masters* (1880), and George Bourne [*sc.* Sturt], *Change in the Village* (1912).

one idea for which he has been blessed by those who benefited and damned by those who had to carry it out. He thought it would be nice if there were to be an RHS Bibliography of British history,[75] a vast engine of misery under whose pistons have since perished many good men and women.[76] But in honesty he had little time for writing any history himself and his many articles for the *Quarterly* were about other things. In fact George Prothero had begun to drift, like his brother, towards becoming a public figure known to those who controlled the state, once it became clear that he would not be elected provost of King's in 1905 – another disappointment.[77] When the Master of the Rolls needed a new member for an advisory committee on the publication of public records in 1912, he turned to Prothero who by then had become a man known to club-room and west-end society.[78] The deepening crisis over German nationalism Prothero already knew well from his days with Sybel; and his evaluation of the German character turned into a harsher form of Germanophobia. Rowland, for his part, entered the House of Commons at a by-election in 1914 just as his old tennis partner at Balliol was declaring that the lights were going out all over Europe. Their own lights were about to do the same. Once sportsmen together, Rowland Prothero and Edward Grey went blind together.

IV

The war terminated the age of Prothero but it would have terminated anyway because its brightest lights were now in their sixties and presiding over the historical work of new dynasties. To R. L. Poole, father of Austin, one should now add a younger generation – that of H. W. C. Davis, father of Ralph, of Bernard Pares father of Richard, of Robert Seton-Watson, father of Hugh, of Albert Pollard of this College, UCL, of H. A. L. Fisher, of Maurice Powicke, of Harold Temperley, of the younger Toynbee and Lewis Namier born within a year of one another. London's hosting of the then International Congress of Historical Sciences in 1913 under the presidency of James Bryce and the organising energy of Harold Temperley presented an opportunity for much of this talent,

---

[75] G. W. Prothero, 'Presidential Address', *Transaction of the Royal Historical Society*, new series, 17 (1903), ix–xxxiv.

[76] For a more balanced judgment see Ian Archer's account of the project and its history available at www.history.ac.uk/makinghistory/resources/articles/RHSB.html.

[77] An agonised narrative appears in the diary through March 1905. He only allowed his name to go forward at the last minute, again because of the reluctance of his wife to move to Cambridge but also because he feared that her health would not tolerate the public life associated with a Head of House. 'I shall regret it as long as I live' (27 Mar.). They elected Montague James.

[78] H. Cozens-Hardy to George Prothero, 29 Nov. 1912, Prothero MSS, bundle 4.

including Prothero's, to find a role.[79] But war with the Central Powers supplied a final occasion and duty to rally to the support of their own state. Rarely does one read a biography of an historian from these generations without watching its subject disappear into the maw of Whitehall after 1914 to work in intelligence or propaganda or supply expert knowledge of little-known territories. For George Prothero it brought a late but real recognition. He turned his facile pen against Berlin in a series of powerful broadsides presenting the British case for resistance and deploying historical knowledge as his most effective weapon.[80] Eighteenth-century connecton came into its own as Prothero maintained a huge correspondence with overseas countries, especially the United States. Not every historian had their war relieved by letters from inside the Washington embassy. Still fewer received letters beginning 'Dear Uncle George'.[81] But Prothero's writ ran far beyond family, thanks to his Harvard visit, in an extensive interchange with Lawrence Lowell, Charles Elliott and especially the historian of Europe, Roger B. Merriman. Historians in France, meanwhile, kept him abreast of events there, especially Henri Omont who, bunkered in the Bibliothèque Nationale, took a magnificently archival view of the carnage on the Western Front in 1915. '[H]euresement les vieux manuscrits de Rheims, Soisson et Arras ont pu être mis en sureté.' Meanwhile at home connection could oil wheels which might otherwise jam. Witness the delicious *majesté* of Victoria, Lady Wemyss, who was married to the Admiralty and used its writing-paper as her own.

Dear Mr. Prothero,

I spoke to my husband about your projected visit to the Fleet and I am sure he will do everything to have matters facilitated for you. . .[82]

So, when the new historical section of the Foreign Office needed an impresario to guide their pamphlets on the peace, Prothero's status as a public figure made him an obvious choice. Had the notorious 'flu' not got him in 1919 he would have been in the thick of things at Versailles as were so many of his historical colleagues declaiming to deaf ears what they ought to learn from the lessons of the Congress of Vienna a century before.[83] The end of the war brought the end for both Protheros, too,

[79] For the London Congress, see K.-D. Erdmann, *Die Ökumene der Historiker: Geschichte des Internationalen Historikerkongresse und des Comité Internationale des Sciences Historiques* (Göttingen, 1987), 86–96.

[80] E.g. *Our Duty and Our Interest in the War* (1914); *German Policy before the War* (1916); *A Lasting Peace* (1917).

[81] Thomas Spring-Rice to Prothero, 30 Mar. 1916, Prothero MSS IV/1.

[82] Lady Wemyss to Prothero, 2 Sept. 1918, Prothero MSS, with bundle 4.

[83] Harold Temperley, Charles Webster and Harold Nicolson were cases in point.

and history would make its next moves in different hands but ones which their generation had trained.

Standing back from these two generations it becomes a simple matter to see them as part of a process, as Charles Crawley did when he looked back to his uncle's 'typify[ing] the process of transition among English historians from the amateur to the professional'.[84] We have a similar implication in the common view that the age represents a transition from whig history to something better. I have quarrelled with this latter judgement in a recent book and shall not repeat that quarrel here. If I have to differ from Crawley's view let me at least differ from his use of a poisonous notion. No age is 'transitional' – a word we might profitably delete from our lexicon. George Prothero had translated Ranke and would have known the great man's mantra *jede Epoche ist unmittelbar zu Gott*, best rendered into English by the Augustinian thought that every age is equidistant from eternity. The period of Maitland and Firth and Tout and Poole was not some groping apprenticeship, trying to master the basics of modernisation theory. It behoves us to consider it in its own terms as an exciting and accomplished moment in British historiography. The age had its silences, its failures, as does ours. It committed itself to a vision of knowledge that we may feel it necessary to question and revise. It brought to bear an unconscious apparatus of criticism and social observation about empire and race and class that feels strange and sometimes uncomfortable to us. But it also broadcast an image of intelligence, humanity and above all service that can teach resonantly to an over-professionalised, celebrity-ridden historical culture that permits itself various styles of stupidity as the assumed cost of disinterest, and imposes forms of self-harm as an assumed requirement of intellectual hygiene. It is not in despite of its own terms but rather because of them that a later, very different historical community might wish to reconsider the age of Prothero. Those historians who comprised it – their perspectives, their diligence, their narratives, their values, for all their blind-spots and shortened horizons – those historians merit and more than merit our collective recall.

---

[84] Crawley, 'George Prothero and his Circle', 119.

ROYAL HISTORICAL SOCIETY
REPORT OF COUNCIL
SESSION 2009 – 2010

Officers and Council

- At the Anniversary Meeting on 27 November 2009 the Officers of the Society were re-elected.
- The Vice-Presidents retiring under By-law XVII were Professor A Curry and Dr A Foster. Professor M C Finn, BA, PhD and Professor P Mandler, BA, AM, PhD were elected to replace them.
- The Members of Council retiring under By-law XX were Professor P G Burgess, Professor S Foot and Professor G Stone. Professor S M Dixon, BA, PhD, Professor K C Fincham, MA, PhD and Dr J J Lewis, BA, PhD were elected in their place.
- The Society's administrative staff consists of Sue Carr, Executive Secretary and Melanie Ransom, Administrative Secretary.
- Kingston Smith were re-appointed auditors for the year 2009–2010 under By-law XXXIX.
- Brewin Dolphin Securities were re-appointed to manage the Society's investment funds.

Activities of the Society during the year

The Annual Report contains individual reports of the activities of the seven Committees which support the work of Council – Research Policy, Teaching Policy, General Purposes, Publications, Finance, Membership and Research Support – and the remarks which now follow are a preface to these more detailed reports.

Throughout the year the Society has maintained its prominent role in defending and advancing the interests of the discipline and the profession.

A major concern of Council through the year has been the impact of government's attitude towards academic research and teaching, as manifested in spending decisions and prescriptions for the future Research Excellence Framework (REF). As noted last year, the government's research funding strategy, announced in April 2009, protected science funding and seriously disadvantaged some high-scoring History Departments and their institutions. In 2009–10 we have seen individual institutions' reactions to the difficult financial situation, including threats to posts in history and related disciplines, and we can expect further developments in 2010–11. Council takes this situation very seriously, especially where it appears to endanger the broad study of history, research-led teaching, and the career development of young historians, and the President has written publicly as well as privately in defence of these values.

The shape of the future REF remains an important topic, though the date and criteria have remained uncertain for most of the year, thanks to the long-expected general election in May 2010 and the different pre-election statements and promises of the parties. Officers and Council members have continued to contribute to discussions and debates on the subject, including a round-table session at the North American Conference on British Studies in Louisville, Kentucky, in November 2009, and meetings at the British Academy. The Society submitted a formal response to HEFCE's consultation over the REF, supporting the ongoing primacy of peer review, and suggesting recalibration of the assessment criteria to give greater weight to peer review and research environment as opposed to impact. The Society also strongly recommended postponing the exercise. While the final criteria have yet to be published (pilot studies are still under way), the date of the REF has now been set for 2014 (submissions in 2013), and the Society is responding to the call for nominations of panel members and sub-panel chairs. The Honorary Secretary and Ms Joanna Innes, Vice-President and Chair of the Research Policy Committee, attended a forum for representatives of learned societies and subject associations at the British Academy in May, focusing on the needs and contributions of the humanities and social science research base in the context of the next government spending review. The President attended the launch of the British Academy's report, *Past, present and future, the Public Value of the Humanities and Social Sciences*, drawing on consultations across the sector, in June.

The Society is maintaining a range of contacts with the AHRC. The Honorary Secretary attended a meeting with Rick Rylance, Director of the AHRC, organised by AHUG (Arts and Humanities User Group), in March 2010. The President attended a meeting with the AHRC and subject assocations in June, at which Impact and future research funding were discussed, and the AHRC's new strategic areas were outlined. He attended a further meeting on Public Engagement in the Arts and Humanities, funded by the AHRC and put on by the National Co-ordinating Committee for Public Engagement, also in June. The Society's meetings with The National Archives in July and September 2009 over proposed cuts at TNA resulted in agreement to set up a Strategic Academic Stakeholders' Forum to facilitate communication between the historical research community and senior management at TNA, of which the President is a member. This forum met in February 2010, but has now been overtaken by the proposal from the Lord Chancellor's Advisory Council on National Records and Archives to constitute a sub-committee to focus on historical manuscripts and academic research. Membership of this sub-committee has yet to be announced, but the Society will press for representation. Collaboration with TNA also continues in the form of the Gerald Aylmer seminar, held this year on 21 April at UCL, on the theme 'Diverse Histories – One Archive'. A full day of talks, discussion and 'interactive activities', chaired by Baroness Lola Young, explored the problems of identifying sources for diverse histories and their archival preservation and cataloguing. The President and members of Council held a positive meeting with senior management at the British Library in May, at which planned reorganisation there was explained and discussed, and further meetings and contacts proposed. The Honorary Secretary attended a symposium for local history and local record-publishing societies organised by the Victoria County History in May.

The online Bibliography of British and Irish History, a partnership with the Institute of Historical Research and Brepols, was successfully launched on a subscription basis 1 January 2010. The termination of the free service is regretted by Council, especially its impact on the independent researcher, but the take-up of subscriptions has been very encouraging. In accordance with the agreement with our partners, the new honorary post of Academic Editor of the BBIH will be created and an appointment made with effect from 2011.

Council is keenly aware of the importance of communicating with Fellows and Members of the Society and responding to their concerns and suggestions. In autumn 2009, a questionnaire concerning the full range of the Society's activities was circulated to the membership. The President reported on the findings in the May Newsletter. Respondents were appreciative of the work of the Society, and noted the need for a strong voice for history in present times. They also stressed the Society's role as a national body, and the importance of visits and contacts outside south-east England. Perhaps surprisingly, the extent of the Society's support for young researchers was not always well-known or taken up. A number of ideas are now being taken forward, including experimenting with podcasting the Society's lectures, and making more and better use of the Society's website for communications. Council also supports moves to increase Membership of the Society among early career researchers, by offering a reduced rate for postgraduate research students. Further important developments at the operational level include the decision to hold a joint meeting of Research Policy and Teaching Policy Committees once a year, and to increase the number of committees on which individual Councillors serve.

Officers and members of Council made a very successful visit to Glasgow Caledonian University on behalf of the Society on 14 April, on the occasion of a symposium organised by The Centre for the Social History of Health and Healthcare of Glasgow Caledonian and Strathclyde Universities entitled 'Science and the Human Subject in History'. The Society sponsored the keynote lecture from Professor Hal Cook of Brown University on 'Medical Specifics and the reconfiguration of the Body in Early Modern Europe'. Council members held meetings with academic and research staff and postgraduate research students associated with the Centre, and were later entertained to a reception and dinner on behalf of the University.

The Society continues to work closely with the IHR and its Director, Professor Miles Taylor, on a number of issues, most notably the Bibliography of British and Irish History. Termly meetings of representatives of the Society, the IHR, the HA, and History UK have been held at the IHR. The Honorary Secretary participated in the interviews for Postgraduate Fellowships at IHR in June, including the Society's Centenary and Marshall Fellowships. A joint reception was held following the Prothero Lecture on 30 June.

The President, Dr Andrew Foster, Vice-President and Chair of Teaching Policy Committee, and other members of Council met with representatives from several UK examination boards on 29 September 2009, to discuss recent developments in the A-level History curricula and examinations.

Council and the Officers record their gratitude to the Society's administrative staff: the Executive Secretary, Sue Carr and the Administrative Secretary, Melanie Ransom. We thank them for their expert and dedicated work on the Society's many activities.

RESEARCH POLICY COMMITTEE, 2009–10

The Committee is maintaining an interest in the implications of the new government's funding plans for the higher education sector. The chair represented the Society at a meeting of subject associations held at the British Academy, which was addressed by representatives of UUK and the Academy, among others. The meeting considered what representation should be made to government, and how.

The Committee has taken a close interest in redundancies planned in certain History departments, and has carefully considered the role it can play in such cases. While it cannot appropriately comment on the details of what universities and departments do, it is thought appropriate for it to emphasise certain principles which it would wish to see observed, and to express concern about the wider ramifications of local planning.

The Committee monitors the activities of the AHRC, informed by comments from Fellows and Council and the Society's representatives on its panels and committees. Concern expressed at the setting of a per capita quota for travel expenses claimable by postgraduate award holders was taken up with the AHRC. It transpires that no reduction in expenditure on this head is planned; the new policy is part of the larger strategy of devolution to institutions, who may allocate the money allotted between students as they think best. The AHRC has made serious efforts to communicate both with universities and with award-holders; universities however are failing to pass information on to departments. The AHRC will do more thinking about its information strategy.

The Committee carefully follows REF arrangements, including the new impact agenda. It is submitting a balanced set of nominations for the Humanities main panel and History sub-panel.

The Committee has continued to nurture its relationship with TNA. Unfortunately a planned reorganisation means the almost immediate phasing out of the new academic stakeholder forum. The Committee will seek opportunities to carry forward the working relationship it was hoped to develop in that context.

The Committee has also begun to develop a relationship with the British Library. A meeting has been held between BL collections staff and members of the society, at which matters including the Library's IT strategy, planning to pass on expertise to a new generation of staff in the light of forthcoming retirements, and the Library's response to overcrowding of its facilities were discussed. Further meetings are planned.

The Committee has been reviewing its own structure and activities and has produced a new statement of purpose. In order to increase opportunities to discuss Research and Teaching Policy matters, and to improve coordination between the two committees, a joint meeting was held in July, which it is intended to repeat in future years. Sarah Richardson also attended that meeting, as Director of the History Subject Centre of the Higher Education Academy, and there was discussion about the ways in which the activities of different bodies representing History in this field can best be coordinated.

TEACHING POLICY COMMITTEE, 2009–10

The Teaching Policy Committee considers all aspects of history in education from schools to postgraduate level, although naturally it relies very much on other organizations to take the lead in areas where they have specific expertise – for example, the Historical Association for schools and History UK (HE) for universities. To this end the committee co-opts representatives from the HA, HUK and also from the Higher Education

Academy's History Subject Centre, so that it might serve as a meeting-point for the various bodies that share an interest in this area. The Society is grateful to Professor Rosemary O'Day, Dr Jason Peacey, Dr Andrew Foster (after he retired as chair of the committee), and Dr Sarah Richardson for acting in this capacity.

One area where this clearing-house function has proved especially useful is in fostering relations between professional historians and the school examination Boards. The committee has organized regular meetings between representatives of historical bodies and the exam boards, particularly to discuss A-Levels and other university-entrance examinations (IB, Pre-U). Constructive ideas have been generated about improving the flow of information in both directions between schools and universities. Another meeting is scheduled for September 2010.

The greatest expansion in student numbers in higher education in recent years has been at Master's level – numbers have grown by a third in the last decade, part-time as much as full-time. The committee considered recent reports by the Department for Business, Innovation and Skills (the Smith report on postgraduate education, March 2010) and by the Quality Assurance Agency (QAA) on the characteristics of Master's degrees (April 2010).

This year's announced and predicted cuts in higher-education provision were high on everyone's mind. The committee monitored closely the effects that job cutbacks might have on the coherence and standards of undergraduate History programmes, and representations were made where they were thought to be useful. Attention was drawn to the QAA History benchmark statement, a document that represents the subject community's views on the standards any undergraduate History degree ought to meet (see www.qaa.ac.uk/academicinfrastructure/benchmark/statements/history07.pdf). At the time of writing the future of such benchmarks, and indeed of the Quality Assurance Agency itself, is also under review as part of government economies. The same applies to the Qualifications and Curriculum Development Agency (which performs a similar role for schools curricula) and to the HEA and its Subject Centres. The committee's chair, Professor Peter Mandler (pm297@cam.ac.uk), is always anxious to hear from Fellows of the Society with experience of such quangoes about their views as to what is worth defending (and what is not) in their current briefs.

The joint meeting between the Teaching and Research Policy Committees held in June 2010 did focus on the overarching question of how the Society could help raise public consciousness of the value of historical research, especially at a time when governments of all stripes were stressing utilitarian considerations of 'impact'. This joint meeting will be repeated next year.

GENERAL PURPOSES COMMITTEE, 2009–10

The remit of this committee ranges across many activities of the Society. It receives suggestions from Fellows and Council for paper-givers and makes recommendations to Council on the card of session, taking into account the need for a balanced programme in terms of chronological and geographical spread. In addition to the regular sessions held at UCL and outside London, it is also responsible for the Prothero Lecture, the Colin Matthew Lecture and the Gerald Aylmer Seminar.

The programme of lectures and visits for 2010 was confirmed, including visits to Glasgow Caledonian University in April (reported above) and York University, in October. Proposals for 2011 have been discussed and speakers invited. Regional symposia and visits to Lancaster and the University of Wales are planned, and participation in a conference in Cambridge to mark the centenary of J.H. Plumb's birth in July. The Committee continues to review the purpose and success of both lectures and visits, and to consider ways of increasing their reach, for example through podcasting and repeat lectures. The Committee was pleased to receive several proposals for regional symposia, and would like to encourage more departments to make such proposals. The 2010 Gerald Aylmer Seminar was held in April, on 'Diverse Histories – One Archive' (reported above) and discussions with TNA and other interested parties for the 2011 seminar are under way. The President and the Honorary Treasurer held further talks about possible joint events with the Dulwich Picture gallery.

The Committee is also responsible for the appointment of assessors for the Society's prizes, and receives their reports and proposals for award winners. It regularly reviews the terms and conditions of the awards. It is grateful to members of Council for their hard work in reading entries and selecting the prize winners. Attracting entries for the Alexander Prize and the Rees Davies Prize continues to be problematic.

This year the Committee has also considered broader administrative and developmental issues aimed at raising the Society's profile within the academic community. Several initiatives have resulted from the questionnaire circulated to the membership. Work on the website and on the database of Fellows and Members, past and present, has continued.

Meetings of the Society

Five papers were given in London this year.

At the ordinary meetings of the Society the following papers were read:

'The Age of Prothero: British Historiography in the long *fin-de-siècle*, 1870–1920', Professor Michael Bentley (1 July 2009: Prothero Lecture)

'The Purpose of Religion: Monks and the City in Late Medieval Italy', Dr Frances Andrews (25 September 2009)

'The Reformation of the Landscape: Religion, Identity and Memory in Early Modern Britain and Ireland' Professor Alex Walsham (7 May 2010)

At the Anniversary Meeting on 27 November 2009, the President, Professor Colin Jones delivered his first address on 'French Crossings I: Tales of Two Cities'.

The Colin Matthew Memorial Lecture for the Public Understanding of History was given on Wednesday 11 November 2009 by Professor Charles Saumarez Smith on 'The Institutionalisation of Art in Early Victorian England'. These lectures continue to be given in memory of the late Professor Colin Matthew, a former Literary Director and Vice-President of the Society.

Prizes

The Society's annual prizes were awarded as follows:

The Alexander Prize for 2009 attracted six entries and was awarded to George Molyneaux for his article 'The Old English Bede: English Ideology or Christian Instruction?' in *English Historical Review*, 124 (2009).

The judges' citation read:

George Molyneaux's article subjects the Old English translation of Bede's *Historia Ecclesiastica* to close scrutiny. By studying the strategies adopted by the translator, not least his numerous omissions or abbreviations, doubt is cast on the notion that the English were believed to be a single chosen people who enjoyed a special relationship with God. Learned, penetrating and unfailingly lucid, this is a highly impressive article. The author analyses with great skill a body of material that is diverse, fragmented and technically very difficult to master, expressing the fruits of his scholarship in a clear, elegant, narrative voice. His conclusions will contribute much to the debate about the nature and political significance of English consciousness in the ninth and tenth centuries.

The David Berry Prize for an article on Scottish history for 2009 attracted two entries and was awarded to Sandip Hazareesingh for his article 'Interconnected synchronicities: the production of Glasgow and Bombay as modern global ports c. 1850–1880', in *Journal of Global* History, 4 (2009).

The judges' citation read:

The article critically examines the Cain/Hopkins proposition that imperialism was focussed on the City of London, and suggests instead that imperial projects could involve 'a far wider range of networked commercial actors interacting with both the imperial and the colonial state'. It does so largely through a case-study of the port of Bombay, showing how a network of mainly Scots with Glaswegian connections tried to impose their model on India. It achieves its object convincingly, both at a theoretical and at an empirical level; it has impressive intellectual breadth, and it tackles something quite new in Scottish historical studies. It also provides a model example for further work on the Scottish contribution to the British Empire which deserves to be widely read.

The Whitfield Book Prize for a first book on British history attracted 29 entries. The prize for 2009 was awarded to:

Nicholas Draper, The Price of Emancipation: Slave-ownership, Compensation and British Society at the End of Slavery (Cambridge University Press, 2009).

The judges citation read:

When in 1833 the imperial parliament agreed to abolish slavery in British dominions, slave owners were offered compensation. Nicholas Draper's highly original and illuminating monograph draws on documentation generated by this process to develop a social and cultural history of slave owners in mainland Britain. At the core of his study lies a painstaking analysis of who the slave owners were; around this central relationship often accreted other legal and financial complications, which makes this task harder to discharge accurately than some previous scholars have realised. Draper shows that, while slave ownership was characteristic of a distinct community, the passage of property in slaves through family gifts and inheritance means that individuals within this community were diverse, and their relations with the slave economy often highly mediated. He makes a significant and original contribution to women's history by showing that family strategies often placed property in slaves in the hands of women. He also offers a nuanced account of ways in which slave owners represented themselves in different contexts, an account of parliamentary debates around the issue of compensation, and of the administration and workings of the compensation process. His is a broadly conceived, empirically dense yet lucid study, at once hard headed and humane, which offers striking new perspectives on several key topics in modern British history.

The judges nominated a proxime accessit:

Guy Ortolano for The Two Cultures Controversy: Science, Literature and Cultural Politics in Postwar Britain (Cambridge University Press, 2009).

The Gladstone Book Prize for a first book on non-British history attracted 15 entries.

The Prize for 2009 was awarded to:

Alice Rio, Legal Practice and the Written Word in the Early Middle Ages: Frankish Formulae c. 500–1000 (Cambridge University Press, 2009).

The judges' citation read:

This work is a formidable achievement on many levels. It is methodologically innovative, forging a new path for our understanding of early medieval Merovingian and Carolingian society. Written in a crisp and readable style, it adopts an engaging approach which renders its subject relevant for historians of any period. Drawing upon meticulous research in French, German, Italian and Latin, Alice Rio asks us to rethink the utility of a source often dismissed as unusable: legal formulae, the compilations made by scribes in which data about historical context were stripped out to create instructive case studies for contemporaries or later generations. While critiquing the way these sources were catalogued by nineteenth-century German scholars, Dr Rio provides an ambitious alternative methodology. She then demonstrates the rewards of a flexible approach, testing her theories in a case study of early medieval slavery or 'unfreedom'. The judges felt that the book engaged with major historical questions and was also highly reflective about the practice of history as a whole. In short, it is a work which transcends its time period and offers salutary lessons for any historian.

The judges nominated a proxime accessit:

Maurizio Isabella for Risorgimento in Exile. Italian Émigrés and the Liberal International in the Post-Napoleonic Era (Oxford University Press, 2009).

The Society's Rees Davies Essay Prize was not awarded in 2009.

In order to recognise the high quality of work now being produced at undergraduate level in the form of third-year dissertations, the Society continued, in association with *History Today* magazine, to award an annual prize for the best undergraduate dissertation. Departments are asked to nominate annually their best dissertation and a joint committee of the Society and *History Today* select in the autumn the national prizewinner from among these nominations. The prize also recognizes the Society's close relations with *History Today* and the important role the magazine has played in disseminating scholarly research to a wider audience. 35 submissions were made.

The Prize for 2009 was awarded to:

Eleanor Betts (Queen Mary, University of London) for her dissertation 'Who Will Help? The Impact of the 1866 cholera epidemic on the children of East London'.

An article by the prize-winner presenting her research will appear in *History Today* in 2010.

The German History Society, in association with the Society, agreed to award a prize to the winner of an essay competition. The essay, on any aspect of German history, including the history of German-speaking people both within and beyond Europe, was open to any postgraduate registered for a degree in a university in either the United Kingdom or the Republic of Ireland.

The prize for the winning essay in 2009 was awarded to:

Mark Hobbs (University of Glasgow), for his essay 'Weimar Berlin's house-building programme: a case study'.

The Frampton and Beazley Prizes for A-level performances in 2009 were awarded to the following nominations from the examining bodies:

Frampton Prize:

Welsh JEC: Natalie Williams (Blaengwawr Comprehensive School, Aberdare)
OCR: Lucy Parker (Oxford High School, Oxford)

Beazley Prize:

SQA: Arthur Learoyd (Morrison's Academy, Perthshire)
CCEA: Emily Hamilton (Methodist College, Belfast)

The Director of the Institute of Historical Research announced the winners of the Pollard Prize 2010 awarded annually to the best postgraduate student paper presented in a seminar at the IHR, and the Sir John Neale Prize for the best essay on the study of 16th century England by a postgraduate student.

The Pollard Prize for 2010 was awarded to Julie Mumby for her paper 'The descent of family land in later Anglo-Saxon England' given to the Economic and Social History of the Premodern World, 1500 – 1800 seminar.

The Sir John Neale Prize for 2010 was awarded to Charlotte Panofré (St Edmund's College, Cambridge) for her essay 'Radical Geneva? The publication of Knox's "First Blast of the Trumpet" and Goodman's "How Superior Powers oght to be Obeyd" in context'.

Publications

PUBLICATIONS COMMITTEE, 2009–10

The transition from the Royal Historical Society Bibliography to the Bibliography of British and Irish History (BBIH) passed smoothly on 1 January 2010. A very good working relationship between the Society, the Institute of Historical Research, and Brepols has been established, and the publishers have already responded to user feedback in implementing compatibility with the freely available bibliographic software, Zotero. BBIH works according to the routines established by the RHS Bibliography, and we have already exceeded our annual target of 10,000 new records: the total currently stands at over 17,500. We have recruited two new section editors, Dr Matthew Kelly and Dr Beth Hartland, to cover the Irish material. Although the climate is not good for library subscriptions, the take up of the service has well exceeded our expectations. We remain concerned about users not in Higher Education Institutions, and we hope that in the medium term we will be able to negotiate a more favourable deal for them.

Lists of local record society publications (formerly known as *Texts and Calendars*) are now available through the Society's website, and will be updated annually. The Committee is grateful to the Executive Secretary for her work on this invaluable resource.

Another project that has come to fruition over the past year is the digitisation of the entire back list of Camden volumes through the Digital Archive at Cambridge Journals On-Line. The Society is very grateful to Daniel Pearce and his colleagues at the Press for driving this forward.

The Publications Committee remains responsible for the ongoing programme. Professor Arthur Burns represents the Society's interests on the Studies in History Editorial Board, while Dr Ian Archer edits *Transactions*, and they share responsibility for Camden volumes.

Transactions, Sixth Series, Volume 19 was published during the session, and *Transactions*, Sixth Series, Volume 20 went to press, to be published in November 2010.

In the Camden, Fifth Series, Stuart Dynastic Policy and Religious Politics, 1621–1625, ed. Michael Questier (vol. 34) and The Political Diaries of the Fourth Earl of Carnarvon, 1857–1890: Colonial Secretary and Lord Lieutenant of Ireland, ed. Peter Gordon (vol. 35) were published during the session and The Life of John Rastrick, 1650–1727, ed. Andrew Cambers (vol. 36) and British Envoys to Germany, 1816–1866. Vol. IV: 1851–1866, eds. Markus Mösslang, Chris Manias, Torsten Riotte (vol. 37) went to press for publication in 2010–11.

The *Studies in History* Editorial Board continued to meet throughout the year. The second series continued to produce exciting volumes. Professor Daniel Power and Dr Bernhard Rieger joined the Editorial Board. The following volumes were published, or went to press, during the session:

○ *The Political Life of Josiah C Wedgwood. Land. Liberty and Empire, 1872–1943*, Paul Mulvey
○ *Pathways of Power in late-Carolingian Catalonia: charters and connections on a medieval border*, Jonathan Jarrett
○ *Law and Kinship in Thirteenth Century England*, Samantha Worby
○ *Trade and Trust in the Eighteenth-Century Atlantic World: Spanish Merchants and their Overseas Networks*, Xabier Lamikiz

As in previous subscription years, volumes in *Studies in History* series were offered to the membership at a favourably discounted price. Many Fellows, Associates and Members accepted the offer for volumes published during the year, and the advance orders for further copies of the volumes to be published in the year 2010–2011 were encouraging.

A very welcome development in 2011 will be the reissue of nineteen recent volumes from the series in paperback. The Boydell Press have initiated the reissue (which is very welcome to the Society) at their own risk, but will pay both authors and the Society royalties. If it is a success, it is hoped to extend the reissue to other volumes

The Society acknowledges its gratitude for the continuing subventions from the Economic History Society and the Past and Present Society to the *Studies in History* series.

Finance

FINANCE COMMITTEE 2009–10

The Finance Committee approves the Society's accounts each financial year and its estimates for the following year. This year, as before, the accounts were very professionally audited by Kingston Smith. They are presented elsewhere in *Transactions*, together with the Trustees' Annual Report. Since that Report discusses the main financial developments of the year, there is very little more to say here.

The value of the Society's investments has recovered from £1.97m in June 2009 to £2.16m. The total return for the year, when withdrawn dividend income is taken into account, is 12.68%. The portfolio continues to be managed by Brewin Dolphin for the longer term, and is now practically fully invested. The proportion in fixed interest securities remains higher than in most recent years at 25.7%, owing to the corporate bond and other purchases in 2008–9. Dividend income declined, mainly because of the travails of the financial sector and BP, but also because of a deliberate slight shift away from the very defensive investment strategy that had been pursued in recent years. Even so, at £78,000, dividends still practically matched our withdrawals for income.

Moreover in future it would be possible for the Society, if it chooses, to withdraw smaller sums each year, owing to the cushion that it now has in the shape of the COIF current account that was set up in 2008. This new account also allows us to save money that will be required to meet the expenses of the Bibliography of British and Irish History in future years. We will need to budget to spend between £20,000 and £30,000 a year on the Bibliography for the six years of the new contract, 2010–15.

Income and expenditure have been in line with our estimates at the beginning of the year, and there were no major surprises on either side. However there was a pleasing increase in income from the joint publishing agreement with Cambridge University Press, mainly owing to initial sales of the new digital archive.

Paul ffolkes Davis resigned as an external member of the Finance Committee in February. His advice on the management of the portfolio over the last few years has been very useful and we are very grateful for his service. Dr Nick Draper joined the Committee as an external member in the course of the year, and we hope to make another appointment in September 2010.

- Council records with gratitude the benefactions made to the Society by:

  - The Bibliographical Society
  - Professor C R Cole
  - Sir Patrick Cormack
  - Professor J R Cramsie
  - Economic History Society
  - Professor Sir Geoffrey Elton
  - Miss B F Harvey
  - Dr A Hessayon
  - Professor T Hitchcock
  - Professor A P Jenkins
  - Professor P M Kennedy
  - Dr M T Lofthouse
  - Dr M Lynn
  - Dr E Magennis
  - Professor S E Marks
  - Professor P J Marshall
  - Professor J A North
  - Professor P O'Dochartaigh
  - Professor H Ono
  - Past & Present Society
  - Sir George Prothero
  - Dr L Rausing
  - Miss E M Robinson
  - Professor H Schulze
  - Professor Lord Smith of Clifton
  - Professor D P Smyth
  - Mr H M Stuchfield
  - Dr G P Tapsell
  - Mr T V Ward
  - Mr H Williams

Membership

MEMBERSHIP COMMITTEE, 2009–10

The Committee reviews all applications for Fellowship and Membership received by the Society, and makes recommendations to Council. We reported last year that we were advising the President and Council in a review of the Society's criteria for admission to both categories, partly for greater transparency but also to encourage more applications. We are very pleased that this policy has been successful, especially in maintaining a considerable increase in the numbers of new Members. We are always glad to receive applications in either category, and we would like to emphasise that we favour a broad definition of history in assessing candidates.

The following were elected to the Fellowship:

Maher Abu-Munshar, PhD
Martin R Allen, PhD
Craig R Armstrong, BA, PhD
Jonathan A Arnold, BA, MA, PhD
Geoff Baker, BA, MA, MRes, PhD
Gregory A Barton, PhD
Bernardo Batiz-Lazo, BSc, MSc, PhD
James B Bell, BA, MDiv, DPhil
Francis R Bongiorno, BA, PhD
Mercedes M Camino, PhD
Hugh Chignell, BA, MA, PhD
Gillian G Cockram, BA, MA, PhD
Patrick T Cormack, BA
John H Darch, BA, MA, PhD
Kenneth R Dark, BA, PhD
Andrew M Davies, BA, PhD
John D Davies, MA, DPhil
William J Davies, MA
Michael Davis, BA, MA, Juris Doctorate
Russell Deacon, BA, PhD
Kent Gang Deng, PhD
Caroline Dodds Pennock, BA, MSt, DPhil
Helen Doe, MA, PhD
Wayne Dooling, PhD
Alex Drace-Francis, BA, MA, PhD
Gillian M Draper, BA, MA, PhD
Jonathan C Edmondson, MA, PhD
Michael J Edwards, BA, MPhil, MA, PhD
Christiane Eisenberg, DPhil
Benjamin J Elton, MA, PhD
Joel Felix, BA, MA, Doctorat
Katherine L French, BA, MA, PhD
Philip W Gardner, BA, MA, DPhil, PGCE, FRSA
Keith Gildart, BA, DPhil
Jacqueline Glomski, BA, MA, MSc, PhD
Andrew M Godfrey, MA, LLB, PhD

Ingrid A Gregg, BA, MSc, PhD
Mark S Hagger, MA, MLitt, PhD
Peter W Hammond, BA, BSc
Stephen A Hart, BA, MA, PhD
Barbara Hately-Broad, BA, MA, PhD
Bridget M Heal, BA, MA, PhD
Irving R Hexham, BA, MA, PhD
Konrad Hirschler, PhD
Katrina Honeyman, BA, PhD
Caroline Humfress, BA, MA, PhD
Norman Ingram, BA, MA, PhD
Robert Ingram, BA, MA, PhD
Anthony P Jenkins, BA, MA
Keith G Jones, BA, MA, PhD, MBIM
Peter T Kirby, BA, PhD
Christian Koller, MA, PhD
Helen E Lacey, BA, MA, PhD
Ryan L Lavelle, BA, MA, PhD
Avi Lifschitz, MA, DPhil
Cheng Liu, MPhil, DPhil
John W Lockington, BA, BD, MTh, PhD, DD
Anthony R Margrave
Benjamin J Marsh, BA, MPhil, PhD
Shin Matsuzono, BA, MA, PhD
Stephen A Mileson, BA, MSt, DPhil
Peter Mitchell, BA, MA, PhD
Kevin W Mitchinson, BA, MA, PhD, PGCE
Jorg Monar, PhD PhD
Anne L Murphy, BA, MA, PhD
James H Murphy, BA, BD, PhD, Dlitt
Claire V Noble, BA, MA, PhD
John A North, MA, DPhil
Pol O'Dochartaigh, BA, PhD, BA
Allen G Packwood, BA, MPhil
James T Palmer, BA, MPhil, PhD
Elizabeth Parkinson, BSc, MA, PhD
Julie Peakman, PhD
Mark Peel, BA, MA, PhD
Michael A Penman, MA, PhD
Hilary D Perraton, MA, PhD, DUniv
David R Pratt, MA, PhD
Jennifer Regan-Lefebvre, MA, PhD
James E Renton, BA, PhD
Stephen A Royle, MA, PhD, MRIA, C.Ceog, FRGS

Alexandra Sanmark, BA, MA, PhD
Clare T M Shawcross, BA, MPhil, DPhil, Maitrise
Caroline Shenton, MA, DPhil
James G Shields, MA, PhD, DLitt
Deborah L Simonton, BA, MA, PhD
Sujit Pradin Sivasundaram, MA, MPhil, PhD
Christopher J Skidmore, BA, MSt
A R Kristina Spohr Readman, BA, MPhil, PhD
Alan L Strathern, BA, MA, DPhil
John Swift, BA, MA, PhD
James C Taylor, BA, MA, PhD
Geoffrey C Tyack, MA, MLitt, PhD
Karine N Varley, BA, MA, PhD
Anna von der Goltz, BA, MPhil, DPhil
Paul Ward, BA, PhD
Daniel Wildmann, Lic.phil, Dr.phil
Glenn R Wilkinson, BA, PhD
Clive Wilkins-Jones, BA, PhD
Samuel B A Willis, BA, MA, PhD
Jon E Wilson, BA, MA, PhD
Philip J Withington, BA, PhD

The following was announced in the Queen's Honours' Lists during the year:

Professor Michael Prestwich – Fellow – O.B.E. for services to Scholarship

The following were elected to the Fellowship of the British Academy:

Mr Robin Briggs – Fellow, Professor Brucc Campbell – Fellow, Mrs Jean Dunbabin – Retired Fellow and Professor Alex Walsham- Fellow.

Council was advised of and recorded with regret the deaths of 11 Fellows, 25 Retired Fellows, 1 Life Fellow and 3 Associates.

These included:

Professor G E Connell-Smith – Retired Fellow
Professor P M Crawford – Retired Fellow
Professor J H Denton – Retired Fellow
Professor S R Dockrill – Fellow
Professor C R Elrington – Retired Fellow
Dr C J Erickson – Retired Fellow
Mr M W Farr – Fellow
Professor R C Finucane – Fellow
Professor N Gash – Fellow

Mr J M Golby – Fellow
Professor M A R Graves – Fellow
Dr G E Gregg – Retired Fellow
Major A G Harfield – Retired Fellow
Miss M C Hill – Life Fellow
Professor G A Holmes – Retired Fellow
Reverend Father T G Holt – Retired Fellow
Dr R F Hunnisett – Retired Fellow
Mr F R Johnston – Associate
Reverend D R Jones – Associate
Professor M Lester – Retired Fellow
Colonel O J M Lindsay – Retired Fellow
Professor H V Livermore – Retired Fellow
Mr J R Lowerson – Fellow
Dr J F A Mason – Retired Fellow
Mr J S Matthews – Retired Fellow
Dr R C Oresko – Fellow
Dr F A Peake – Retired Fellow
Professor J A Ramsden – Retired Fellow
Dr A C Ross – Retired Fellow
Mr A D Saunders – Retired Fellow
Professor J Saville – Fellow
Dr A N E D Schofield – Retired Fellow
Professor B Semmel – Retired Fellow
Professor R E F Smith – Retired Fellow
Miss R Spalding – Fellow
Professor D J Sturdy – Retired Fellow
Mr J Taylor – Fellow
Mr A F Thompson – Retired Fellow
Professor D E Underdown – Retired Fellow
Mr J O Wood – Associate

Over the year ending on 30 June 2010, 101 Fellows and 61 Members were elected, and the total membership of the Society on that date was 2,997 (including 1946 Fellows, 652 Retired Fellows, 15 Honorary Vice-Presidents, 86 Corresponding and Honorary Fellows, 52 Associates and 246 Members).

The Society exchanged publications with 15 societies, British and Foreign.

Representatives of the Society

• The representation of the Society upon other various bodies was as follows:

- Dr Julia Crick on the Joint Committee of the Society and the British Academy established to prepare an edition of Anglo-Saxon charters;
- Professor Nicholas Brooks on a committee to promote the publication of photographic records of the more significant collections of British coins;
- Dr Christopher Kitching on the Council of the British Records Association;
- Mr Phillip Bell on the Editorial Advisory Board of the *Annual Register*;
- Professor Claire Cross on the Council of the British Association for Local History; and on the British Sub-Commission of the Commission Internationale d' Histoire Ecclesiastique Comparée;
- Professor Rosamund McKitterick on a committee to regulate British co-operation in the preparation of a new repertory of medieval sources to replace Potthast's *Bibliotheca Historica Medii Aevi*;
- Professor Richard Rathbone on the Court of Governors of the University of Wales, Swansea;
- Professor Mark Ormrod on the National Council on Archives;
- Professor John Breuilly on the Steering Committee of the British Centre for Historical Research in Germany
- Professor Colin Jones on the board of the Panizzi Foundation and the Advisory Council of the Committee for the Export of Objects of Cultural Interest
- Professor Chris Whatley on the Court of the University of Stirling

Grants

RESEARCH SUPPORT COMMITTEE, 2009–10:

The committee met five times in the course of the year to distribute research funds to early career historians (primarily research students but also recent PhDs not yet in full-time employment) through a process of peer review. In total, the Committee made 115 awards to researchers at over forty UK institutions, of which 15 grants were to support research within the UK, 35 to support research outside the UK, 33 to support attendance at conferences to deliver papers, 31 to allow conference organisers to subsidise attendance of early career researchers at their events and one (the Martin Lynn Scholarship) to support research within Africa. The broad range of topics funded by the Committee attests both to the vibrancy of the discipline in sub-fields that extend from medieval European religious history to contemporary South African history. Successful applicants' end-of-award reports confirm that RHS funding significantly enhances postgraduate students' opportunities to conduct substantial archival research projects and to hone their ensuing dissertation chapters and first publications through participation in national and international workshops and conferences. The calibre of applicants continues to be high, with significantly more qualified applicants than the committee is able to fund – a circumstance that recent and impending reductions of research funding at both university and Research Council-level will likely exacerbate in the coming year. Further, to ensure that its limited funds are allocated to the most appropriate candidates, the Committee devoted considerable time this year to clarifying and streamlining its application process and criteria.

The Royal Historical Society Centenary Fellowship was awarded in the academic year 2009–2010 to Bianca Gaudenzi (Trinity Hall, University of Cambridge) for work on 'Commercial Advertising in Germany and Italy, 1918–1945' and Niels Van Manen (University of York) for work on 'The Climbing Boy Campaigns: Chimney Sweep Apprentices, Cultures of Reform, Languages of Health and Experiences of Childhood in Britain, c. 1770–1840.'

The Society's P.J. Marshall Fellowship was awarded in the academic year 2009–2010 to Valentina Pugliano (Mansfield College, University of Oxford) for work on 'Botanical Artisans: Apothecaries and the Study of Nature in Venice and London, 1550–1630.'

- Grants during the year were made to the following:

Travel to Conferences (Training Bursaries):

- Alexandra Bacopoulos-Viau, University of Cambridge
- Cheiron: the International Society for the History of the Behavioral and Social Sciences (Annual Meeting), Syracuse, New York, 24th-27th June 2010
- Lucy-Ann Bates, University of Durham
- Material Cultures: Technology, Textuality, and Transmission, University of Edinburgh, 16th-18th July 2010
- Sebastian Buckle, University of Southampton
- European Social Sciences History Conference, Ghent, 13th-16th April 2010
- Say Burgin, University of Leeds
- International Sociological Association's World Congress of Sociology: Sociology on the Move, Gothenburg, 11th-17th July 2010
- Marie Chenard, London School of Economics
- The external relations of the EU, historical and contemporary perspectives, Melbourne, Australia, 24th-25th September 2009
- Rebecca Conway, University of Manchester
- Social History Society Conference 2010, Glasgow, 30th March – 1st April 2010

- Benjamin Dabby, University of Cambridge
- Symposium on Fictions of the Industrial Age: Historical Readings of C19th Literature
- Los Angeles, 23rd-24th October 2009
- Robert Decker, University of Leeds
- Locating the hidden Diaspora: The English in the Anglo-phone world, Northumbria University, 8th-10th July 2010
- Ceri-Anne Fidler, Cardiff University
- Social History Society Conference 2010, Glasgow, 30th March – 1st April 2010
- Jasper Heinzen, University of Cambridge
- 33rd Annual German Studies Conference, Washington DC, 8th-11th October 2009
- Lucy Hewitt, University of Edinburgh
- Agency and Action, 34th Annual Meeting of the Social Science History Association
- Long Beach, California, 12th-15th November 2009
- Simon Hill, Liverpool John Moores University
- Consortium on the Revolutionary Era, 1750–1850, Charleston, 25th-27th February 2010
- Jochen Hung, Institute of Germanic & Romance Studies
- Ideology in Motion: on the relationship of sports and politics, University of British Columbia, Vancouver, 4th-5th December 2009
- Mark Hutchinson, Canterbury Christ Church University
- Elizabeth I and Ireland, Connecticut, 12th-14th November 2009
- William Jackson, University of Leeds
- Performing Colonial Modernity: Postgraduate and Early-Career Researchers Conference, University of Edinburgh, 18th-19th May 2010
- Sarah Kelly, University of Cambridge
- Pacific Coast Conference on British Studies (PCCBS), Claremont, 19th-21st March 2010
- Simon Lambe, St Mary's University College
- Propaganda: purpose and practice in the 16th and 20th centuries, Brussels, 23rd October 2009
- Phoebe Luckyn-Malone, University of Cambridge
- Modern Standard Arabic (Upper Intermediate/Advanced) and private tuition
- Arabic Language Institute, Fez, Morocco, 20th June – 31st July 2010
- Natasha Mihailovic, University of Exeter
- The Social Context of Death, Dying and Disposal, 9th Bienniel Conference
- University of Durham, 9th-12th September 2009
- Rachel Milestone, University of Leeds

- Seventh Biennial Music in Nineteenth-Century Britain Conference, University of Bristol, 23rd-26th July 2009
- Liz Mylod, University of Leeds
- International Congress on Medieval Studies, Kalamazoo, Michigan, 13th-16th May 2010
- Samantha Owen, University of Reading
- XX International Association of Italian Studies Conference: Languages, Cultures, Identities of Italy in the World, Pennsylvania, 3rd-6th December 2009
- Zsuzsanna Papp, University of Leeds
- Writing Central Eastern Europe, Jagiellonian University, Krakow, 11th-12th June 2010
- Natalia Petrovskaia, University of Cambridge
- International Medieval Congress, Leeds, 12th-15th July 2010
- Simon Pooley, University of Oxford
- First World Congress on Environmental History, Copenhagen, 4th-8th August 2009
- Charles Rozier, University of Durham
- Leeds International Medieval Congress, University of Leeds, 12th-15th July 2010
- Michelle Sikes, University of Oxford
- Social History Society Conference 2010, Glasgow, 30th March – 1st April 2010
- Emma Sutton, University College London
- Cheiron: the International Society for the History of the Behavioral and Social Sciences (Annual Meeting), Syracuse, New York, 24th-27th June 2010
- Christopher Webb, University of Huddersfield
- Columbia University Oral History Summer Institute, Columbia University, New York, 7th-18th June 2010
- David Willimott, University of East Anglia
- VIII International Council for Central and East European Studies World Congress
- Stockholm, 26th-31st July 2010
- Sara Wolfson, University of Durham
- The 16th Biennial New College Conference on Medieval and Renaissance Studies
- Sarasota, 10th-14th March 2010
- Alexander Wragge-Morley, University of Cambridge
- History of Science Society Annual Meeting, Phoenix, 19th-22nd November 2009
- Reza Zia-Ebrahimi, University of Oxford
- 8th Biennial Iranian Studies Conference, Los Angeles, 27th-30th May 2010

Research Expenses Within the United Kingdom:

o Kristen Brill, University of Cambridge
o Archives in Bristol, 14th-18th June 2010
o Denis Clark, University of Oxford
o Archives in London, Cambridge, Edinburgh and Carlisle, 14th September – 14th December 2009
o Tommy Dickinson, University of Manchester
o Archives in London and Edinburgh, March 2010 – March 2014
o Mark Gjessing, University of Leeds
o Archives in Greenwich, Cambridge and Southampton, 31st May – 18th June 2010
o Richard Hammond, University of Exeter
o Archives in London, Middlesex and Hampshire, October 2009 – March 2010
o Vincent Hiribarren, University of Leeds
o Archives in London, 7th-11th September 2009
o Deborah Jewison, De Montfort University
o Archives in London, 27th June – 2nd July 2010
o Giulio Marchisio, University of Durham
o National Archives London, 11th-16th January 2010
o Katie McDade, University of Nottingham
o Archives in Bristol, 28th January – 21st May 2010
o Benjamin Mountford, University of Oxford
o Archives in Scotland, Hatfield and London, May – August 2010
o Rebecca Roberts, University of Teesside
o Centre for Kentish Studies Maidstone, March 2010
o Allison Stagg, University College London
o Archives in Newcastle upon Tyne, 25th-26th August 2009
o Helen Walsh, Manchester Metropolitan University
o Archives in Farnham and London, 7th – 18th June 2010
o May Witwit, University of Bedfordshire
o Archives in Cambridge, Newcastle, London and Strathclyde, August – December 2009
o Jacqueline Young, University of Glasgow
o Archives in London, March 2010

Research Expenses Outside the United Kingdom:

o George Adamson, University of Brighton
o Archives in Boston, USA, October 2010
o John Burman, University of Cambridge
o Archives in Istanbul, 14th October – 13th November 2009
o Berris Charnley, University of Leeds

- Archives in Canberra, Australia, 17th-27th July 2009
- Robert Decker, University of Leeds
- Archives in Boston, New York and Washington, August – October 2010
- Daniel De Groff, Queen Mary, University of London
- Archives in France, March 2010
- Arabella De Steiger Khandwala, University of Exeter
- Archives in Granada and Cordoba, Spain, 10th-23rd September 2009
- Christopher Dennis, Cardiff University
- Archives in Paris, 12th-16th January 2010
- Jonathon Earle, University of Cambridge
- Archives in Uganda, October 2009 – June 2010
- Edina Eszenyi, University of Kent
- Archives in Rome and Venice, 1st June – 31st August 2010
- Jennifer Farrar, University of Sheffield
- Archives in Paris, December 2009
- Mark Gjessing, University of Leeds
- Archives in Canberra, Melbourne, Sydney and Jervis Bay, 1st July – 3rd September 2010
- Matthew Graham, University of Sheffield
- Archives in South Africa, 1st September – 15th October 2009
- Robert Hearn, University of Nottingham
- Archives in Italy, September 2009 – September 2010
- Lars-Christopher Huening, University of Sheffield
- Interviews in Kinshasa, 20th June – 8th July 2010
- Lars-Christopher Huening, University of Sheffield
- Archives in Belgium, October 2009 – January 2010
- Leslie James, London School of Economics
- Archives in Washington, D.C., 13th-27th June 2010
- Emmanouil Kalkanis, University of Durham
- Archives in Los Angeles, June – July 2010
- Rei Kanemura, University of Cambridge
- Archives in San Marino, California, 18th July – 23rd September 2010
- Claire Knight, University of Cambridge
- Archives in Moscow, 15th June – 15th August 2010
- Kate Law, University of Sheffield
- Archives in South Africa, March – April 2010
- Esther Meininghaus, University of Manchester
- Archives in Syria, March – June 2010
- Marie Molloy, Keele University
- Archives and libraries in USA, 9th May – 9th June 2010
- Ana Otero-Cleves, University of Oxford
- Archives in Washington, D.C. and New York, June – August 2010
- Kenneth Parker, Royal Holloway, University of London
- Archives in Cairo, 29th October – 14th November 2009

- o Shirley Pemberston, School of Advanced Study, University of London
- o Archives in St Kitts/Nevis, 6th March – 20th April 2010
- o Anna Pilz, University of Liverpool
- o Archives in New York, 1st February – 31st March 2010
- o Bryan Roby, University of Manchester
- o Archives in Jerusalem, 25th May – 1st September 2010
- o Melania Savino, School of Oriental and African Studies, University of London
- o Archives in Turkey, October 2009 – May 2010
- o Kate Smith, University of Warwick
- o Archives in Delaware, 29th March – 22nd April 2010
- o Daniel Spence, Sheffield Hallam University
- o Archives in Trinidad and the Cayman Islands, 9th June – 21st July 2010
- o David Stokes, University of St Andrews
- o Archives in Vienna, 23rd November – 5th December 2009
- o Aya Tsuruta, University of Edinburgh
- o Archives in Brussels and Tervuren, 3rd July – 7th August 2010
- o Stephen Tuffnell, University of Oxford
- o Archives in Massachusetts, Connecticut and Rhode Island, 22nd July – 25th September 2010
- o Christopher Vaughan, University of Durham
- o Archives in France, 4th-17th October 2009
- o Elizabeth Vigurs, University of Leeds
- o Archives at Pforzheim, Karlsruhe and Natzweiler/Sruthof, October – November 2009

Conference Organisation (Workshop):

- o James Ainsworth
- o "New Research into the History of Warfare: An International Graduate Conference"
- o Cambridge, 7th-8th August 2010
- o Katie Barclay
- o "New perspectives on seventeenth and eighteenth century Scotland", Economic and Social History Society of Scotland Annual Conference, Dundee, 7th-8th May 2010
- o Richard Blakemore
- o "Education and Learning in Early Modern Britain", Trinity Hall, Cambridge, 24th September 2010
- o Matthew Broad
- o "European Integration and the Cold War, 1945–1989", History of European Integration Research Society, 15th-16th April 2010
- o Anne Byrne

- "From Coronation to Chari-vari: the many uses of ritual and ceremony in the early modern world", Birkbeck, University of London, 23rd-24th September 2010
- Isabel Divanna
- "Intellectual Networks and Exchanges", Wolfson College, Oxford, 1st-2nd July 2010
- Michael Finn
- "Third Annual History of Science, Technology and Medicine Postgraduate Workshop and Tyndall Correspondence Symposium", University of Leeds, 22nd-24th June 2010
- Maria Fusaro
- "New Researchers in Maritime History", University of Exeter, 12th-13th March 2010
- Graeme Gooday
- "Managing Knowledge in the Techno-sciences, 1850–2000", University of Leeds, 5th-8th July 2010
- Rachel Hammersley
- "Ageing and Health in French History", Society for the Study of French History Annual Conference, Newcastle University, 27th-29th June 2010
- Bridget Heal
- "Reformation Studies Colloquium", University of St Andrews, 7th-9th September 2010
- Diane Heath
- "Bad Behaviour in Medieval and Early Modern Europe," one-day postgraduate colloquium, University of Kent, 3rd December 2009
- Karen Heath
- "Historians of the Twentieth Century United States: Third Annual Conference"
- University of Sussex, 1st-3rd July 2010
- Emma Jones
- "Politics and Practices: The History of Post-war Women's Health", University of Manchester, 22nd-23rd October 2010
- Axel Korner
- "Rewriting Histories – The Transnational Challenge", University College London, 30th April – 1st May 2010
- Christoph Laucht
- "British Nuclear Culture: Themes, Approaches, Perspectives", University of Liverpool, 17th-18th June 2010
- Matthew McHaffie
- "Gender and Transgression Postgraduate Conference", St Andrews Institute of Medieval Studies, 23rd-24th April 2010
- Alison Montgomery
- "Body on Display, from Renaissance to Enlightenment (c.1400-c.1800)", University of Durham, 6th-7th July 2010

- o Jason Peacey
- o "Making the British Empire, 1660–1800" (including Neale Lecture by Professor Steve Pincus 'Reconceptualising the Origins of the British Empire'), University College London, 19th-20th March 2010
- o Kirsty Reid
- o "Writing the empire: scribblings from below", University of Bristol, 24th-26th June 2010
- o Jessica Reinisch
- o "The Forty Years' Crisis: Refugees in Europe, 1919–1959", Birkbeck, University of London, 14th-16th September 2010
- o Sarah Richardson
- o "Performing the Self: Women's Lives in Historical Perspective", University of Warwick, 10th-12th September 2010
- o Thomas Roebuck
- o "John Selden, 1584–1654", Magdalen College, Oxford, 24th-26th June 2010
- o Laura Stewart
- o "The Early Modern State: Comparative Perspectives", Birkbeck, University of London, 13th-14th July 2010
- o Katherine Tubb
- o "Beyond Glitter and Doom: New Perspectives on the Weimar Republic"
- o Institute of Germanic & Romance Studies, 30th September – 1st October 2010
- o Laura Ugolini
- o "Distribution Networks for Textiles and Dress, c.1700–1945", University of Wolverhampton, 8th-9th September 2010
- o Nicola Verdon
- o "Rural History 2010": An International Conference, University of Sussex, 13th-16th September 2010
- o Tiago Viula de Faria
- o "English and Portuguese in Exchange (1100–1500)": A workshop on forms of 'international' contact in medieval Western Europe, University of Oxford, 28th May 2010
- o Paul Ward
- o "Identity and the 'Other British Isles'", University of Huddersfield, 23rd-25th June 2010
- o Sethina Watson
- o "York 1190: Jews and Others in the Wake of Massacre", University of York, 22nd-24th March 2010
- o Dhan Zunino Singh
- o "Blocked Arteries: Circulation and Congestion in History", Institute of Historical Research, 25th-26th November 2010

Martin Lynn Scholarship:

○ Nana Antwi-Ansorge, University of Oxford
○ Archives in Liberia, October – December 2009

Royal Historical Society Postgraduate Speakers Series (RHSPSS):

○ Bath Spa University
○ University of Warwick
○ Cardiff University

FINANCIAL STATEMENTS
FOR THE YEAR ENDED
30 JUNE 2010

THE ROYAL HISTORICAL SOCIETY
REPORT OF THE COUNCIL (THE TRUSTEES)
FOR THE YEAR ENDED 30 JUNE 2010

The members of Council present their report and audited accounts for the year ended 30 June 2010. The information shown on page 1 forms a part of these financial statements.

STRUCTURE, GOVERNANCE AND MANAGEMENT

The Society was founded on 23 November 1868 and received its Royal Charter in 1889. It is governed by the document 'The By-Laws of the Royal Historical Society', which was last amended in January 2008. The elected Officers of the Society are the President, six Vice-Presidents, the Treasurer, the Secretary, the Director of Communications and not more than two Literary Directors. These officers, together with twelve Councillors constitute the governing body of the Society, and therefore its trustees. The Society also has two executive officers: an Executive Secretary and an Administrative Secretary.

Appointment of Trustees

The identity of the trustees is indicated above. All Fellows and Members of the Society are able to nominate Councillors; they are elected by a ballot of Fellows. Other trustees are elected by Council.

The President shall be *ex-officio* a member of all Committees appointed by the Council; and the Treasurer, the Secretary, the Director of Communications and the Literary Directors shall, unless the Council otherwise determine, also be *ex-officio* members of all such Committees.

In accordance with By-law XVII, the Vice-Presidents shall hold office normally for a term of three years. Two of them shall retire by rotation, in order of seniority in office, at each Anniversary Meeting and shall not be eligible for re-election before the Anniversary Meeting of the next year. In accordance with By-law XX, the Councillors shall hold office normally for a term of four years. Three of them shall retire by rotation, in order of seniority in office, at each Anniversary Meeting and shall not be eligible for re-election before the Anniversary Meeting of the next year.

At the Anniversary Meeting on 27 November 2009, the Vice-Presidents retiring under By-law XVII were Professor A Curry and Dr A Foster. Professor M Finn and Professor P Mandler were elected to replace them. The Members of Council retiring under By-law XX were Professor G Burgess, Professor S Foot and Professor G Stone. In accordance with By-law XXI, Professor S Dixon, Professor K Fincham and Dr J Lewis were elected in their place. Professor N Miller was re-elected in accordance with By-law XXII for one year from the Anniversary Meeting in November 2009.

Trustee training and induction process

New trustees are welcomed in writing before their initial meeting, and sent details of the coming year's meeting schedule and other information about the Society and their duties. They are advised of Committee structure and receive papers in advance of the appropriate Committee and Council meetings, including minutes of the previous meetings. Trustees are already Fellows of the Society and have received regular information including the annual volume of *Transactions of the Royal Historical Society* which includes the annual report and accounts. They have therefore been kept apprised of any changes in the Society's business. Details of a Review on the restructuring of the Society in 1993 are available to all Members of Council.

MEMBERSHIP COMMITTEE:
Professor D Palliser – Chair)
Professor G Burgess (to November 2009)
Professor T Hitchcock (to November 2009)
Professor C Given-Wilson (from November 2009)
Professor C Whatley (from November 2009)

RESEARCH SUPPORT COMMITTEE:
Professor M Finn – Chair (from November 2009)
Professor G Bernard – Chair (to November 2009)
Professor S Barton (from November 2009)
Professor K Fincham (from November 2009)
Professor S R I Foot (to November 2009)
Professor T Hitchcock (to November 2009)
Professor N Miller (from November 2009)
Professor M Ormrod (to November 2009)

FINANCE COMMITTEE:
Professor G Bernard – Chair
Professor S Connolly

Risk assessment

The trustees are satisfied that they have considered the major risks to which the charity is exposed, that they have taken action to mitigate or manage those risks and that they have systems in place to monitor any change to those risks.

OBJECTS, OBJECTIVES, ACTIVITIES AND PUBLIC BENEFIT

The Society has referred to the guidance in the Charity Commission's general guidance on Public Benefit when reviewing its aims and objectives and in planning its future activities. In particular, the trustees consider how planned activities will contribute to the aims and objectives they have set.

226 TRANSACTIONS OF THE ROYAL HISTORICAL SOCIETY

The Society remains the foremost society in Great Britain promoting and defending the scholarly study of the past. The Society promotes discussion of history by means of a full programme of public lectures and conferences, and disseminates the results of historical research and debate through its many publications. It also speaks for the interests of history and historians for the benefit of the public.

The Society offers grants to support research training, and annual prizes for historical essays and publications. It produces (in conjunction with Brepols Publishers and the Institute of Historical Research) the Bibliography of British and Irish History, a database of over 490,000 records, by far the most complete online bibliographical resource on British and Irish history, including relations with the empire and the Commonwealth. The Bibliography is kept updated, and includes near-comprehensive coverage of works since 1901 and selected earlier works.

The Society's specific new objectives for the year are set out in 'Plans for Future Periods' below.

The Society relies on volunteers from among its Fellows to act as its elected Officers, Councillors and Vice-Presidents. In many of its activities it also relies on the goodwill of Fellows and others interested in the study of the past. It has two salaried staff, and also pays a stipend to the Series Editor of Studies in History and to certain individuals for work on the Society's Bibliography.

ACHIEVEMENTS AND PERFORMANCE

Grants

The Society awards funds to assist advanced historical research, by distributing grants to individuals. A wide range of people are eligible for these research and conference grants, including all postgraduate students registered for a research degree at United Kingdom institutions of higher education (full-time and part-time). The Society also considers applications from individuals who have completed doctoral dissertations within the last two years and are not yet in full-time employment. It operates five separate schemes, for each of which there is an application form. The Society's Research Support Committee considers applications at meetings held regularly throughout the year. In turn the Research Support Committee reports to Council. This year the grants budget was maintained at £30,000, and this was fully allocated, though the accounts show a higher sum expended, as grants paid after last year's travel are also included.

The Society was also able to award its Centenary and Marshall Fellowships this year. Those eligible are doctoral students who are engaged in the completion of a PhD in history (broadly defined) and who will have completed at least two years' research on their chosen topic (and not more than four years full-time or six years part-time) at the beginning of the session for which the awards are made. Full details and a list of awards made are provided in the Society's Annual Report.

Lectures and other meetings

During the year the Society held meetings in London and at universities outside London at which papers are delivered. Lectures are open to the public and are advertised on the website. In 2009–10 it sponsored a session at a colloquium held at Glasgow Caledonian University with the University of Strathclyde. It continues to sponsor the joint lecture for a wider public with Gresham College. It meets with other bodies to consider teaching and research policy issues of national importance. Together with The National Archives, it organised the annual Gerald Aylmer seminar, between historians and archivists, in April. Full details are provided in the Annual Report.

Publications

This year, as in previous years, it has delivered an ambitious programme of publications – a volume of *Transactions*, two volumes of edited texts in the *Camden* Series and six further volumes in the *Studies in History* Series have appeared. It has increased its financial support for the Bibliography of British and Irish History, in its new format as a Brepols publication from January 2010. The Bibliography is offered to all universities at institutional rates, and made available free to members consulting it at the Institute of Historical Research.

Library

The Society continues to subscribe to a range of record series publications, which, with its other holdings, are housed either in the Council Room or in the room immediately across the corridor, in the UCL History Library. A catalogue of the Society's private library holdings and listings of record series and regional history society publications (Texts and Calendars) have been made available on the Society's website. The record series publications as well as the Society's private library are available for consultation by the Society's membership, and to non-members by appointment.

Membership services

In accordance with the Society's 'By-laws', the membership is entitled to receive, after payment of subscription, a copy of the Society's *Transactions*, and to buy at a preferential rate copies of volumes published in the *Camden* series, and the *Studies in History* series. Society Newsletters continue to be circulated to the membership twice annually, in an accessible format. The membership benefits from many other activities of the Society including the frequent representations to various official bodies where the interests of historical scholarship are involved.

Investment performance

The Society holds an investment portfolio with a market value of about £2.16 million (2009: £1.97 million). It has adopted a "total return" approach to its investment policy. This means that the funds are invested solely on the basis of seeking to secure the best total level of economic return compatible with the duty to make safe investments, but regardless of the form the return takes.

The Society has adopted this approach to ensure even-handedness between current and future beneficiaries, as the focus of many investments moves away from producing income to maximising capital values. The total return strategy does not make distinctions between income and capital returns. It lumps together all forms of return on investment – dividends, interest, and capital gains etc, to produce a "total return". Some of the total return is then used to meet the needs of present beneficiaries, while the remainder is added to the existing investment portfolios to help meet the needs of future beneficiaries.

During the year Brewin Dolphin plc continued to act as investment managers. They report all transactions to the Honorary Treasurer and provide three-monthly reports on the portfolios, which are considered by the Society's Finance Committee which meets three times a year. In turn the Finance Committee reports to Council. A manager from Brewin attends two Finance Committee meetings a year.

The Society assesses its portfolio against the FTSE APCIMS balanced benchmark. During the year the portfolio generated a total return of 12.68% against 16% for the benchmark. This slight underperformance reflects the defensive nature of the portfolio in a period of market recovery. Fees are 0.5% of the value of the portfolio. The estimated yield on current values is 3.7%. This is a reduction from last year, reflecting not only the increase in capital value but also a policy decision to move to a slightly less defensive portfolio together with a short-term reduction in income from some formerly reliable blue chip stocks. The Society has a policy of not drawing down more than 3.5% of the market value of the portfolio (valued over a 3-year rolling period) in any one year. Though the Society operates a total return investment policy, in fact dividend income this year virtually matched capital withdrawals.

FINANCIAL REVIEW

Results

The Society generated a modest surplus of £27,222 this year (2009: £50,195). Income from the joint publishing agreement with Cambridge University Press increased, mainly owing to initial sales of the new digital archive. Council has reviewed the joint publishing arrangement and has resolved to renew it for another five years. Subscription income was maintained. However, there was a decline in investment income, as discussed above.

Expenditure was broadly similar to last year's. As noted in last year's report, from January 2010 the Society bears substantially increased costs for the production of the Bibliography of British and Irish History. The cost to the Society is estimated to average £25,000 per year over the next three years. These costs will be more visible in next year's accounts. The Society has set up a new cash investment account, partly in order to ensure that it has reserves immediately available to meet this cost. At the year end there is £58,000 in the account, in line with our targets.

Fixed assets

Information relating to changes in fixed assets is given in notes 5 and 6 to the accounts.

Reserves policy

Council has reviewed its policy towards its investment portfolio. It considers it to be primarily an investment fund held to produce income which is required for the Society's day-to-day operations. It needs sufficient reserves to generate an investment income of £70,000-£80,000 a year. A conservative annual draw-down policy has been adopted, in order to maintain the real value of the capital funds over the long-term and thus to balance the needs of current and future beneficiaries as required by charity law. In view of the relatively stable nature of the Society's subscription income, and the conservative drawdown policy in relation to the portfolio's capital value, Council has determined that it requires only a small additional free cash reserve. It has set this additional cash reserve at £75,000, one-third of normal annual expenditure. At 30 June 2010 its cash reserves amounted to £88,587. Council is satisfied with this level. The reserves policy is reviewed annually.

The Society's restricted funds consist of a number of different funds where the donor has imposed restrictions on the use of the funds which are legally binding. The purposes of these funds are set out in notes 11-13.

PLANS FOR FUTURE PERIODS

Council plans to set up a new Communications Group, supervised by the Hon. Director of Communications, to ensure that the Society communicates as effectively as possible with Fellows and Members and remains of maximum benefit to them. The new website, updated during the year, will play an important part in this strategy. Council proposes to introduce a new Membership category, for postgraduate students, to encourage more early career researchers to join the Society. Council also plans to continue its extensive involvement in public discussions about teaching and research issues. It will continue to offer support for wide-ranging seminar/lecture events outside London each year, some to be held at universities, and some run by consortia of local universities and other academic institutions. Council will continue to review the role, function, and membership of its committees, focusing first on the Teaching Policy and Research Policy Committees.

The Society intends to maintain the level of its current financial support to postgraduate and other young historians. It will increase the stipend for the Centenary and Marshall Fellowships from October 2010, and will continue to be actively involved in the selection procedure for the Fellowships, organised by the Institute of Historical Research. From 2010, the Bibliography of British and Irish History is available to the public on a subscription basis, in order to provide the resources necessary to continue to update it; the Society will increase its own subsidy of the operation.

STATEMENT OF COUNCIL'S RESPONSIBILITIES

The Council members are responsible for preparing the Trustees' Report and the financial statements in accordance with applicable law and United Kingdom Accounting Standards (United Kingdom Generally Accepted Accounting Practice.)

The law applicable to charities in England & Wales requires the Council to prepare financial statements for each financial year which give a true and fair view of the state of the affairs of the charity and of the incoming resources and application of resources of the charity for that period. In preparing these financial statements, the trustees are required to:

- select suitable accounting policies and then apply them consistently;
- observe the methods and principles in the Charities SORP;
- make judgements and estimates that are reasonable and prudent;
- state whether applicable accounting standards have been followed, subject to any material departures disclosed and explained in the financial statements;
- prepare the financial statements on the going concern basis unless it is inappropriate to presume that the charity will continue in business.

The Council is responsible for keeping proper accounting records that disclose with reasonable accuracy at any time the financial position of the charity and enable them to ensure that the financial statements comply with the Charities Act 1993, the Charity (Accounts and Reports) Regulations 2008 and the provisions of the Royal Charter. It is also responsible for safeguarding the assets of the charity and hence for taking reasonable steps for the prevention and detection of fraud and other irregularities.

In determining how amounts are presented within items in the statement of financial activities and balance sheet, the Council has had regard to the substance of the reported transaction or arrangement, in accordance with generally accepted accounting policies or practice.

AUDITORS

Kingston Smith LLP were appointed auditors in the year. They have indicated their willingness to continue in office and a proposal for their re-appointment will be presented at the Anniversary meeting.

By Order of the Board

Honorary Secretary

Professor V Harding

24 September 2010

THE ROYAL HISTORICAL SOCIETY

STATEMENT OF FINANCIAL ACTIVITIES
FOR THE YEAR ENDED 30 JUNE 2010

	Note	Unrestricted Funds £	Endowment Funds £	Restricted Funds £	Total Funds 2010 £	Total Funds 2009 £
INCOMING RESOURCES						
Incoming resources from generated funds						
Donations, legacies and similar incoming resources	2	9,792	–	1,000	10,792	18,086
Investment income	6	76,346	–	2,343	78,689	103,996
Incoming resources from charitable activities						
Grants for awards	–	–	10,000	10,000	11,000	
Grants for publications		8,000	–	–	8,000	6,000
Subscriptions		103,147	–	–	103,147	102,685
Royalties		53,986	–	–	53,986	39,890
Other incoming resources		666	–	–	666	2,614
TOTAL INCOMING RESOURCES		251,937	–	13,343	265,280	284,271
RESOURCES EXPENDED						
Cost of generating funds						
Investment manager's fees		10,456	–	323	10,779	10,519
Charitable activities						
Grants for awards	3	56,479	–	13,007	69,846	62,725
Lectures and meetings		14,900	–	–	14,900	13,513
Publications		71,643	–	–	71,643	78,773
Library		5,161	–	–	5,161	4,245
Membership services		47,781	–	–	47,781	45,080
Governance		18,309	–	–	18,309	19,220
TOTAL RESOURCES EXPENDED	4a	224,728	–	13,330	238,418	234,076
NET INCOMING/(OUTGOING) RESOURCES BEFORE TRANSFERS		27,208	–	13	26,862	50,195
Gross transfers between funds		(670)	–	670	–	–
NET INCOMING/(OUTGOING) RESOURCES BEFORE GAINS		26,538	–	683	26,862	50,195
Other recognised gains and losses						
Net (loss)/gain on investments	6	196,624	6,081	–	202,705	(395,450)
NET MOVEMENT IN FUNDS		223,162	6,081	683	229,567	(345,255)
Balance at 1 July		1,976,355	56,195	2,912	2,035,462	2,380,716
Balance at 30 June		2,199,517	62,276	3,595	2,265,029	2,035,462

The notes on pages 11 to 17 form part of these financial statements.

THE ROYAL HISTORICAL SOCIETY

BALANCE SHEET AT 30 JUNE 2010

	Note	2010 £	2010 £	2009 £	2009 £
FIXED ASSETS					
Tangible assets	5		794		907
Investments	6		2,162,298		1,970,280
COIF Investments			57,671		71,097
			2,220,763		2,042,284
CURRENT ASSETS					
Debtors	7	46,901		2,118	
Cash at bank and in hand		30,916		16,601	
		77,817		18,719	
LESS: CREDITORS					
Amounts due within one year	8	(33,191)		(25,541)	
NET CURRENT ASSETS			44,626		(6,822)
NET ASSETS			2,265,389		2,035,462
REPRESENTED BY:					
Endowment Funds	10				
A S Whitfield Prize Fund			41,697		37,643
The David Berry Essay Trust			20,579		18,552
Restricted Funds	11				
A S Whitfield Prize Fund			1,551		1,762
P J Marshall Fellowship			–		–
The David Berry Essay Trust			1,044		1,150
The Martin Lynn Bequest			1,000		–
Unrestricted Funds					
Designated – E M Robinson Bequest	12		108,115		98,514
General Fund	13		2,091,403		1,877,841
			2,265,029		2,035,462

The accounts have been prepared in accordance with the Financial Reporting Standard for Smaller Entities (effective April 2008).

The notes on pages 11 to 17 form part of these financial statements.

The financial statements were approved and authorised for issue by the Council on . . . . and were signed on its behalf by:

. . . .

Professor C Jones – **President**   Professor J Parry – **Honorary Treasurer**

THE ROYAL HISTORICAL SOCIETY

NOTES TO THE FINANCIAL STATEMENTS FOR THE YEAR ENDED 30 JUNE 2010

1. ACCOUNTING POLICIES

Basis of accounting
The financial statements have been prepared under the historical cost convention, as modified to include the revaluation of fixed assets including investments which are carried at market value, in accordance with the Statement of Recommended Practice (SORP 2005) "Accounting and Reporting by Charities", published in March 2005, with applicable accounting standards and the Financial Reporting Standard for Smaller Entities (effective April 2008).

Depreciation
Depreciation is calculated by reference to the cost of fixed assets using a straight line basis at rates considered appropriate having regard to the expected lives of the fixed assets. The annual rates of depreciation in use are:
Furniture and equipment   10%
Computer equipment   25%

Stock
Stock is valued at the lower of cost and net realisable value.

Library and Archives
The cost of additions to the library and archives is written off in the year of purchase.

Subscription Income
Subscription income is recognised in the year it became receivable with a provision against any subscription not received.

Investments
Investments are stated at market value. Any surplus/deficit arising on revaluation is included in the Statement of Financial Activities. Dividend income is accounted for when the Society becomes entitled to such monies.

Donations and Other Voluntary Income
Donations and other voluntary income are recognised when the Society becomes legally entitled to such monies.

Royalties
Royalties are recognised on an accruals basis in accordance with the terms of the relevant agreement.

Grants Payable
Grants payable are recognised in the year in which they are approved and notified to recipients.

Funds
Unrestricted: these are funds which can be used in accordance with the charitable objects at the discretion of the trustees.
Designated: these are unrestricted funds which have been set aside by the trustees for specific purposes.
Restricted: these are funds that can only be used for particular restricted purposes defined by the benefactor and within the objects of the charity.
Endowment: permanent endowment funds must be held permanently by the trustees and income arising is separately included in restricted funds for specific use as defined by the donors.
The purpose and use of endowment, restricted and designated funds are disclosed in the notes to the accounts.

Allocations
Wages, salary costs and office expenditure are allocated on the basis of the work done by the Executive Secretary and the Administrative Assistant.

Pensions
Pension costs are charged to the SOFA when payments fall due. The Society contributed 12.5% of gross salary to the personal pension plan of two of the employees.

2. DONATIONS AND LEGACIES	2010 £	2009 £
G R Elton Bequest		424
Donations via membership	1,254	1,134
Gladstone Memorial Trust	600	600
Browning Bequest		–
Vera London	–	7,997
Lisbet Rausing trust	5,000	5,000
Martin Lynn scholarship	1,000	
Sundry income	–	–
Gift Aid reclaimed	2,938	2,931
	10,792	18,086

3. GRANTS FOR AWARDS

	Unrestricted Funds £	Restricted Funds £	Total funds 2010 £	Total funds 2009 £
RHS Centenary Fellowship	10,000	–	10,000	10,000
Research support grants (see below)	32,932	1,087	34,019	27,141
A-Level prizes	300	–	300	400
AS Whitfield prize	–	1,000	1,000	1,000
E M Robinson Bequest				
Grant to Dulwich Picture Library	4,000	–	4,000	4,000
Gladstone history book prize	1,000	–	1,000	1,000
P J Marshall Fellowship	–	10,670	10,670	10,663
David Berry Prize	–	250	250	250
Staff and support costs (Note 4a)	8,247	–	8,247	8,271
	56,479	13,007	69,487	
30 June 2009	48,421	14,304		62,725

During the year Society awarded grants to a value of £34,019 (2009 – £27,141) to 131 (2009 – 123) individuals.

GRANTS PAYABLE

	2010 £	2009 £
Commitments at 1 July	1,300	–
Commitments made in the year	61,239	55,754
Grants paid during the year	(54,469)	(54,454)
Commitments at 30 June	8,069	1,300

Commitments at 30 June 2010 and 2009 are included in creditors.

4a. TOTAL RESOURCES EXPENDED

	Staff costs £ (Note 4b)	Support costs £ (Note 4b)	Direct costs £	Total £
Cost of generating funds				
Investment manager's fee	–	–	10,779	10,779
Charitable activities				
Grants for awards (Note 3)	5,890	2,357	61,240	69,487
Lectures and meetings	5,890	1,178	7,832	14,901
Publications	10,471	4,715	56,457	71,643
Library	2,618	1,179	1,365	5,162
Membership services	32,721	11,787	3,273	47,781
Governance	7,853	2,357	8,098	18,308
Total Resources Expended	65,443	23,574	149,043	238,059
30 June 2009	63,267	25,772	145,036	234,075

4b. STAFF COSTS

	2010 £	2009 £
Wages and salaries	53,360	51,687
Social security costs	5,390	5,194
Other pension costs	6,691	6,386
	65,440	63,267

4c. SUPPORT COSTS

	2010 £	2009 £
Stationery, photocopying and postage	12,669	12,788
Computer support	490	460
Insurance	920	923
Telephone	254	255
Depreciation	113	583
Bad debts		–
Other	9,126	10,763
	23,572	25,773

The average number of employees in the year was 2 (2009 – 2). There were no employees whose emoluments exceeded £60,000 in the year.

During the year travel expenses were reimbursed to 20 (2009: 24) Councillors attending Council meetings at a cost of £3,311 (2009 – £2,201). No Councillor received any remuneration during the year (2009 – £Nil).

Included in governance is the following:

	2010 £	2009 £
Auditors Remuneration – current year	7,461	7,100
Auditors Remuneration – in respect of prio years	88	524
Auditors Remuneration for non-audit services	550	1,398

5. TANGIBLE FIXED ASSETS

	Computer Equipment £	Furniture and Equipment £	Total £
COST			
At 1 July 2009 and 30 June 2010	33,224	2,307	35,531
DEPRECIATION			
At 1 July 2009	33,224	1,400	34,624
Charge for the year	–	113	113
At 30 June 2010	33,224	1,513	34,737
NET BOOK VALUE			
At 30 June 2010	–	794	794
At 30 June 2009	–	907	907

All tangible fixed assets are used in the furtherance of the Society's objects.

6. INVESTMENTS

	General Fund £	Designated Robinson Bequest £	Whitfield Prize Fund £	David Berry Essay Trust £	Total £
Market value at 1 July 2009	1,812,658	98,514	39,405	19,703	1,970,280
Additions	725,577	39,434	15,776	7,887	788,674
Disposals	(735,412)	(39,968)	(15,987)	(7,994)	(799,361)
Net loss on investments	186,489	10,135	4,054	2,027	202,705
Market value at 30 June 2010	1,989,312	108,115	43,248	21,623	2,162,298
Cost at 30 June 2010	1,906,917	103,637	41,455	20,727	2,072,736

	2010 £	2009 £
UK Equities	999,392	1,335,916
UK Government Stock and Bonds	551,602	283,132
Overseas Equities	575,604	304,545
Uninvested Cash	35,700	46,687
	2,162,298	1,970,280
Dividends and interest on listed investments	78,092	102,281
Interest on cash deposits	597	1,715
	78,689	103,996

7. DEBTORS

	2010 £	2009 £
Other debtors	2,261	650
Royalty debtor	42,366	1,017
Prepayments	2,274	451
	46,901	2,118

8. CREDITORS: Amounts due within one year

	2010 £	2009 £
Sundry creditors	13,486	6,408
Taxes and social security	1,210	1,444
Subscriptions received in advance	6,345	5,289
Accruals and deferred income	12,150	12,400
	33,191	25,541

Included within Sundry creditors is an amount of £398 (2009: £358) relating to pension liabilities.

9. LEASE COMMITMENTS

The Society has the following annual commitments under non-cancellable operating leases which expire:

	2010 £	2009 £
Within 1–2 years	9,846	–
Within 2–5 years	–	9,846

10. ENDOWMENT FUNDS

	Balance at 1 July 2009 £	Investment Gain £	Balance at 30 June 2010 £
A S Whitfield Prize Fund	37,643	4,054	41,697
The David Berry Essay Trust	18,552	2,027	20,579
	56,195	6,081	62,276

A S Whitfield Prize Fund

The A S Whitfield Prize Fund is an endowment used to provide income for an annual prize for the best first monograph for British history published in the calendar year.

The David Berry Essay Trust

The David Berry Essay Trust is an endowment to provide income for annual prizes for essays on subjects dealing with Scottish history.

11. RESTRICTED FUNDS

	Balance at 1 July 2009 £	Incoming Resources £	Outgoing Resources £	Transfers £	Balance at 30 June 2010 £
A S Whitfield Prize Fund	1,762	1,563	(1,774)	–	1,551
P J Marshall Fellowship	–	10,000	(10,670)	670	–
The David Berry Essay Trust	1,150	780	(886)	–	1,044
Martin Lynn Bequest	–	1,000	–	–	1,000
	2,912	13,343	(13,330)	670	3,595

A S Whitfield Prize Fund Income

Income from the A S Whitfield Prize Fund is used to provide an annual prize for the best first monograph for British history published in the calendar year.

P J Marshall Fellowship

The P J Marshall Fellowship is used to provide a sum sufficient to cover the stipend for a one-year doctoral research fellowship alongside the existing Royal Historical Society Centenary Fellowship at the Institute of Historical Research.

The David Berry Essay Trust Income

Income from the David Berry Trust is to provide annual prizes for essays on subjects dealing with Scottish history.

The Martin Lynn Bequest

This annual bequest is used by the Society to give financial assistance to postgraduates researching topics in African history.

12. DESIGNATED FUND	Balance at 1 July 2009 £	Incoming Resources £	Outgoing Resources £	Investment Loss £	Transfers £	Balance at 30 June 2010 £
E M Robinson Bequest	98,514	3,905	(4,439)	10,135	–	108,115

E M Robinson Bequest

Income from the E M Robinson Bequest is to further the study of history and to date has been used to provide grants to the Dulwich Picture Gallery.

13. GENERAL FUND	Balance at 1 July 2009 £	Incoming Resources £	Outgoing Resources £	Investment Loss £	Transfers £	Balance at 30 June 2010 £
	1,877,841	248,032	(220,289)	186,489	(670)	2,091,403

14. ANALYSIS OF NET ASSETS BETWEEN FUNDS

	General Fund £	Designated Fund £	Restricted Funds £	Endowment Funds £	Total £
Fixed assets	794	–	–	–	794
Investments	1,989,312	108,115	2,595	62,276	2,162,298
COIF investments	57,671	–	–	–	57,671
	2,047,777	108,115	2,595	62,276	2,220,763
Current assets	76,817	–	1,000	–	77,817
Less: Creditors	(33,191)	–	–	–	(33,191)
Net current assets/(liabilities)	43,626	–	1,000	–	44,626
Net Assets	2,091,403	108,115	3,595	62,276	2,265,389